"Monsignor Buelt's reflections help n ed
assembly to more deeply appreciate tl
pastorally practical and spiritually nou ... help to highlight
how the deacon at the liturgy and in pa... life can lead us more deeply into
the mystery of Christ's love for us."

—Monsignor James P. Moroney
Saint John's Seminary
Brighton, Massachusetts

"Let us be honest. In many parishes the deaconate has become somewhat
'tired.' Some deacons feel taken for granted, others lack direction and drift,
and zeal for ministry fades. Deacons today need a deeper spirituality, their
own spirituality. This can be found in the treasury of the church. Drawing
on the classical sources, Msgr. Edward Buelt provides a fresh vision of the
deacon's ministry in the word, at the altar, and through charity. His book is
invaluable for deacons and all who work with them."

—Bishop Peter J. Elliott
Author of *Ceremonies of the Modern Roman Rite*

"Monsignor Buelt draws on his impressive learning and extensive pastoral
and personal experiences to guide us in a deep reflection on what it means to
answer the call to diaconal ministry. His book makes a valuable contribution
to the proper understanding of the person and role of the deacon and the
unique place this newly revitalized ministry has in the mission of the church
in our time."

—The Most Rev. Salvatore J. Cordileone
Bishop of the Diocese of Oakland, California

A New Friendship

The Spirituality
and Ministry of the Deacon

Edward L. Buelt

*Foreword by the Most Reverend Charles J. Chaput, OFM Cap,
Archbishop of Denver*

LITURGICAL PRESS

Collegeville, Minnesota

www.litpress.org

Nihil Obstat: Mr. William Beckman, *Censor Deputatus*
Imprimatur: ✠ Most Reverend Charles J. Chaput, O.F.M. Cap., *Archiepiscopus Denveriense*, Denver, Colorado, February 12, 2010

Cover design and photo by David Manahan, OSB.

Excerpts from documents of the Second Vatican Council are from *Vatican Council II: Volume 1, The Conciliar and Post Conciliar Documents*, by Austin Flannery, OP © 1996 (Costello Publishing Company, Inc.). Used with permission.

Scripture texts in this work are taken from the *New Revised Standard Version Bible: Catholic Edition* © 1989, 1993, Division of Christian Education of the National Council of the Churches of Christ in the United States of America. Used by permission. All rights reserved.

1   2   3   4   5   6   7   8

Library of Congress Cataloging-in-Publication Data

Buelt, Edward Louis.
  A new friendship : the spirituality and ministry of the deacon / Edward L. Buelt ; foreword by Charles J. Chaput.
       p.   cm.
    Includes bibliographical references (p.   ).
    ISBN 978-0-8146-3363-2 (pbk.) — ISBN 978-0-8146-3943-6 (e-book)
    1. Deacons. I. Title.

  BV680.B84   2011
  262'.142—dc22   2010042472

To Wilfred and Mary Ann Buelt, my parents,
who loved me as a son,
and James Francis Cardinal Stafford,
who taught me as a father.

Contents

Foreword

For many Catholics, deacons seem like an innovation of the Second Vatican Council, especially since the council decreed that married men could be ordained deacons. But the diaconate is as old and new as Christianity itself. The institution of the diaconate is found in the Acts of the Apostles, chapter 6. Acts also tells us of the witness of St. Stephen, one of the first seven deacons and the church's first martyr, and that of St. Philip, who evangelized and baptized the Ethiopian eunuch. From these two deacons in Sacred Scripture the essential role of the deacon is made evident: through his ministry of *diaconia*, the deacon both witnesses to Christ and brings people to him. When Vatican II restored the historic diaconate as a permanent order in the church, it sought to reinvigorate the church so that the church, with the same ardor shown by Stephen and Philip, might be both witness and evangelizer.

Exactly a decade after the close of the council, Pope Paul VI wrote an apostolic exhortation on evangelization, titled *Evangelii nuntiandi*, to encourage the church in her evangelical mission. The pope taught that "the Church exists in order to evangelise." Evangelization, the pope affirmed, is the "service rendered to the Christian community and also to the whole of humanity." From these two statements the importance of the diaconate becomes clear. If the service that the church provides to the world is evangelization, then the deacon, who is ordained in the service of the church, must be a model of evangelization. This is expressed beautifully in the diaconal ordination rite. As the bishop hands the ordinand the Book of the Gospels, he prays, "Receive the Gospel of Christ, whose herald you now are. Believe what you read, teach what you believe, and practice what you teach."

The church's message regarding the form of true service needs to be heard again today. Some people try to reduce the service of the church to nothing more than social activism. On the other hand, powerful forces exist in our culture, such as relativism, materialism, and excessive individualism, which are enemies of authentic service. Contrary to these two voices of counterfeit service and anti-service, the church proclaims the Lord's message of true service. True service is revealed in love, which Jesus himself teaches requires the laying down of one's life for another. This is the mission of the deacon, not simply to serve, but to serve as Jesus did, laying his life down for all of us.

From this perspective we can see that without the ministry of the deacon, the church would be in a far weaker position to preach the Gospel. Pope John Paul II referred to the crucial mission of the deacon when in Detroit in 1987 he met with the deacons of the United States and their wives: "By the standards of this world, servanthood is despised, but in the wisdom and providence of God it is the mystery through which Christ redeems the world. And you are ministers of that mystery, heralds of that Gospel."

It is with this understanding of the importance of the diaconate to the life of the church that I am grateful to Monsignor Edward Buelt for this important book, *A New Friendship: The Spirituality and Ministry of the Deacon*. This book is the fruit of a retreat that Monsignor Buelt gave at my invitation to men who were being ordained to the diaconate. I hope it will be very widely shared, so that through its success, the ministry of deacons to serve sinners and the poor will be advanced.

In the first six chapters, Monsignor Buelt discusses the deacon in relation to the Persons of the Blessed Trinity and how this relationship unfolds in the deacon's office of teaching, sanctifying, and serving. Jesus Christ has revealed that the love within God is fundamentally diaconal—each divine Person "serves" the other. Through an understanding of the deacon in relation to trinitarian *communio*, we see that true *diaconia* has its source in the very mystery of trinitarian love and self-surrender.

The second half of his book considers the deacon in his role as an icon of Christ the Suffering Servant. Monsignor Buelt makes two essential points. The first is the relationship of the deacon to the episcopate and the presbyterate. Deacons are members of the clergy. After ordination they are no longer laymen, although they are ordained "not to the priesthood, but for service." At his own ordination, the bishop is anointed with the "Spirit of governance" in order to continue the work of the apostles. The priest is anointed with a "Spirit of holiness" in order to offer sacrifice.

The deacon is anointed with the Holy Spirit's gift of sevenfold "grace to carry out faithfully the work of the ministry." As such the deacon is not ordained *in persona Christi capitis ecclesiae*, that is, in the person of Christ, Head of the church. Rather, through his ordination the deacon is configured to Christ the Servant. Nevertheless, since the service of Christ is one, these orders are interrelated. This unity is expressed in the fact that practically speaking the bishop governs and the priest offers sacrifice while it is the role of the deacon to care for the needy and to ensure that the poor are brought to the communion of the church so that they too take part in that sacrifice handed down by the apostles.

The second key point made by Monsignor Buelt is the unity of the diaconal ministry through the deacon's threefold mandate of Word, liturgy, and service. In his ministry of *leitourgia, martyria,* and *diaconia,* the deacon is called to preach the Good News of salvation to the poor. As an icon of the Suffering Servant, the deacon brings the very person of Jesus Christ, the love of God made flesh, to sinners and those in need and then gathers them to partake of the eucharistic sacrifice.

In the Archdiocese of Denver, we are blessed with many faithful deacons and their wives who give extraordinary witness. I am—and always will be—deeply grateful for their service. Monsignor Buelt describes the deacon as "an icon of Christ the Suffering Servant." An icon is more than a picture; Orthodox Christians understand the icon as acting like a sacrament. Through visible means, an icon makes present a mystical reality. In this light, a deacon is not just an image of Christ the servant who came to serve and to offer his life as a ransom. The deacon, through his ministry, is the service of Christ and the church sacramentalized and a constant reminder to the church and the world that Jesus Christ is among us always "as one who serves" (Luke 22:27).

Most Reverend Charles J. Chaput, OFM Cap
Archbishop of Denver

Preface

A few years back, at the invitation of Archbishop Chaput of Denver and Bishop Ricken of Cheyenne, I led the ordination retreat of fourteen men whom they were calling to the diaconate. We gathered at the Abbey of Saint Walburga, set at the base of majestic mountain peaks northwest of Fort Collins, Colorado. As the retreat master my goals were simple. First, I wanted to help the candidates summarize four years of formation. Second, building on the foundations laid by their formators, I sought to help each of the candidates to articulate his own vision of diaconal ministry. Finally, I wanted to offer the retreatants some practical considerations for carrying out their diaconal tasks. When the retreat concluded they encouraged me to make it more widely available to their wives and families, pastors, spiritual directors, formators, confreres, and any who might aspire to the diaconate or have questions concerning it. Two years on, the archbishop of Denver granted me a six-month sabbatical from my pastoral ministry. During that time I set about to complete this present text. I thank the archbishop for his kindness and support of this project, and for his episcopal leadership.

I invite the reader to engage these reflections as a type of retreat. As in any retreat, there are four actors.

The first and primary actor is the Blessed Trinity. At the outset of the retreat I encouraged the candidates to compose their own simple profession of faith in the Trinity and to pray it each day as a sort of morning offering. I invite the reader to do so even now. I offer two examples of my own composing. The first is: "The Father has created me in his own image and likeness and revealed himself to me; he loves me. The Son is before all else that is and has redeemed me; he loves me. The Holy Spirit is the Lord and Giver of all life and my life; he loves me. By his power I have been called to serve the church and my brothers and sisters." The other one is: "Lord Jesus, may my every thought, deed, and word today be true worship of your Father, proclaim you to be Lord, welcome your Holy Spirit, build up your church, and serve your brothers and sisters, and mine, in truth and charity."

The second actor at work in a retreat is the church. In the creed we profess our belief in one, holy, catholic, and apostolic church. The Latin text of this profession is in the ablative case, not the dative. The meaning of the Latin, unfortunately easily lost in the English, is more than that we believe *in* the church, as if we were simply acknowledging that the church exists. Rather, in the creed we profess that we *believe* the church. We believe what she is; we believe what she says; we believe what she is about. Christ has endowed the church with the fullness of unity and all the means of salvation. For her part, faithful to her Divine Bridegroom, the church proclaims the truth of the faith revealed by him, and she serves others as he has first served her. Both as a baptized Christian and especially as an ordained minister, the deacon is to believe the church, in whose service he gives his life.

Complementary to these reflections, therefore, one should consider and familiarize oneself with the church's teaching on the diaconate, in particular her foundational documents, including the *Directory for the Ministry and Life of Permanent Deacons* and the *Basic Norms for the Formation of Permanent Deacons*. In the United States, too, one should consult the United States Conference of Catholic Bishops' *National Directory for the Formation, Ministry, and Life of Permanent Deacons in the United States.*

I am the third agent of the retreat, acting on behalf of the church. I bring to bear my own knowledge and relationship with the Trinity and with the church, and my own history and experience of life and ministry. I come to this task as the pastor for the past thirteen years of a large, suburban parish community. As such I have been privileged to work with deacons and to call them brothers in ministry; they have taught me much.

I have seen firsthand the enormous potential for the new evangelization that the diaconate holds out. Deacons can bring Christ and the church to places and locales where before they might not have been welcomed. Above all, however, I have come to see that deacons can build up the church and serve sinners and the poor in ways the Second Vatican Council, in restoring the diaconate as a permanent ministry, could not have imagined. To those ends, that is, to building up the church and serving others, I hope simply to offer some markers and pointers, road signs if you will, for deacons and other ministers, for those interested in diaconal life and ministry, and for those who are intrigued and want to learn more about this apostolic ministry.

Fourth, you, the reader, act, not simply in opening yourself to the action of the Spirit and the church but by responding generously and selflessly with the giving of your life in service to others, whatever your vocation may be. A deacon, for his part, is called to make a gift to the Lord and the church of all that goes into making him who he is. Like anyone else, a deacon is a person formed by experiences both under his control and beyond it. Upon him others have acted, for his good or to his detriment. He himself has acted upon others, for their good or for their ill. Freed from original sin at baptism, yet he comes to the sacrament of orders as a sinner. He professes his faith in Christ, who lived and died for him, yet at times he uses his freedom to lade heavy burdens on others. In short, he is a man—not a superman—who, despite all his failings and unworthiness, should know that Christ loves him and has called him to be an icon of his suffering, an icon of the Suffering Servant.

The structure of these reflections is dialogical. Each odd-numbered chapter is an extended Bible study of a passage or passages that in some way give us insight into being a servant, disciple, and especially deacon. Each even-numbered chapter seeks to deepen one's understanding of a deacon's life and ministry through more theological and pastoral reflections on various elements of his relationship with the Trinity and with the church, and on specific functions a deacon carries out. The last chapter is a practical consideration offered to the wives of deacons, candidates, aspirants, or inquirers into the diaconate.

A word about the title, *A New Friendship*.

Newness is a great grace. "[C]lothe yourselves with the new self, created according to the likeness of God in true righteousness and holiness," the author of the letter to the Ephesians urges us (4:24). St. John was given the vision of "a new heaven and a new earth" (Rev 21:1). Seated on his heavenly throne, the Lamb of God proclaims, "See, I am making all things new" (Rev 21:5).

Friendship is also a great grace. Sirach teaches us that a faithful friend is a sturdy shelter, a treasure beyond price, and a life-saving remedy (see 6:14-16). Jesus loved his apostles, and the night before he died he called them "friends" (John 15:15).

These two sources of grace came together for me when I lived in Cuernavaca, Mexico. Each day on my way to and from the school where I was studying Spanish I walked past a vacant lot next to a Catholic church. The lot was enclosed by a chain-link fence, unkempt, littered with trash, and overgrown with weeds. On that fence, at the lot's only entrance, someone had hung a painted metal sign that read, simply, "Una Nueva Amistad (A New Friendship)." It had no further reference, no context to make sense of its meaning, no clue as to why it had been hung. For me it became a sort of "shingle" that Christ was hanging out for the church's neighbors, in particular its young people. He was inviting them to join him in making of that empty lot a home of new friendship with him, with the church, and with one another. I could not stay long enough to see if the invitation was ever accepted. But the metaphor never left me.

I apply it now to the life and ministry of the deacon. Being ordained, a deacon receives a great grace, that of a new friendship with the Lord. The deacon is as that sign, the Lord's shingle, that reads, *A New Friendship*. Chain-link-fenced lots abound in our communities and neighborhoods, next to our churches, everywhere. They are found especially in people's hearts and in their relationships. On the fences of all these lots Christ has hung out his shingle, and through the deacon he is extending *una nueva amistad*.

Finally, I want to thank the many persons who have assisted me with this project. I am grateful first to the fourteen men who made the retreat in May 2007 and to their wives and families. I thank those who read earlier drafts of this text and offered helpful comments, including Benedict Neenan, OSB; Deacon Charles Parker; Anthony Lilles; Owen Vyner; and Bill Beckman. I thank Martha Rasmussen and Carol Rasmussen for their editorial advice. I was supported throughout by the staff of Our Lady of Loreto Parish, who encouraged me to give the retreat in the first place and who shouldered an extra load of pastoral ministry since then and along the way. Finally, I thank Liturgical Press for the confidence it places in me and in the text on behalf of deacons and in service to the church.

chapter one

The Father
and the Prodigal Son

We begin with a prayerful study of Luke 15:11-32, the parable of the Prodigal Son. I want to focus particularly on the relationship between the father and the younger of his two sons. The young man's journey from sonship to slavery back to sonship can give us some insight into how God the Father relates to his deacons both as sons and servants. Additionally, from the servants in the parable we can gain some insight into diaconal life and ministry.

We are quite familiar with the story of the Prodigal Son. A son demands the share of his father's inheritance owed to him, and in so doing declares his father to be as good as dead. Eventually, having squandered his inheritance and sunk to dining degradingly with pigs (Actually, the pigs dined better than he!), the Prodigal Son really did come to believe that the man he knew to be his father was dead. That is, having so thoroughly shamed and humiliated his father and suffering now the consequences of his actions, he came to believe that his father would never forgive him, that he would never return home as the man's son. The Prodigal Son could only hope that even though his father might not forgive and accept him, he would need him for the efficient maintenance of his estate and deign to contract with him commercially, to establish with him nothing more than an agreement in which the utilitarian interests of each might be served.

1

Clinging to this desperate hope, he heads home. Upon arriving home, however, his father welcomes him with arms open beyond his wildest expectations and, contrary to every expectation, he discovers that the father whom he once declared to be dead was undeniably very much alive. Notwithstanding his insolent and disrespectful behavior toward his father—behavior truly unworthy of a son—his father had not ceased loving him, had not declared his son to be dead. Let's read the passage.

Then Jesus said, "There was a man who had two sons. The younger of them said to his father, 'Father, give me the share of the property that will belong to me.' So he divided his property between them. A few days later the younger son gathered all he had and traveled to a distant country, and there he squandered his property in dissolute living. When he had spent everything, a severe famine took place throughout that country, and he began to be in need. So he went and hired himself out to one of the citizens of that country, who sent him to his fields to feed the pigs. He would gladly have filled himself with the pods that the pigs were eating; and no one gave him anything. But when he came to himself he said, 'How many of my father's hired hands have bread enough and to spare, but here I am dying of hunger! I will get up and go to my father, and I will say to him, "Father, I have sinned against heaven and before you; I am no longer worthy to be called your son; treat me like one of your hired hands."' So he set off and went to his father. But while he was still far off, his father saw him and was filled with compassion; he ran and put his arms around him and kissed him. Then the son said to him, 'Father, I have sinned against heaven and before you; I am no longer worthy to be called your son.' But the father said to his slaves, 'Quickly, bring out a robe—the best one—and put it on him; put a ring on his finger and sandals on his feet. And get the fatted calf and kill it, and let us eat and celebrate; for this son of mine was dead and is alive again; he was lost and is found!' And they began to celebrate.

Now his elder son was in the field; and when he came and approached the house, he heard music and dancing. He called one of the slaves and asked what was going on. He replied, 'Your brother has come, and your father has killed the fatted calf, because he has got him back safe and sound.' Then he became angry and refused to go in. His father came out and began to plead with him. But he answered his father, 'Listen! For all these years I have been working like a slave for you, and I have never disobeyed your command; yet you have never given me even a young goat so that I might celebrate with my friends. But when this son of yours came back, who has devoured your property with prostitutes, you killed the fatted calf for him!' Then the father said to him, 'Son, you are always with me, and all that is mine is yours. But we had to celebrate and rejoice, because this brother of yours was dead and has come to life; he was lost and has been found.'"

"Father," the younger son demanded, "give me the share of the property that will belong to me." We can only imagine what the father felt at this impertinent request. In the telling of the parable, we learn that he was an extraordinarily good father. He kept nothing for himself and he held nothing back from his sons; as he affirmed for his older son, "all that is mine is yours." Being a good father he had taught his sons that they were free. Now the younger of the two chose to exercise his freedom and to leave. Although the father undoubtedly could not agree, he did not argue; indeed, there is no hint that he sought to prevent his departure or block his way. He acknowledged his son's right and resolve to leave home, even if, as he might have suspected, it meant he would never see him again. He divided up his property.

We can imagine that the younger son was apportioned a considerable sum, and it must have been an extraordinary undertaking for the father to account, liquidate, and divide his holdings. We know that the father was a landowner and therefore an elite member of the agrarian (and probably political) class of his community, what we would call today the upper class. He managed an estate, the demands of which were met by many servants, slaves, and hired hands. His wealth was substantial, hinted at by his possession of fine robes, jewelry, fatted calves, and the like, even after having dispersed a great deal of his estate to the younger son. His influence was great. Surely he was the patron of many and many were beholden to him and in his debt, for he was able to slaughter a fatted calf, organize a banquet feast with singing and dancing, and host a celebration of his own household and the whole populace, so quickly in fact that it began even before his older son had heard the news of his younger sibling's return and returned home himself. (Compare this father's social status with that of the man in the previous chapter of the gospel who threw a large dinner for many guests, none of whom even bothered to show up [Luke 14:15-24].)

Complying with his younger son's demands surely weakened the father's economic position. But it resulted in even greater damage to his social standing. In the honor-shame culture in which Jesus' listeners lived, the son's behavior would have brought considerable dishonor on his father, family, and tribe. Any other son who dared to treat his father as this son treated him might very well have been handed over to the elders of the community, led outside the city walls, and stoned to death (see Deut 21:18-21). No respectable father would have indulged such a disrespectful and ungrateful son and given in to such belligerent and rebellious demands.

Worst of all, complying with his young son's demands severed the blood bond between them, at least from the perspective and in the thinking of the son. His father was as good as dead, of no "use" to him. We can imagine the son shouting "good riddance" as he turned his back and rode off into the sunset.

The younger son heading off on his horse and the parable continuing on its course, the disaster that everyone could see looming on the horizon unfolded. Such an impulsive young man could not manage even the simplest of his personal affairs, let alone the vast property he had demanded and now possessed. In very short order he squandered the entirety of his possessions and all his money. In the Greek, Jesus says that the young man wasted his *ousian,* that is, the son wasted his substance, his essence, his very being. (Is this not always the case? In sin, is it not our essence, our very being, that we squander and waste?)

Moreover, Jesus tells us that the young man wasted his being *on dissolute living*. The Greek word Jesus uses for "dissolute" is *asōtōs*. This is the only time in the whole of the New Testament that this word is used. Jesus is clearly making a point. For the younger son, cutting himself off from his father and living dissolutely led to the loss of his very being. So low did the Prodigal Son fall that he lost his very humanity. Not, though, when he was eventually forced to feed the pigs. No, the Prodigal Son actually lost his humanity even earlier, from the moment, that is, that he declared his father to be dead and departed from home. The irony is that the son's humanity was the one thing he had inherited from his father and possessed in his own right from birth, something he "owned" without having to kill his father in order to possess it. It was the one thing for which he needed to make neither demand nor claim of his father.

Be that as it may, things eventually went from worse to desperate for the profligate son. Even nature itself turned against him, and a huge famine broke out across the land. In light of this, it comes as a bit of an understatement, then, that Jesus tells us simply that the younger son was "in need." We might have expected Jesus to have been a bit more colorful, describing the young man, perhaps, as starving, desperate, on the verge of death, or hanging on to life by a thread. But Jesus describes the young man's situation simply as "to be being in want" (*hustereisthai*; in the present passive tense). Jesus had an important point to make by describing the young man's situation this way. What did the son want? What did he need? Having squandered his inheritance, having lost his essence, the son's need was for something far greater than food and nourishment. His need was for *being*. He needed to recover his being, and to do that he needed a father.

The son, however, was not yet able to admit his sin and return home. How could he? How can one ever face another whose death he has desired? How does one confess to another that he had been complicit in attempting that person's death? How does a son admit to his father that in willing his death, the death of the one who brought him to life, he himself instead was the one who died? The Prodigal Son could not. So he sought to escape the whole tragic affair by going even further away from home and entering into a commercial relationship with another who, not unlike his own father, owned many lands. Although the text is often translated he "hired himself" or "attached himself" to one of the propertied class, the original Greek is in the aorist (a past) passive tense. In other words, Jesus was telling his hearers not that the son actively hired himself out but rather that he "was attached" passively to the property owner. How could it have been otherwise? The son had squandered everything, even his own being. How could he have arranged even a relationship of menial servitude, of slavery? Born a free man, he is now indentured to another. Born a Jew, a son of the Covenant, he was now a slave to a Gentile. Having exiled himself from the freedom of the Promised Land, he now seeks to survive in pagan territory, assigned the feeding of pigs, for a Jew one of the most unclean of animals. He who had shamed his own father was now without dignity. Now he "would gladly have filled himself with the pods that the pigs were eating." In the son's starvation for being, his very hunger is perverted for pig food.

On a side note, does this not describe exactly the desperate situation of so many of our brothers and sisters, sons and daughters? Having detached themselves from our Father, how many live dissolute lives and waste their humanity, their being? How many people, little more than empty husks, look to "the propertied class" to save them, that is, to whatever seems to promise more and whomever seems to possess more—manipulative relationships, money, entertainment and popular media, fashion, popularity or celebrity, success in business, sports, entertainment, sex and erotica, addictions to drugs, technology, digitalization, and the like? For how many is their hunger for being perverted into hunger for the food of unclean animals? Do we not all, sinning against our Father and against heaven, seek our redemption in relationships and in realities that enslave rather than free us, thus forcing us, if we are honest with ourselves, to live worse off even than pigs? Anything and everything to which we attach ourselves that is not of our Father is as if found in a foreign, pagan land and cannot save us.

Back to the parable. Regarding this younger son, Jesus tells us that sitting in his pigsty "no one gave to him." Jesus doesn't say that "no one gave him anything," simply that "no one gave to him." On one hand, sure, no one provided the lad with corporal or material assistance. On the other hand, and this is more to the point Jesus wants to make, not a single person gave to him even of himself or herself; all refused to give themselves to him as gift. Whereas his father had held nothing back from him, sharing everything—all that he possessed, his legal share of the inheritance, himself, even life itself—in this pagan land all refused to gift themselves. No one cared.

Only when the son understood that no one cared for him did he come back to himself. In the Greek, Jesus uses the verb *elthōn*, "coming to himself," in the aorist active tense. In essence Jesus is saying that the young man was returning to himself, coming back into himself, beginning anew to care for himself. He was not yet there, but the journey home—to himself and at the same time to his father—had begun.

Although by law his right to do so, in truth for the son to have demanded his inheritance from his father made no sense. To have "killed off" his father, although by right his to do, made no sense. Even though no one was the boss of him, to have squandered his very essence on dissolute living made no sense. Even though it seemed there was nothing else to do, to have attached himself to a pagan landowner in a Gentile land really made no sense. Finally, though, when the son understood that no one cared for him and, in fact, that they cared more for pigs, the only thing that made sense was to return to his father's house and reclaim some measure of humanity, of being. He had no legal claim to make of his father, having squandered his share of the inheritance. He had no moral claim to make of him, having dissolved the blood bonds that bound them. He had no claim even for mercy, having shamed his father in the sight of all. All for which he could hope was that the man he had once known as his father was still a smart businessman and in need of one more hired hand.

Here Jesus gives us a clue as to what true poverty is—both physical poverty and poverty of spirit. Even when materially destitute after having squandered his inheritance, the son was not completely impoverished. Even when a natural crisis erupted in the form of famine, he still hadn't reached rock bottom. Even when longing to eat the same husks he was feeding to the pigs, he still wasn't completely broken. Lower still than all these depths, than all these poverties, his deepest poverty lay in the fact that no one cared for him. One is truly poor when no one cares. The true inheritance the younger son wasted was neither his money nor his possessions. It was his father's care. Only when he understood that no one else cared for him did he understand how much his father did.

In the company of pigs the young man remembered his father's just treatment of his workers. "But when he came to himself he said, 'How many of my father's hired hands have bread enough and to spare, but here I am dying of hunger!'" The word that Jesus uses for "hired hands" is *misthios*, not *doulos* (slave). The *misthios* were not part of the master's household and did not benefit from his patronage. They were day laborers, the lowest "blue collar" workers of Jesus' time. A landowner might require the services of day laborers, for example, when the harvest was due, when a construction project was under way, because the condition of one's ordinary pool of labor was such as to compromise the estate's efficient management or productivity, or when one had a job so menial or dangerous to do that it was deemed to be a threat to or below the condition even of one's own slaves. The Talmud, for instance, records one instance in which a wealthy man hired a day laborer simply to run before his horse (b. Ket. 67b Bar.). The *misthios* enjoyed neither security nor social stability. In resolving to ask to be hired as a *misthios*, the son was not asking to be restored to his father's household, even as a slave. All he hoped for was to render what servitude might be required so that day to day he could eat. Such, he believed, was his only hope.

Let's take one final look at the son in the pigsty before turning our attention to the father back at home. In verse eighteen Jesus tells us that the younger son in coming to his senses said to himself simply, "Rising." The verb Jesus uses is *anastas*, in the aorist active tense. Here it qualifies "going," which he uses in the future tense. The literal translation of what the son said to himself is, "Having been rising, I will be going to my father." Two verses later, in verse twenty, Jesus again uses *anastas* in the aorist active tense. Here it qualifies "coming," which he also uses in the aorist tense. Its literal translation would be: "Having been rising, he came to his father." Jesus' meaning becomes clear. The son's rising is both the reason that he can return home and also what he experiences when he gets there. His rising is the grace that enables him both to return to his father *and* what his father gives to him when he has made his way back home. Returning to his father the son was being resurrected to new life. He lost his essence when he stood up to and left his father. He is resurrected when he stands up to pigs and returns home to his father.

When the son returns home he calls out from a distance *"Pater*, Father." *Pater* is how he addressed his father at the beginning of the parable when he demanded his claim of the inheritance. Then he used it in a manipulative and dishonorable way. Now, arriving home, the Prodigal Son again calls out *"Pater."* It might strike us as odd that he does so, for he had once declared this man to be dead and now hopes from him not the restoration of sonship but at best his hiring as an employee. Be that as it may, this time, coming from a broken heart and spoken with cracking voice, *"Pater"* sounds respectful and even tenderly affectionate. Tears should come to any father's eyes, imagining the circumstances out of which it is uttered and the brokenness of its expression.

In the end, perhaps all that a son or daughter has left is the calling out of "Father," "Daddy," "Dad." I have a parishioner whose adult daughter has a developmental disability. One day the daughter was involved in a serious car accident. Awakening from her unconsciousness at the hospital, she looked at her father and with tears in her eyes asked, "Daddy, am I dead?" Isn't this, in some sense, the question on the lips of the Prodigal Son? Isn't this the question every child at some point asks of his or her parent? Isn't that the question that we all, awakening from the sleep of death and seeing our Father for the very first time, will ask of him?

The Prodigal Son also showed his father great honor when next he actually confessed that he had sinned, both against God as well as against him. Taking responsibility for his actions, he began to undo the shame he had brought upon his father and family, and he showed he was still alive, if only barely. He signaled to his father that there was still some humanity left within him, that he was not dead.

Jesus then shifts the focus of his parable to the father. Living in the honor-shame culture in which they did, Jesus' audience would have brought their own expectations of how the father should have responded to and treated his belligerent son. These same expectations Jesus' hearers certainly would have projected onto God, his own heavenly Father. Confronting these judgments and overturning them is the whole point of the parable. And that is exactly what Jesus did.

Telling us that the father caught sight of his son while the son was still a long way off, Jesus is telling us that the father never stopped looking for him to return. The father didn't write his son off or simply wait for him to come back, as Mary did her little lamb in the familiar nursery rhyme. The father desired his son's return; he hoped for it; he willed it. His "seeing" him even from afar acts as a sort of gravitational pull upon his son; it was even the cause of the son's coming to himself and arising. As the psalmist proclaimed, "Truly the eye of the Lord is on those who fear him, on those who hope in his steadfast love, to deliver their soul from death, and to keep them alive in famine" (Ps 33:18-19). In this earthly father's "seeing," Jesus reveals that our heavenly Father is always looking for, hoping for, desiring, and willing our return, that his love is the cause, no matter how far we have wandered from him and the circumstances of our life, of our coming back to ourselves and rising to return home.

Note that the father never left his property, never set foot off it, never once ventured out in search of his son. Acknowledging his son's freedom, even though his son so grossly abused it, the father let him go. But out of his own freedom, a fatherly freedom, he had never stopped longing for his son to return. Even though physically he did not go after him, each day he ventured forth in his prayer and hope that someday he would see his son's return. Remaining true to himself and to his fatherhood, he proved himself true to both his lost son and to his whole household. (How different this parable is from Jesus' parable of the Good Shepherd, who leaves ninety-nine sheep that have not wandered astray to find the single one that has.)

When the father saw his son returning, his response violated every notion of honor and shame, respect and dignity that governed familial behavior at the time. In that context, first, the father certainly would not have been waiting for his son's return. The norms of honor and shame dictated that if such a son ever dared to return, his father should treat him as if he no longer had a son, as if the son instead was the one who was dead. At the very most, a father might deign to wait for the son to grovel and beg for mercy, demand that he pay back what he had taken, and then maybe consider how else to humiliate and punish him. Worse, he indeed might have actually treated him as a hired hand.

Not so this father. Seeing his son from afar, he ran to embrace him. In Jesus' time, running was child's play; no dignified adult ran. Running as eagerly as this father did over that great distance would have only lowered the father's standing in the judgment of his family, tribe, and associates and, if any further humiliation was even possible, added to the embarrassment and shame already brought upon him by his son. Now, however, exhausted by the grief from which he suffered at his son's departure, worn from his prayerful hoping, overwhelmed by the joy he felt seeing him alive, he could not help but do what would seem to us to be most natural in such circumstances—his own pride and others' expectations be damned! "Filled with compassion," Jesus tells us, the father yanked up his garments and took off running. (Traditional Palestinian dress then and now certainly did not facilitate athletic grace!) Reaching him, unable to control himself, he launched himself onto his son and began to kiss him fondly.

The Greek word for "kisses fondly" is *kataphileō*. It is the same word that St. Luke uses in chapter seven to describe the penitent woman kissing Jesus' feet at the banquet hosted by Simon the Pharisee. There Luke contrasts it with *philēma*, the kiss of welcome and respect Simon had failed to extend to Jesus upon his arrival at his home (7:45). Luke uses *kataphileō* in the Acts of the Apostles to describe the grieved weeping of the priests of Miletus at Paul's departure for Jerusalem (20:37). *Kataphileō* means more than a simple peck on the cheek. *Kataphileō* is uncontrolled, repeated, emotional, and affectionate kissing, kissing over and over and over again. It is slobbering all over another with one's kisses.

I used to have an Aunt Caroline. She was an eccentric woman, flamboyant in makeup and manner, and she lived in Milwaukee. She was one of my father's favorite aunts. Whenever she visited us in Denver, upon her arrival she mercilessly threw her arms around us children, smothered us in her enormous bosom (at least it seemed so to us!), and slobbered our faces with fat, wet kisses. We couldn't wait to break away and wash off her slobbering. This type of kissing is the same type of kissing with which the father kissed his Prodigal Son upon his return. He hung himself on his son's neck and affectionately, repeatedly slobbered him with fat, wet kisses. With his own saliva the father bathed his son, cleansed him from the dirt of his sins, and baptized him. (He gave the first spit bath ever recorded in history!) The mother of the Prodigal Son had first birthed him from the womb into the world; now his father brought him to a new birth from sin and death to life.

Let's pause a moment and consider something else going on between this father and his son. A person cannot breathe and speak at the same time. When one speaks he can only breathe out. To breathe in one must be silent or, at the very least, pause between words. At the beginning of our parable, the younger son was the only one of these two protagonists to speak; the father said nothing. The son, demanding his share of the inheritance, could only breathe out. He could not breathe in (preventing his father, in any case, from getting even a single word in edgewise), and so refused to breathe in his father's spirit. By not breathing in his father's spirit, he suffocated his father's spirit within himself. Unwilling to receive what his father desired to give to him, the son demanded inheritance and money instead. His father wanted to speak, to breathe into him his spirit. But the son refused to allow him to do so; he refused his father's word and so refused his father's spirit.

When, though, his own being had been reduced below that of pigs in squalor, the son heard his father's voice. He finally breathed in and received his spirit. Now, upon his return home, it is the father who refuses to allow his son to speak. The only words he permits his Prodigal Son to breathe out are words of confession. Then, perhaps having anticipated what his son would request of him, he interrupted him. The father would not allow him to breathe even a single word requesting servanthood. Servanthood would not be life for his son. Rather than the son breathing out words requesting servanthood, the father could finally breathe new life into him, could finally breathe his fatherly spirit into his son.

Continuing on, the father then performed three rites that completed and confirmed his son's "baptism" and reinitiation into the household.

First, having squandered everything, having lived with pigs, being one for whom no one cared, when he returned home the younger son was undoubtedly in rags, shamed even in nakedness. His father, though, didn't simply want to clothe him and cover his body. For that he could have taken off his own robe and placed it on him. After all, he had endured enough shaming as it was; his own nakedness would add no more. But the father, despite having been clothed in shame since his son's departure, chose to remain clothed in shame a little longer and to clothe his son with honor instead. So he ordered the servants to clothe the boy in the *prōtēn stolēn*, the "first robe." Not simply the "finest" (New American Bible) or "best" robe (New Revised Standard Version and The Jerusalem Bible), the *prōtēn stolēn* is the first robe, a new skin, new flesh, a new "housing" for his body. Jesus uses this image to teach that the father's love and forgiveness restored his son's humanity, his essence, his very being, resurrecting from the dead the boy who was now alive, and breathing into him a new spirit, making of him a new man. (When God the Father himself raised Jesus from the dead, it was certainly the *prōtēn stolēn* with which he clothed him.)

Additionally, the verb Jesus uses to describe the act of clothing, *enduō*, is the same word that the author of the letter to the Ephesians uses when he writes that we must "put away your former way of life, your old self, corrupt and deluded by its lusts, . . . cloth[ing] yourselves with the new self, created according to the likeness of God in true righteousness and holiness" (4:22-23). In that passage the epistle's author is drawing on the image of the Jewish *mikvah*, the ceremonial bathing pool into which a Jew was required to enter and bathe before approaching the temple. A Jew stripped completely naked, descended into the *mikvah* until all parts of his or her body, including one's hair, touched the water, and exited by a separate set of stairs. He or she then donned a white robe and, having been purified, entered into the temple precincts, into the dwelling place of God.

If Jesus' audience had been shocked by the behavior of the father heretofore, what he did next would have left them utterly speechless. The father ordered the servants to put a ring on his son's finger. In our own culture, the giving of a ring is usually motivated by reasons of romance and affection, as when, for example, engaged or married couples exchange rings, or children give their moms a birthstone keepsake. In ancient Mediterranean culture, however, the giving of a ring symbolized the giving of authority. For example, by placing a signet ring on Joseph's finger, Pharaoh bestowed on him the entire kingdom of Egypt (Gen 41:42). King Ahasuerus established Mordecai's authority over Haman's household by giving to him the latter's signet ring (Esth 8:2).

Having clothed his son with a new humanity, the father, in putting a signet ring on his son's finger, gave him authority over his entire household. Admittedly, we do not know what authority, if any, the son exercised in his father's household before he claimed his inheritance and departed. For all we know, he could have exercised none at all. Now, though, the father closed his ears to his son's request that he be hired day by day as a laborer. And he did not require his son to restore the property he had lost or work until he had paid back the full sum of what he had squandered. The father placed no conditions on the son's return and his acceptance back into the family. Quite to the contrary, to him who had demonstrated a complete incompetence to manage even his own possessions, the father now gave charge over the affairs of the estate. This son was certainly not that "faithful and wise slave, whom his master has put in charge of his household" (Matt 24:45), or the servant invited to share his master's joy because, having proven himself "good and trustworthy" in small matters, he was given charge of greater affairs (Matt 25:21-25). This was the nonsensical one, the ingrate, the yahoo who had heaped shame and scandal upon his father and family, who had compromised their social standing if not even threatened their very livelihood. Yet none of that diminished the father's love for his son; if anything, it increased it. Here was his beloved son; in him the father took great delight. Simply because he was his son the father placed on his son's finger a signet ring. Regardless of what the son had done, he would be neither a slave nor a day laborer. To the contrary, he would share in the governance of his household.

Fine, Jesus' audience might have said. As incredible as that sounds, we'll give you that one. But certainly the father, to protect himself and everyone else, must have ensured that never again would this impetuous one behave in such a way as to hurt the father and harm the household. Surely the father set up safeguards or imposed some conditions or restrictions on his son's return and on his authority. No, Jesus answers. God's ways are not man's ways, and this father's ways are not those of either business or commerce. What son would be a son if he were not free? He would indeed be nothing more than a slave. If the father was to have his son back, if the boy who was dead were to live again, then he must be free. So he ordered that he be shod with new sandals. Sandals are a symbol of freedom. Slaves were not shod, for if they were they could run away. Here the father of the Prodigal Son showed what risk he was taking in welcoming his son home. He risked that the son would again, at some point in the future, behave exactly as he had done before. In risking this, what the father truly risked was not simply that his son would again leave, not simply that his son would again shame him, but that the day would come when again his son would forget and cease to be grateful.

What, if anything, does a son or daughter owe to a father? Parents choose to bring children into the world; children do not choose to be born. The 1967 movie, *Guess Who's Coming to Dinner*, tells the story of Doctor Prentice, a black man, and Joanna, a white woman, who are engaged. Neither had introduced the other to his or her own parents. Nor are the parents aware of the race of their soon-to-be son- or daughter-in-law; all four are blissfully ignorant until introduced at a hastily arranged dinner party at Joanna's parents' home. It is not easy for any of the parents to accept that their children have chosen to wed outside their race, let alone a black man and a white woman. As such, Doctor Prentice's father at a certain point takes his son aside and asks him to call off the marriage. When he refuses, his father attempts to shame him into doing so by claiming that he owes it to his mother and to him. The young Doctor Prentice responds, "You tell me what rights I've got or haven't got and what I owe to you for what you've done for me. Let me tell you something. I owe you nothing. If you carried that bag a million miles you did what you were supposed to do because you brought me into this world and from that day you owed me everything you could ever do for me, like I will owe my son if I ever have another. But you don't own me. You can't tell me when or where I'm out of line or try to get me to live my life according to your rules."

Doctor Prentice's response to his father gives us an insight into the irony of the parable of the Prodigal Son. The father chose to bring his son into the world; the son didn't choose to be born. In demanding the inheritance, the younger son acted as a son had a legal right to act. Moreover, he showed total ingratitude for everything his father had been or had ever done for him. He broke the fourth commandment and dishonored him. All of this being true, still the father was a father. If he was to remain true to himself as a father, the burden was on him to give life again, even if the young son wasn't exactly choosing to be reborn, hoping to become a hired hand, wanting simply to eat and survive. The father didn't own him but never stopped owing him everything, that is, he never stopped owing him his fatherhood. And so, despite the son's ingratitude for all his father was and did for him, the father nonetheless was grateful that the young man was his son. He took the risk of losing him a second time, but it was a risk he had to take. If he were to be a true father, he had to restore his son's freedom without parole and without conditions.

Before moving on and turning our attention to the ministry of the deacon, teasing out of this parable a few insights that might prove valuable in understanding his relationship as a deacon to his heavenly Father, a relationship at one and the same time of both sonship and servanthood, let's note a few final things about the relationship between the father and his Prodigal Son.

First, note that in the entire parable the father never actually spoke to the younger son, not even a single word. The younger son twice called his father *"Pater."* But nowhere did the father address his younger son as "Son" or actually declare him restored to sonship. Why not? From the perspective of the father, the son had never died, he had never ceased being his son. Understandably, until he caught sight of him upon his return, he mourned his son's departure. Jesus tells us that upon the son's return the father was "filled with compassion" (vs. 20). The word that Jesus uses, *esplagchnisthē*, is the same verb that in Greek is used to describe a mother's joy at giving birth to her baby. The father had been in labor pains until his son came to his senses and returned home. Nothing more needed to be said or done to restore the relationship between them.

Second, although nothing was required to restore the son's sonship, for he had never lost it, the father nonetheless ritualized his son's new life. In giving him the first robe, the father restored his son's humanity and dignity; giving him a signet ring restored his place and authority in the family; putting sandals on his feet, the father restored his son's freedom. Through these three rites he taught his son that his true freedom lay not in being free from his father, but rather, precisely, in being his father's son and at his father's side. The young son, in demanding his father's goods, had really rejected his father's goodness. The father, in reconciling, showed himself to be not simply wealthy in the ownership of land and possessions, but truly rich in goodness and free to share from its abundance. Reconciling his son to himself, the father invited the young man to accept the dignity of sonship.

Finally, the Prodigal Son demanded his share of the father's inheritance and wound up living in the squalor of pigs. For his part, Christ demanded nothing of his Father's glory. He so honored his Father that he even accepted the Father's mission to rescue Adam, his own Prodigal Son, living in the squalor of the pigsty known as hell. The Prodigal Son demanded what was rightfully his by earthly law and wound up losing everything. The eternal Son demanded nothing of what was rightfully his by heavenly law, and received everything in return. Christ, clothed in the first robe of his resurrection, wearing the signet ring of the kingship of heaven and earth, and shod with the sandals of divine sonship now willingly shares it all with all who come to their senses, leave the squalor of sin, and return home to their Father.

Actions Speak Louder than Words

From the father's quiet behavior toward his Prodigal Son, from the son himself, and even from the father's household servants, a deacon can learn much about his own relationship with God, about his new friendship with the Father.

First, because God calls one to be a deacon, the deacon does not cease to be first of all God's son. From the Prodigal Son, then, a deacon can learn to not go looking to his heavenly Father for anything other than the Father's fatherhood and the deacon's sonship. He should not look for the wrong things, for what is really too little, for what he doesn't really need, for what fails to satisfy his deepest spiritual needs. Instead, the deacon must let Jesus, in whose image he has been ordained, breathe into him his own Spirit, his Spirit of suffering servanthood. To do that, unlike the Prodigal Son, the deacon has to let Jesus "get a word in edgewise," speak, and breathe into him his Spirit. A deacon has to have faith that the Father is good, in the Father's goodness, and declare his Father to be very much alive. God already knows what one needs even before one asks (see Matt 6:8). A deacon will not be able to teach sinners and the poor to rely fully on God as their Father if he and his household do not do so. A good deacon, therefore, recognizes his own poverty and trusts God to provide for all of his needs.

Like the son in the parable, though, unfortunately, deacons too are sinners. Simply because he is ordained a deacon he does not cease to be a sinner; sinlessness is not one of the graces of diaconal ordination. In truth, the deacon must remember that as a deacon he is even more the target of Satan's machinations and temptations. The devil is among the first to understand the potential of this sacrament for the new evangelization. He is not pleased with the restoration of the diaconate as a permanent state of life and ministry in the church, nor is he pleased with anyone's ordination to the diaconate. The last thing he wants is for the light of Christ, the Suffering Servant, to burn more ardently and widely across the world and in the hearts of the poor.

A good deacon, therefore, abhors even the thought of evil and is repentant. Repentance requires coming to one's senses, that is, honesty in self-knowledge and the courage of self-acceptance. Despite whatever sin, a deacon, like the Prodigal Son, must, "rising," "come to himself" and, through frequent use of the sacrament of reconciliation, return to his Father's home. He is a better deacon to the extent that he is a repentant son. And he is a humble son to the extent that when lost in sin he allows himself to be found, when dead he allows himself to be raised.

Moreover, a deacon can learn several important lessons from the servants in the father's household. In the parable, it was the father and not the servants who saw the Prodigal Son from afar, it was the father and not the servants who ran out to meet him. Then, having welcomed his son back home, the father turned to his slaves and ordered them to clothe him, to put a signet ring on his finger, to shoe his feet, and to prepare the celebratory banquet. These servants teach us that a deacon's role is to affirm and celebrate reconciliation between God and his sons and daughters, which through the cross of Jesus Christ has already been achieved, and to aid his brothers and sisters to live in the freedom and dignity that divine reconciliation engenders. God the Father calls the deacon to be the light that enables sinners and the poor to escape from whatever dissolute living and squalor they are in and from whatever foreign land into which they may have wandered. The deacon is called to be the light in which sinners and the poor arise as sons and daughters of God and return to their Father and their Father's house, the church. It pertains to the deacon, as it did to the servants in the parable, to clothe sinners and the poor, put signet rings on their fingers, shoe their feet, and prepare the banquet celebrating their new life.

Regarding the *prōtēn stolēn*, the first robe—Christ himself has clothed the deacon in the *prōtēn stolēn* of Christian dignity in virtue of his being baptized and confirmed, reconciled through penance, nourished with the Eucharist, and by the laying on of hands. In turn, the deacon clothes the poor in the *prōtēn stolēn*, helping them to be faithful to their baptismal promises, to know their dignity in Christ, and to be reconciled from sin. In his ministry, the deacon will more and more come to understand that sin is the cause of every poverty, especially the squalor of that spiritual poverty we bring on ourselves when we enter into our own self-imposed exiles from our Father and our Father's house. Therefore, the deacon must, in the first place, confront sin. For this reason God commissions him to help the poor address the causes that give rise to the spiritual poverty of their lives, their own sinfulness. He is to partner with the poor so as to acquire a new way of thinking, to put on that new man who is Jesus Christ, and approach the living God. But God also commissions the deacon to address the structures of sin and injustice that give rise to the many forms of emotional, material, and social poverty in our world.

As did the servants in the father's household, in his ministry a deacon places the signet ring of authority on those he serves. By the fact that all human persons are created in the image and likeness of God, in order to be fully human we need to reflect the divine Creator's image to others. This is the authority we exercise over ourselves and over one another. When we do not reflect the image of the One who created us, the result is that we actually alienate ourselves from ourselves, we create a rift within our own personhood, and we break apart. This lack of self-unity, which is the shame Adam and Eve felt before God and the other, is one of the rotten fruits of original sin and a bitter fruit of every sin. Deacons are called to restore to sinners, the poor, and the suffering their dignity, helping them both to recover their unity of self and personhood, their personal integrity and dignity lost due to sin, and to be reconciled and reunited with the church and with her members in its community, restored to their rightful place in the household of God. A deacon helps sinners and the poor to know, in other words, that the church loves and cares for them.

Finally, in the parable of the Prodigal Son, the servants in the father's household are servants of the son's freedom. To restore another's freedom in Christ is the very *raison d'être* of diaconal service. This requires the deacon to be a man of great humility. Humility is the virtue by which one shows himself or herself to be most open to the other, to the other's very being, to *communio* with another. Humility is also that virtue which prevents one's diaconal service (and all ministerial service) from becoming simply the exercise of "technique" rather than the expression of genuine love. For true love is always humble.

In the parable, the father's servants could only obey his order to put sandals on his young son's feet when they themselves had first knelt down on the ground and bowed before the lad who had sinned against and shamed their beloved master. Likewise, the deacon must be willing, as the author of Ephesians exhorted his readers, to bow before others out of reverence for Christ (Eph 5:21), and especially to kneel before sinners and the poor. Through his servitude, sinners and the poor may come to know their own true freedom as sons and daughters of God.

How did the servants in the parable come to be so loyal and obedient? They must have seen in the Father as their master what both of his sons failed to see in him as their father and so judged him to be merely a master. They saw that even though he was their master he loved them as a father. The younger son failed to see it, and so he left his father's house. The older son failed to see it and so, having returned from the fields, just as shamefully refused to enter into his father's joy. Both sons refused to acknowledge their dependence on the father and so, paradoxically, neither came to know true freedom.

The younger son embraced the false freedom of autonomy. Believing he could only be free when his father was dead, the younger son enslaved himself to unholy people (Gentiles) and to unclean animals (pigs). Having squandered his freedom, in the end he wound up simply living as an animal. The older son also embraced a false freedom, which he believed to be the escape from his self-imprisoned victimhood. He believed that he could only be free when everyone saw how his father treated him, how he suffered at his father's hands, and that his father never even gave him a kid goat with which to celebrate with his friends. He wanted everyone to believe (contrary to the truth) that he himself was a victim and to pity him. (Isn't this how it is with so many in their relationship with God? They ask, rhetorically, "Why does God do this to me? If only I could understand why God was punishing me like this, wouldn't I then be free of God?") The older son had enslaved himself to ingratitude, to what he believed was an injustice toward him, to anger, and to his own unwillingness to forgive.

Herein, then, lies the difference between the father's sons and his servants. As any slaves, these slaves were dependent on their master and his benevolence. Before the tragic events of this parable, these servants must have observed how the father lovingly treated his sons. Certainly after those events played out, they watched as he longingly, hopefully, waited for the Prodigal Son to return. Even as slaves they had come to know their owner-master as a father. They too had come to love him as a father. Even though they were slaves, because he was a father they had come to know that they were truly free. There is no way else to understand their quick obedience of his commands, their successful gathering of family and community for the celebration, and their proclamation to others of the good news of the father's joy at having his younger son home. They shared their master's joy. The author of the letter to the Ephesians exhorted slaves, and deacons are wise to heed his counsel: "[D]o the will of God from the heart. Render service with enthusiasm, as to the Lord and not to men and women" (Eph 6:7).

In the parable, the younger son had fled his father's house ungrateful. Ungrateful, too, was the older son, who never left the property but nonetheless refused to enter in. As God's sons deacons must make gratitude their attitude of mind and heart; they must be always grateful. They must be grateful that Christ has clothed them with the robes of Christian dignity and the vestments of diaconal office and ministry, that he has accorded them diaconal authority over his own household and their fellow servants, that Christ has himself set a banquet of finest food for the deacon and for all. Gratitude is the mother of humility and one of the characteristics of life that a candidate must evince to demonstrate the sincerity of his vocation and that after ordination marks a genuinely lived diaconal life. In being grateful, then, a deacon shows that he is both God's son and God's servant, both a son of the church and the church's deacon. He shows that he has earned the first title with which the bishop addressed him at his ordination: "My son." In gratitude he shows himself to be God's new friend. In gratitude he teaches sinners, the poor, and the suffering how to be grateful sons and daughters of God.

Finally, the father ordered his servants to kill the fatted calf and prepare a banquet, the celebration meal of his rebirth. We can intimate from this order something of the deacon's role in the Eucharist, and regarding this role I will say more later. But for now, let me note simply that it pertains to the deacon to celebrate life and to assist the whole community to do the same. He himself must love life and be in love with living. He must love people and enjoy their community. St. Irenaeus of Lyons taught that the glory of God is man fully alive. If this is true, a deacon gives glory to our Father in heaven when on earth he leads the poor to a life that is full and in the celebration of life. Notice in the gospel parable what the father did not require of his Prodigal Son. After the son confessed his sin, the father did not chastise him. He did not demand an accounting of his life or of the lost property. Nor did he require his son to repay the squandered inheritance. He would have none of that. No, he was a father and so he celebrated.

Immediately preceding our parable of the Prodigal Son, Jesus told another story of a woman who, finding a lost coin, called her friends and neighbors together to rejoice. Like this poor woman, the deacon, in the name of Christ the Suffering Servant and because of his unique iconic vocation to love, should know joy in life, be joyful because of life, and gather the lost into the joyful celebration of new life. The deacon restores to the Father and to the church what has been lost. Having been found, he leads them to the celebration of their Father's joy.

Let the party begin.

chapter two

The Deacon, Servant of the Father Who Speaks

The Father Speaks; the Son is Spoken.
The Deacon Hears the Father's Voice and Proclaims the Word.
The Deacon's Munus Docendi, *the Office of Teaching.*

In this chapter I want to consider the relationship between God the Father, who speaks, and the deacon. How are we to understand the relationship between the two? First, we must consider the nature of the Trinity itself. Next we will look to Mary, who is the model par excellence of all relationships with God and of all Christian discipleship. Then we will look briefly at that part of the ordination rite, the presentation of the candidate, through which a deacon gives himself to the Lord and the church for their service. We will also explore those ministries of the deacon at the Eucharist that serve God's Word being spoken. Finally, we will conclude this reflection by considering a few spiritual aids to keep God's Word alive in a deacon's heart.

The Trinity: *Communio* of Love and Honor

Since we are considering the relationship of the deacon to each of the persons of the Trinity, we should begin by considering the Trinity itself—

who is it; what is its nature? Unfortunately, this is neither the time nor the place for an extended doctrinal consideration of this central mystery of our Christian faith. Here I can offer only limited consideration of a few foundational points on which to build our more extended reflections on the diaconate.

If someone were to ask us to define the Trinity, we would be hard-pressed to do so. An all-embracing definition of the Trinity is impossible; it is a mystery and therefore of its nature incomprehensible. We could have no insight into the Trinity except for the fact that Jesus Christ has revealed it to us. But what Jesus has revealed we can come to love. Although we cannot fully comprehend the Trinity, we can love it. What we are unable to grasp, we can nonetheless allow to grasp us; we can give ourselves over to it.

Some of us may remember what the *Baltimore Catechism* taught about the Trinity, in questions 27–30.

> Q. What do you mean by the Blessed Trinity?
>
> A. By the Blessed Trinity I mean one God in three Divine Persons.
>
> Q. Are the three Divine Persons equal in all things?
>
> A. The three Divine Persons are equal in all things.
>
> Q. Are the three Divine Persons one and the same God?
>
> A. The three Divine Persons are one and the same God, having one and the same divine nature and substance. Though they are one and the same, we sometimes attribute different works to them. For example, works of creation we attribute to God the Father; works of mercy to God the Son; and works of love and sanctification to the Holy Ghost; and you will often find them thus spoken of in pious books; but all such works are done by all the Persons of the Trinity; because such works are the works of God, and there is but one God.
>
> Q. Can we fully understand how the three Divine Persons are one and the same God?
>
> A. We cannot fully understand how the three Divine Persons are one and the same God, because this is a mystery. "Fully"—entirely. We can partly understand it. We know what one God is and we know what three persons are; but how these two things go together is the part we do not understand—the mystery.

"How these things go together is the part we do not understand" is an understatement, indeed!

The *Catechism of the Catholic Church*, quoting the Council of Florence, teaches us that in the Trinity "everything . . . is one where there is no opposition of relationship. Because of that unity the Father is wholly in the Son and wholly in the Holy Spirit; the Son is wholly in the Father and wholly in the Holy Spirit; the Holy Spirit is wholly in the Father and wholly in the Son" (255). The *Catechism* sums up its introduction to the Trinity with these words: "Inseparable in what they are, the divine persons are also inseparable in what they do" (267).

One of the words—perhaps the preferred word—the church uses to describe this inseparability of being and acting is *communio*. The Trinity is a *communio* of persons. Looked at positively, the three divine persons exist and act for the sake of the other. This being and acting for each other's sake is total, fecund, and eternal. It is *total*. The Trinity's very *being* is a *communio* of love. We call this the immanent Trinity, meaning the Trinity that exists in and for itself without reference to acting outside of itself when it creates, redeems, and sanctifies. It is *fecund*. Its *acting* is love that gives life beyond itself. We call this the economic Trinity, meaning the Trinity that pours out its love onto what it creates, redeems, and sanctifies. Its creatures therefore participate in the Trinity's life not by nature but by grace. It is *eternal*. Because the Trinity is love and loves, there is no limitation of either space or time to its divine being or its acting. "Love looks to the eternal," Pope Benedict XVI teaches in his encyclical *Deus caritas est* (6). Looked at negatively, *communio* in the Trinity means, as the *Catechism* teaches, that between the three persons there is "no opposition of relationship."

What is *communio*? Let's consider what *communio* means by making reference to marriage vows, something familiar to the vast majority of deacons. In a gospel passage proclaimed at many wedding ceremonies, Jesus teaches, "This is my commandment, that you love one another as I have loved you. No one has greater love than this, to lay down one's life for one's friends" (John 15:12-13). In fulfillment of this command, a groom and a bride vow to each other, "I promise to be true to you. . . . I will love you and honor you all the days of my life." In any authentic friendship, and especially in the unique friendship that is marriage, these three elements—truth, love, and honor—must always be present. These are the three elements that make up *communio*.

At their simplest, or better yet, at their foundational level, love is giving and honor is receiving. To love is to give oneself as gift; to honor is to receive as gift the other who gives oneself. A married couple deeply in love, however, especially one that has loved for many years of better and worse, sickness and health, richness and poverty, knows that loving and honoring go well beyond the sense of transactional exchange that giving and receiving can imply. Loving and honoring by their very nature must be wedded to truth. When they are, they create between the lovers what St. Thomas Aquinas called "friendship love."

One who loves with friendship love doesn't simply give to the other. In friendship love one yearns for, delights in, gratefully gazes upon, and possesses the other in joy. One accepts in humble reverence the wonder of the other's very being and treasures the other simply because he or she is. One loves the reality of the other's being, not the experience of it for oneself. To love with friendship love is, on one hand, to will that the other know truth, and, on the other hand, to will the other's holiness and goodness in truth. True love wills not simply that one's beloved receive good things but that one's beloved be good. One who truly loves wills not simply that one's beloved receive justice but that one's beloved know the true freedom that sets us free (see John 8:32, 36). One who loves the other gives to the other the integrity of the truth. One who loves with friendship love, in a word, wills that the other be holy, as the Father in heaven is holy (see Matt 5:48).

To honor in friendship love means in the first place to receive, to welcome, the other. Honoring another goes well beyond simply tolerating the other's existence or merely accepting his or her person. (This is the extent of that tolerance that is the pseudo virtue of the politically correct. It neither invites nor offers *communio*.) Rather, when one honors another one receives and welcomes the other. One receives the other into oneself because the other makes the recipient better. And one receives the other not solely for one's own sake, but for the sake of others besides. When one honors another he or she recognizes the good of the other, appropriates that goodness for oneself, and expresses the truth about the one whom one honors to others. Honor is like praise. We praise the good of another so as to participate in that goodness ourselves. When we acknowledge the good of another, we are made better for doing so. When we honor another because he or she is good, we are made honorable. In a word, then, to honor is to hold up one's beloved, appropriate the other's goodness for oneself, and declare the other's worth to all.

In his encyclical *Humanae vitae*, Pope Paul VI taught that married love that is "total [is] that very special form of personal friendship in which husband and wife generously share everything, allowing no unreasonable exceptions and not thinking solely of their own convenience. Whoever really loves his partner loves not only for what he receives, but loves that partner for the partner's own sake, content to be able to enrich the other with the gift of himself" (9). That is why, in part, a husband pays his wife the highest honor when he desires that she be the mother of his children, and she pays him the highest honor when she desires that he be the father of hers. On one hand, to call forth the fatherhood or the motherhood of one's beloved is to call forth the richest image of God himself, whom Jesus reveals to us to be a life-giving Father. On the other hand, to hold up one's spouse to one's children as an exemplar of holiness and goodness is the greatest act of honor one can pay to the other.

Apply these images to the Trinity. The Father loves his only-begotten Son and delights in him. He yearns for him, he treasures him, he rejoices in him. Everything that the Father is and has he gives to his Son, emptying himself, pouring himself out to his Son and for his Son. The Son honors his Father and he empties himself so as to receive him, to receive all he is and has. He even goes so far in honoring his Father that he accepts his Father's will and by the power of their Holy Spirit takes on our human nature. The Father, both at Jesus' baptism and at the Transfiguration, revealed his own personal delight in Jesus, honoring him with the titles of "Beloved Son" (Mark 9:7; Matt 17:5) and "Chosen" (Luke 9:35). On the cross, too, the Father glorified Christ, desiring him to be alive in human flesh, and so raised him from the dead in the Spirit, seating him at his own right hand.

The Trinity shares its truthful loving and honoring, its divine *communio*, with what it creates through the great mysteries of creation, redemption, and sanctification. This sharing is willed by the Father, accomplished in Jesus Christ, and perpetuated by the Holy Spirit. From the outset it must be made clear that creaturely participation in uncreated *communio* is only possible through and by the grace poured out in Jesus Christ. "No one," Christ himself proclaimed, "comes to the Father except through me" (John 14:6). Christ, St. Paul wrote,

> is the image of the invisible God, the firstborn of all creation; for in him all things in heaven and on earth were created, things visible and invisible, whether thrones or dominions or rulers or powers—all things have been created through him and for him. He himself is before all things, and in him all things hold together. He is the head of the body, the church; he is the beginning, the firstborn from the dead, so that he might come to have first place in everything. For in him all the fullness of God was pleased to dwell, and through him God was pleased to reconcile to himself all things, whether on

earth or in heaven, by making peace through the blood of his cross. (Col 1:15-20)

In moving outside of itself—in moving, if you will, from immanence to economy—the Trinity reveals that it doesn't create simply so that its creatures might be. God doesn't create his creatures simply that they might be alone. God has created and so redeemed and sanctified the whole of creation and all creatures with the capacity to participate in the divine *communio* out of which and for which he creates them. The Trinity creates whatever it creates so that its creatures might live with him, participate in his own *communio*, be, in other words, in a total, fecund, and eternal relationship with him *and* with all else that he has willed into being. *Communio* has both a vertical dimension, that is, with each of the persons of the Trinity, and a horizontal dimension, that is with everything else the Trinity creates. "For what can be known about God is plain . . . , because God has shown it. . . . Ever since the creation of the world his eternal power and divine nature, invisible though they are, have been understood and seen through the things he has made" (Rom 1:19-20). Indeed God wills that "Christ is all and in all" (Col 3:11).

This capacity for *communio* is uniquely true of the human person, who alone of all earthly creatures God created in his own divine image and likeness. In Christ Jesus, through whom and for whom all things were made (see Col 1:15-17), the human person, innocent and pure, that is, as he was created before the Fall and restored to that state through baptism into the death and resurrection of Christ, is by God's grace made capable of and invited into *communio* with God. Moreover, God loves us to such an unfathomable degree—"For indeed our God is a consuming fire" (Heb 12:29)—that in sharing his divine *communio* with us, as the burning bush in the desert out of which God revealed his name, his being, to Moses was aflame but not consumed, God does not consume us in loving us. As at the sight of the burning bush Moses turned from his earthly preoccupations and daily work to discover why the bush was not burned up, how the flame and the bush could exist together, so too does our Creator invite us to the flame of divine *communio* and to discover that we are not to end up in ashes.

Adam and Eve were seduced into believing that in their relationship with God they would be consumed and left in ashes. They refused to love and honor God and they sinned. They rejected *communio* with God. Still, "where sin increased," St. Paul said, "grace abounded all the more" (Rom 5:20). God did not turn from Adam and Eve. To the contrary he turned even more intently toward them. Again God gave himself by sending Jesus in the likeness of Adam and Eve, offering his *communio* to their children, and teaching them that if they loved, if they accepted divine *communio*, they would be not consumed but freed. Once redeemed, so that men and women might not again turn away from but live for him who redeemed them, yet again the Father and the Son offered humans *communio* and gave them their Holy Spirit.

Let's summarize. The Trinity is a *communio* of persons who eternally, entirely, and with fecundity love and honor one another. Because the Father, the Son, and the Holy Spirit are truly unique, their unity is a real "friendship love" of giving and receiving, of being and acting for the other. In being for the other, each divine person mutually and freely chooses the other out of love and honor and is freely chosen by the other. Then, as the Trinity abounds in the delight that each of the persons takes in the other, it overflows: it creates, reveals, redeems, and sanctifies, sharing its very delight with all creation. Surprisingly, incredibly, the Trinity enables and invites its creatures to share in its personal, divine, intimate *communio*, to share in the delight it takes in each of the other of the divine persons. *Communio*, then, both for God and analogously for human beings, is not just a style of living. *Communio*, sharing the divine delight, is the very essence of being and the way of all creation. As Thomas Merton said, commenting on Jesus' prayer at the Last Supper that all may be one as he is one with the Father, "Jesus is saying that those who reach perfect union with God, in Himself, will be as much One with God by grace as He is One with the Father by Nature" (*The Ascent to Truth*, p. 194).

Communio, then, is a deacon's being and ministry. The deacon is the icon of the Son's suffering love even as the Son himself is the icon of the Father's honoring love. The deacon is called to be in and to live this *communio*, and to lead others, especially sinners and the poor, into their own intimate relationship with God. This is the essence of diaconal life and ministry, that, as the icon of Christ's suffering servanthood he serves others so as to lead them into divine *communio*—with the Trinity, the church, and all creation.

The Trinity and the Blessed Virgin Mary

It is important for a deacon to be in a loving relationship with the Blessed Virgin Mary, the mother of the Suffering Servant of God. She is the "burning bush" whom God has consumed in love and whose very being proclaims his greatness; from the moment of her conception she was enraptured by divine *communio*. Through her glorious assumption into heaven the blessed Trinity has welcomed her totally and eternally into its *communio*. She is the Mother of the church, who gathers in her mantle the *anawim*, the poor dispersed ones of the Lord. She is the model of all *diaconia*. We do well, then, to look to her, contemplate her relationship to the Trinity, and consider her service to *communio*.

Let's begin our consideration of Mary by asking: Would it have made any sense for God to create so as to share his divine *communio* with his creature without endowing the creature with the capacity for *communio* in the first place? In other words, would it have made sense for God to create his creatures without the capacity to receive what he wanted to give to them?

To answer our questions we need to return to the beginning. The book of Genesis reveals that, except for the second day, at the end of each of the first six days of creating, God judged what he had created on each of those days to be good. On the sixth day, God "saw everything that he had made, and indeed, it was very good" (Gen 1:31). This creaturely goodness is itself the capacity to know and enter into divine *communio*. But of what does this judgment of goodness consist? What does it mean to be "very good"?

An original Hebrew understanding of goodness was "to draw near." For example, the psalmist sang, "But for me it is good to be near God; I have made the Lord GOD my refuge" (Ps 73:28). In the Gospel of Mark the rich young man addressed Jesus as "Good Teacher," to which Jesus responded, "Why do you call me good? No one is good but God alone" (10:18). Jesus was affirming that no one is near to God but God himself. So, then, when God judged his creation to be good, God revealed that what he created, he had created to be capable of receiving him and drawing near.

This begs the question, however: With what specifically did the Creator endow his creatures so that they in their own right would be able to receive him and draw near? What did God give to the human person, making it possible to honor God and to love him, and so to share in his *communio*? The answer is freedom. God graced the human person with freedom. Because we are free (I am speaking of our baptismal state of life), we can know that God loves us and we can freely choose to love and honor God in return. Graced by God with human freedom, we are capable of choosing *communio*. It is within the very nature of the human person, endowed with created grace, to be able to cooperate with grace and so appropriate the Trinity's gifts of creation, redemption, and sanctification, sharing in divine *communio*.

St. Paul used another word for this freedom when he wrote to the Ephesians that "in Christ Jesus our Lord . . . we have access to God in boldness and confidence through faith in him" (3:11-12). The Greek word he uses for "boldness" is *parrēsian*. This word can mean freedom in speaking; free and fearless confidence; or a cheerful courage, boldness, or assurance. Paul even applied it specifically to deacons when, in his first letter to Timothy, he wrote that "those who serve well as deacons gain a good standing for themselves and great boldness [*parrēsian*] in the faith that is in Christ Jesus" (3:13). The author of the letter to the Hebrews also wrote, "Therefore, my friends, since we have confidence [*parrēsian*] to enter the sanctuary by the blood of Jesus, by the new and living way that he opened for us through the curtain (that is, through his flesh), and since we have a great priest over the house of God, let us approach with a true heart in full assurance of faith, with our hearts sprinkled clean from an evil conscience and our bodies washed with pure water" (10:19-22).

Let us look specifically at Adam and Eve. Upon creating them, God himself had judged them to be "very good." The three had quite a natural and easy relationship with one another. In fact, so natural was their goodness, their drawing near to each other, that God, Adam, and Eve—all three—at the breezy time of the day walked around naked in Eden's garden. So natural was their goodness, their drawing near to each other, that when Adam and Eve sinned God did not "know" it; nor did God assume the worst. He could not find them until they confessed that they were ashamed of their nakedness and were hiding. Sin had destroyed their natural ease of relating to God; in their shame they hid themselves from him.

The rest of the Old Testament from that point on can be read as the history of God's never-ending search to find them, to find man who, ashamed, hid himself from God. The entire Bible records God's desire to draw near to his human creatures and God's repeated attempts, culminating in Jesus Christ, to grace them so as to recover the natural ease of their relationship, to recover *communio*. As Cardinal Ratzinger wrote, "[In] fact . . . the Old Testament knows of no 'communion' between God and man; the New Testament *is* this communion, in and through the Person of Jesus Christ" (*Behold the Pierced One*, p. 85).

Then one day in God's never-ending search for man, there came to his eye Mary. In Genesis, God judged what he created on the first five days to be good, but what he made on the sixth day was indeed "very good" (Gen 1:31). Analogously, although God loves all that he has created, Mary is his "favored one" (Luke 1:28). In her sinlessness Mary was indeed judged to be "very good." Delighting in what he saw in her, henceforth not only God himself but fittingly "all generations will call [her] blessed" (Luke 1:48).

What specifically about Mary attracted the Lord's eye and "won" her his favor? What was her beauty that caught his attention? It was her freedom, her cheerful courage, her free and fearless confidence. God did not impose himself on her, who was his daughter. Rather he revealed his fatherhood to her and invited her to share fully in his own *communio*. Indeed, so all-encompassing and intimate was this *communio* into which God invited Mary that when she consented to Gabriel's greeting, in the intimacy of her *fiat*, at the moment of the overshadowing of the Holy Spirit and the conception of Jesus, she who was daughter of the Father became also spouse of the Holy Spirit and mother of the Son. As St. Paul said of the deacon, so it can be said of Mary that she gained "a good standing for [herself] and great boldness in the faith that is in Christ Jesus."

Mary's gift of self to the Father for the Son by the Holy Spirit represents humanity's, and therefore all of nature's, greatest act of responsibility. In her *fiat*, Mary proved herself to be the responsible one. The word "responsible" is rooted in the Latin *res* and *pons*, meaning reality (or truth) and bridge. The subject of a responsible act "bridges" himself or herself to the object of the act, uniting together both the subject and the object through the act. (For example, painters who paint "responsibly" construct a bridge between themselves and those who look upon their work, uniting them all, not to the painting as such, but rather to the *res*, the subject, the truth whose image they have re-presented, re-created on canvas.) In her freely given *fiat*, her "let it be done to me according to your word," Mary built a bridge back to being itself, to God, who is love. She united herself as the subject of the act with its object, God himself. She is like the ramp of Noah's ark, over which all creation makes its way onto the ark so that it might be saved from the flood waters brought about by humanity's wickedness and corruption. But she too is the ramp of that same ark over which creation exits, that it might live on the earth, fertile and multiplying, as God had intended from the beginning. Mary's responsibility to God overcame Adam and Eve's lack thereof.

Mary teaches us that at the heart of Christian life, and therefore *diaconia*, is responsibility. Freedom is the ground because of which God judges humankind to be very good and because of which humankind can draw near to him. Responsibility is the bridge over which one exercises one's freedom and gives oneself back to God, who has drawn near to us. In Christ, to be responsible is to use one's freedom, as Mary did, for the sake of *communio*. God created us to be free not so that we can do whatever we want but so that we can draw near to him, know his fatherly goodness, know divine *communio*. The responsible use of one's freedom, then, is to love and honor God *and* to love and honor the other whom God loves and honors. "This was in accordance with the eternal purpose that [God] has carried out in Christ Jesus our Lord, in whom we have access to God in boldness and confidence through faith in him" (Eph 3:12).

The Deacon's Vocational Presence to the Word of God

"Welcome with meekness the implanted word that has the power to save your souls. But be doers of the word, and not merely hearers who deceive themselves" (Jas 1:21-22).

In the Trinity, both immanently and economically, it is the Father who speaks and the Son who is spoken. What does the Father speak? He speaks the *Logos*, the Word that is Jesus. But as we have seen, when the Father speaks, what he speaks is both the *Logos* and his *communio* with the *Logos*. Voicing his Son's sonship the Father voices his own fatherhood. The deacon is called to hear the voice of the One speaking, to be a servant of God who speaks and of God's Word being spoken. The deacon is called to be a servant of God's fatherhood spoken in the Son, Jesus Christ.

Having been freed by Christ in baptism, once ordained, a deacon obediently serves God's Word. Unlike a slave who is captured, sold, and bought, a deacon makes himself freely "present" and takes up the duties and obligations of Christian service responsibly. "Let the same mind be in you that was in Christ Jesus," St. Paul taught. "Though he was in the form of God, [he] did not regard equality with God as something to be exploited, but emptied himself, taking the form of a slave, being born in human likeness" (Phil 2:5-7).

Obedience to God's Word and Christian service are sources of friendship. To the Twelve Christ said, "I do not call you servants any longer, because the servant does not know what the master is doing; but I have called you friends, because I have made known to you everything that I have heard from my Father" (John 15:15). Of himself, too, St. Paul said, "For though I am free with respect to all, I have made myself a slave to all, so that I might win more of them" (1 Cor 9:19). At ordination Christ extends to the deacon a new friendship. But to live in this friendship, the deacon must assume Christ's own attitude of willing and unhesitant service. It is this attitude he must bring to his ordination. This is one of the first characteristics of his new friendship with God.

In the first book of Samuel, chapter 3, we read a story that gives to us the prototype of all ecclesial vocation. It is the story of the prophet Samuel, a young man, who "was ministering to the Lord." Yet, even though ministering to the Lord, Samuel "did not yet know the Lord, and the word of the Lord had not yet been revealed to him" (3:7). Why not? Because "the word of the Lord was rare in those days; visions were not widespread" at that time (3:1). One night, though, the Lord called Samuel. Being unfamiliar with the Lord, Samuel mistakenly believed that it was his master, Eli, who was calling him. "Here I am," the young Samuel affirmed, awakening the sleeping Eli, "for you called me" (3:5).

"Here I am, for you called me." Let us take a look at the ordination rite of the deacon, because it brings out the dynamic of his obedient response to God's Word. Interestingly, in the conversation between the bishop and representatives of the local church by which he offers himself for that church's service, the candidate for ordination has only one word to pronounce, "Present."

Like young Samuel, it is safe to say that a deacon-candidate at the time of his ordination is already a minister to the Lord. In "boldness" and "confidence" he is brought to his ordination and accompanied there by his *ecclesia domestica*, that is, his family, and by his friends in the church. Symbolically, through the entrance procession, they present him—their son, husband, father, grandfather, and friend—to the bishop. (Although not necessary, it is appropriate if one's wife and immediate family accompany the deacon-candidate into the assembled community.) Then, following the proclamation of the gospel, a dialogue that in some sense sums up diaconal ministry begins. A priest calls the deacon-candidate by name. (Ideally the deacon-candidate's pastor as the representative of his local parish community should be the one who presents him to the bishop.) Having been brought by family and friends, now he must speak for himself, making his presence and his resolve his own. He responds with but a single word, "Present." This is the only word he says. With this "Present," however, he says everything. He avers, "I have nothing to offer, nothing to give, but myself. All that I am and all that I have—my history and heritage, my strength and weakness, my faith and fidelity—I give. All that by God's grace I have become and all that I am about I bring here to this place, to this moment, to this community, to this church, to the Lord. Here I am. You called me."

With his "Present" the deacon-candidate affirms three things. First, he professes that he willingly offers his heart in love for the One speaking. Second, he promises to offer willingly his obedience, his careful hearing, to the *Logos* and to the Word that has redeemed and sanctified him and now calls him to the diaconate. Third, he testifies that he is willing to give his life so that Christ, the Suffering Servant, whose icon he will become, may conform him to himself. To these three ends the bishop will then exhort the deacon-candidate and, after ordaining him, entrust to him the Word of God.

The bishop, before whom the deacon-candidate stands, is as the Lord: he is the chief shepherd of the local church into whose service the deacon is ordained. It is through him that the deacon makes of himself a gift both to the Father who speaks and to the Word who is spoken. That is why the ordination ritual itself begins immediately after the gospel has been proclaimed and before the bishop begins his homiletic instruction.

Following the presentation of the deacon-candidate, the priest who has called him forward now addresses the ordaining bishop. "Most Reverend Father," he begins, "holy mother Church asks you to ordain this man, our brother, for service as deacon." The deacon-candidate himself does not ask to be ordained, nor are his family and friends petitioning on his behalf. It is the church, characterized in the dialogue as holy and a mother, who knows her needs and who makes this appeal of the bishop. Holy mother church herself seeks to provide for her children through the deacon's life and service, nurturing her children through his ministry of Word, sacrament, and charity. The deacon has not chosen his mother, the church; she has chosen the deacon. The church has chosen the deacon because she herself loves both her bridegroom and the world created in his own image and likeness. And so she desires to honor the deacon, that is, to hold him up to her bridegroom and to offer the deacon to the world as a living icon of her bridegroom's suffering servanthood.

The bishop too must protect his flock lest a wolf in sheep's clothing be welcomed into the sheepfold. So he asks the priest, "Do you judge him to be worthy?" The priest responds to the bishop, "After inquiry among the people of Christ and upon recommendation of those concerned with his training, I testify that he has been found worthy." The rite does not say what constitutes worthiness. Certainly to be found worthy means that a deacon-candidate has been judged by the church to be, like the first seven deacons, "of good standing, full of the Spirit and of wisdom" (Acts 6:3). His worthiness, too, has been established in the years of his formation, as he completed those requirements established by the church. And worthiness will be clarified further when the bishop questions the deacon-candidate, and especially when he hands to him the Book of the Gospels. Anticipating the bishop's homiletic exhortation, though, in essence the priest is testifying to the bishop that the deacon-candidate is a man of integrity, a man who believes the Scriptures and the church's teaching, who teaches by word and deed what he believes, and who puts in practice in his own life what he teaches to others.

In concluding the deacon-candidate's presentation, the bishop does not answer the testimony of the priest or of the community. Neither does he address the deacon-candidate directly. He turns instead to God. "We rely on the help of the Lord God and our Savior Jesus Christ, and we choose this man, our brother, for the order of deacons." In a cynical moment one (perhaps even the deacon-candidate himself) might interpret the bishop's comment to mean, "Heaven help us all." No. The bishop is testifying to the church and affirming to the deacon-candidate that although the church judges him to be worthy and chooses him for the order of deacons, it is the Lord himself who has called him and it is by the Lord's grace and help that the deacon-candidate will become and be a deacon.

The Deacon's Functions in the Liturgy of the Word

"Here am I, the servant of the Lord; let it be with me according to your word" (Luke 1:38). With these words Mary showed herself to be the responsible one and consented to the Word of God. In this part of our current reflection, I want to consider some ways in which deacons are "responsible" for God's Word, exercising the *munus docendi*, the office of teaching, under the authority of the bishop and in cooperation with priests.

When at ordination the bishop scrutinizes a deacon-candidate concerning his intentions, he addresses the candidate as "my son." The bishop acknowledges that with him the deacon-candidate is about to become a coheir of the ministry that Christ and the church have entrusted to the bishop and that he in turn shares with the deacon. Even more than this, though, the bishop recognizes the deacon-candidate to be a son of God's Word, one born of the fatherhood of the church's Scriptures and the motherhood of her sacred tradition. In the celebration of the Eucharist, a deacon exercises three functions in service to God's Word.

First, before the deacon proclaims the gospel he turns and, either kneeling or standing, bows before the presider to receive a blessing. The

General Instruction of the Roman Missal calls for "a profound bow" (175), not a simple nod of the head. Bowing is a gesture of reverence, honor, and obedience. Facing the bishop or priest, the deacon bows to him who *in persona Christi capitis ecclesiae*, that is, in the person of Christ, the head of the church, presides at the eucharistic sacrifice. But the deacon is also bowing to the gospel he will proclaim, the blessing of which he is receiving, showing in this way his own obedient submission to God's Word. In this gesture of bowing at the waist, the deacon shows himself to be *responsible* for the gospel, making of his own body a sort of bridge between Christ (in the person of the presider) and the gospel he, the deacon, is about to proclaim, as well as between Christ (in the person of the presider) and the assembled faithful to whom he, the deacon, proclaims God's Word.

The blessing the presider gives to the deacon is: "The Lord be in your heart and on your lips that you may worthily proclaim his gospel." The deacon cannot proclaim the gospel worthily with his lips unless he first possesses it in his heart. Mary conceived the Word of God in her heart before conceiving him in her womb and bringing him into the world. She then treasured in her heart all things having to do with her Son. Her motherly heart was pierced because of her filial obedience to the Father. That is why her maternal heart is at the core of her freedom, her cheerful courage exercised responsibly for the Word made flesh. Like Mary, the deacon must conceive, treasure, suffer the Word of God in his heart. For this reason, I commend to deacons Mary under the title of Our Lady of Loreto as a patron of their ministry. Our Lady of Loreto is the Blessed Virgin whom the church venerates for welcoming and making a home for God's Word in her heart from the moment of her own immaculate conception, even before she made a home for the Word of God in her womb and gave birth to God's Word into the world.

Next, having received the blessing, the deacon proceeds to elevate the Book of the Gospels for the adoration of the faithful while they themselves stand and, singing "Alleluia," prepare to hear it. The deacon introduces the gospel to the faithful with the words, "The Lord be with you." These are more than words that introduce the subsequent action. These words are the deacon's prayer that the *communio* of the Trinity, offered to the faithful in his proclamation of the saving Good News of Jesus, be the foundation of the lives of each and all who hear. That is why the deacon does not simply read the gospel but proclaims it, and proclaims not simply words but what he himself is living. Only when he himself sincerely believes, teaches, and puts into practice the words he proclaims to the faithful can he even begin to hope that they themselves treasure them in their own hearts. The deacon cannot pray with integrity that others receive what he himself has not first welcomed, the gift of trinitarian *communio* given to him in God's Word.

Each and every time a deacon proclaims the gospel he should prepare and practice the proclamation beforehand. He should never presume to know the text, no matter how many times he has proclaimed it. If he is unfamiliar with the text, stumbles over or mispronounces its words, merely reads words rather than proclaiming Good News, or if he evinces a laziness, casualness, or over-familiarity with the gospel, he is not serving God's Word. To the contrary, he would be taking for granted the sacred words he then kisses, both as a gesture of his affection for those words and as a prayer that those who hear them will know the forgiveness of their sins. Furthermore, he might very well be distracting his hearers, perhaps preventing them that day from hearing God's voice and softening their hearts so as to enter into God's rest (see Ps 95:7, 11).

Finally, at the Eucharist the deacon may preach the homily. Let's pause a moment and consider here the ministry of preaching in general.

The *Directory* teaches that the bishop commends deacons to the church "by their conduct, their preaching of the mystery of Christ, by transmitting Christian doctrine and by devoting attention to the problems of our time" (23). These are the four avenues of diaconal preaching.

The deacon preaches first and foremost by his conduct of life. He has "renounced the shameful things that one hides; [he] refuse[s] to practice cunning or to falsify God's word; but by the open statement of the truth . . . commend[s himself] to the conscience of everyone in the sight of God" (2 Cor 4:1-2). His life and demeanor are not contentious but hospitable. He has learned from St. Francis of Assisi, himself a deacon, "not to engage in arguments or disputes, but to be subject *to every human creature for God's sake* [1 Pet 2:13] and to acknowledge that they themselves are Christians" (*The Earlier Rule* 16). Francis, for this reason, taught, "Preach the Gospel always. Use words if necessary."

Second, the deacon preaches the Word of God through the homily he occasionally* gives at the Eucharist and when he presides at liturgical

---

* Deacons are not ordinary preachers of the homily at the Eucharist, which on that occasion is reserved to the celebrant, concelebrant, or another priest. Nonetheless, in some dioceses, deacons have become used to preaching at the celebration of the Eucharist on a regular, or even a frequent basis. They should not be. Whereas the *Code*

celebrations. When he does so, his preaching should be diaconal preaching, not priestly or episcopal. What do I mean by that?

At the end of Matthew's gospel, Jesus commissions the apostles to "make disciples of all nations, baptizing them in the name of the Father and of the Son and of the Holy Spirit, and teaching them to obey everything that I have commanded you" (Matt 28:19-20). Jesus' apostolic charge is threefold, namely, making disciples (evangelization), baptizing (celebrating the sacraments), and teaching (catechesis). The successors of the apostles, the bishops, share this commission with priests and deacons, whom they ordain to evangelize, celebrate the sacraments, and catechize.

That having been said, because the deacon is ordained to ministry and not to priesthood, his manner of preaching should be specifically ministerial and not priestly. The deacon's primary function in carrying out the threefold commission of Christ is to "make disciples," although he may baptize (baptism being the only sacrament he may administer) and transmit Christian doctrine. Therefore, a deacon should strive in his preaching to "make disciples" of all who give him a hearing and of the poor. His preaching should be specifically evangelical in character.

Being an icon of Christ the Suffering Servant, in his preaching the deacon should show himself to be compassionate and merciful as Christ is compassionate and merciful. Because the deacon serves *communio*, his

---

of Canon Law establishes that it is proper for presbyters *to proclaim* the Gospel of God (pastors and others entrusted with the care of souls are especially bound to this office), it prescribes that deacons are *to serve* the people of God in the ministry of the word in communion with bishops and priests (c. 757). The Code affirms that deacons "possess the faculty to preach everywhere" given the presumed consent of the rector of the church (c. 764). But the faculty of preaching is not given absolutely, and the ministry of preaching in general should not be confused with the very specific and eminent form of preaching that is giving the homily. The *Introduction to the Lectionary* establishes that preaching the homily is the proper function of the one presiding at the Liturgy of the Word (see 38–41). The *GIRM* instructs that "the homily should ordinarily be given by the priest celebrant himself. He may entrust it to a concelebrating priest or *occasionally, according to circumstances*, to the deacon" (66; emphasis added). The *GIRM* specifies further that the deacon may preach God's word at the Eucharist "from time to time" (94). The *Directory*, in the section "Homily and catechesis," emphasizes that the deacon is a "servant and not master of the word of God," and clarifies that "[w]hen the deacon presides at a liturgical celebration . . . he shall give due importance to the homily" (24, 25; emphasis added). When the *Directory* itself further reviews the role of the deacon at Mass (32), although it refers to him as an "ordinary minister" of Communion and of eucharistic exposition and benediction, it is silent regarding his preaching of the homily.

homilies and sermons should proclaim the Good News that God desires all to come to the knowledge of divine *communio* through the communion of the church. A deacon's preaching should be welcoming and invitatory, not harsh and condemnatory. Like a good father, like the father of the Prodigal Son, who said not a word to his son, the deacon knows when to hug before homilizing and to homilize before hugging, but his words should always embrace. True, the deacon calls sinners and the poor to be faithful to the Gospel, but the truth is always proclaimed in love (see Eph 4:15). As such, in his preaching he does not lord his authority over others (see Mark 10:42), but shows himself to be one with sinners and in solidarity with the poor.

Third, the deacon preaches through catechesis and exhortation.

Finally, the deacon preaches through evangelization, speaking to all whom he meets, Catholic and non-Catholic alike, of the mysteries of God in Christ. He learns from St. Dominic that *now* is always a necessary time for words. He is called to evangelize, even—perhaps especially—in his professional life, both by his presence and ministering as a deacon (see *Directory* 26). Indeed, the bringing of the Gospel to the so-called professional world is one of the primary tasks of evangelization the church entrusts to deacons and should be understood as one of their primary tasks.

"Rekindle the Gift of God"

To love God's Word, obey it, and configure his life to it will daily require a renewal of the grace a deacon receives at his ordination, "which is strength, *vigor specialis*, a gift for living the new reality wrought by the sacrament. . . . Just as in all sacraments which imprint a character, grace has a permanent validity. It flowers again and again in the same measure in which it is received and accepted again and again in faith" (*Basic Norms* 7). I conclude this reflection with a consideration of a few of the aids that the Spirit and the church offer the deacon "to rekindle the gift of God that is within [him]" (2 Tim 1:6), to hear the voice of the One speaking, and to serve the Word of God.

First, the Gospel of St. Luke teaches us that the Holy Family and Christ himself had made the practice of their faith habitual. (The Holy Family should always serve as a particular patron of a deacon's life and ministry, especially a married deacon.) Similarly, it is vital that the deacon's family develop a *habitus vivendi*, and he a *habitus ministrandi*, habits of living and of ministering, characterized by:

- Familiarity with and fidelity to the Word of God. Christ "sustains all things by his powerful word" (Heb 1:3). A deacon cannot hope to be renewed in life and ministry if he is not himself a man of God's Word. He will not be able to proclaim the Gospel to others if he himself does not possess and live what he is claiming to hand on to others. A married deacon together with his wife and family do well to make *lectio divina* a daily habit, prayerfully reflecting on the readings to be proclaimed at the next Sunday's Eucharist, on an approaching holy day or special liturgical day in their life (for example, the anniversary of their marriage or ordination), or even on the daily readings.

- Stillness of life and critical attitude toward popular media. In Psalm 46:11, God himself sings out, "Be still, and know that I am God!" A deacon cannot confess the faith if his life is filled with noise and banter, if it is filled with things that distract and keep him from the God who speaks as "sheer silence" (1 Kgs 19:12). Thomas Merton wrote, "Incapable of the divine activity which alone can satisfy his soul, fallen man flings himself upon exterior things, not so much for their own sake as for the sake of the agitation which keeps his spirit pleasantly numb" (*The Ascent to Truth*, p. 19). Since at ordination the Holy Spirit strengthens his sevenfold gifts within the deacon, the deacon must not allow those gifts and his own spirit to be pleasantly numbed, a very real possibility even for an ordained minister.

  To this end, a deacon must first develop a critical attitude toward the popular media, and he must be constantly on guard against the incursion of entertainment and technology in his life *and* that of his family. He must not be addicted to digital and electronic technology and to entertainment. He must develop the habit of turning off, better yet not turning on, the many screens in life—television, computer, Blackberry, cell phone, iPod, MP3 player, in short, every distraction that, on one hand, keeps him from being fully present both to his *ecclesia domestica* and to his *ecclesia locale*, as at his ordination he professed himself to be, and, on the other hand, simply keeps him from opening up and reading the Word of God, prayerfully listening for the "most sweet" and "altogether desirable" voice of the Lord (Song 5:16), and conversing with God.

- Right attitude toward ministry. Ordination to the diaconate imprints on the individual a permanent character, and he is sanctified by the very ministry he carries out—the ministry of the Word, sacraments, and charity. Through praying, preaching, celebrating the sacraments, and serving sinners and the poor, the deacon never fails to open himself to the grace of the diaconate. He is actually strengthened and renewed by it, not drained and tired, even as he exercises it. Pope John Paul II taught that freedom does not precede or anticipate free acting. Rather, in acting one is either freed, one becomes free, or one is enslaved. Analogously, a deacon rekindles the very gift of God given at his ordination in the very exercise of his ministry. The *Directory* teaches, "Progress in the spiritual life is achieved primarily by faithful and tireless exercise of the ministry in integrity of life" (51). For this reason, even though perchance retired from active ministry, a deacon must never retire from the diaconate, that is, from being a deacon, from serving in everything he is about and does.

- Right attitude toward work. The *Directory* teaches that "the secular work of permanent deacons is in some sense linked with their ministry" (12). Deacons who earn their living and provide for their families in secular employment act honorably. They who are employed in secular work participate in the church's *missio ad gentes* and are called to be missionaries. "The deacon's ministry of service is linked with the missionary dimension of the Church. . . . Mission includes witness to Christ in a secular profession or occupation" (27). His very presence in the world of secular work is a witness to Christ and an opportunity for evangelization. He must "always be ready to make [his] defense to anyone who demands from [him] an accounting for the hope that is in [him]" (1 Pet 3:15). Because he is a deacon, he must carry out his employment with the attitude of Christ, that is, as a servant, acting always in an honest, virtuous, respectful, and helpful way.

    Yet, "one does not live by bread alone, but by every word that comes from the mouth of God" (Matt 4:4). A deacon should be bold and confident in believing that God is his Father and as a Father knows how to give his children good things (see Luke 11:13). A deacon must be cautious lest he place faith in his employer for his livelihood and the well-being of his family or become addicted to work. By a right attitude toward work, he demonstrates that work is a means, not an end. When he fills his mind and heart with the first things, then his mind and heart are focused on the right things. Can a deacon hope to lead sinners and the poor into the rest of God if he himself is not resting in God, not keeping the Sabbath, overly dedicated if not even addicted to work and to its tools and instruments? "Therefore I tell you, do not worry about your life, what you will eat or what you will drink, or about your body, what you will wear. . . . [I]ndeed your heavenly Father knows that you need all these things. . . . [S]trive first for the kingdom of God and his righteousness, and all these things will be given to you as well" (Matt 6:25, 32-33).

In addition to these spiritual aids, the church offers these ecclesial aids for the renewal of a deacon's life and ministry:

- The Liturgy of the Hours. In praying the Liturgy of the Hours daily, the deacon joins his voice in the choir of the church, one with the psalmists and saints of every generation, praising God and petitioning the Lord for the sanctification of the church and the world and for the poor. Praying the Liturgy of the Hours—the psalms of which are ripe with the raw emotions of one sincerely struggling to know God's love and to understand his ways—helps every Christian, but especially the church's ministers, to persevere in vocation and in ministry.

- The church's teachings. The teachings of the church are "like a hiding place from the wind, a covert from the tempest, like streams of water in a dry place, like the shade of a great rock in a weary land" (Isa 32:2). Through its teachings the church witnesses that it has heard the Word of God, is faithful to it, and in turn nourishes and serves God's children with God's Word. Contrarily, a deacon who is either not living the teachings of the church privately—that is, in his marriage, family, and business life—or who dissents from them publicly in word or deed, gives evidence that he lacks oneness of mind and heart and unity of his personhood, that he lacks integrity. He would fail in those qualities to which his family and friends, and the church, too, attested on the day of his ordination. No one will follow another who lacks integrity. Pope John Paul II, when in Denver for World Youth Day 1993, said of young people that they know instinctively when their leaders are not telling the truth and they know instinctively when their leaders are not living the truth they profess.

- If a deacon is married, his vocation as husband, father, and grandfather, faithful to the vows he made at his marriage. Because a married deacon receives the sacrament of marriage before he is ordained, his marriage is brought into the diaconate before his diaconate is brought into his marriage. He can be an effective deacon only to the extent that first he "bow[s his] knees before the Father, from whom every family in heaven and on earth takes its name" (Eph 3:14-15).

Summary

The Trinity creates, redeems, and sanctifies, that we might know his divine *communio*. In ordination a deacon receives a new friendship in the *communio*, that is, the life of the Trinity itself. In service to the Father who speaks and the Son who is spoken, he will be continually renewed by God's Word. In his ministry he proclaims the Father's own divine *communio* and leads others to it—his family first, then the church, sinners, and the poor. Every day, as he did before the bishop at his ordination, he must kneel to receive the Gospel of Christ, whose herald he is, believing what he reads, teaching what he believes, and practicing what he teaches.

chapter three

The Almost-Apostle

In Mark's gospel we read the heartrending story of the encounter between Jesus and an anonymous man, who is not otherwise described for us in the story. We pick up the story in 10:17-31. The man runs up to Jesus and begs him share with him the secret to eternal life. Jesus obliges, instructing him, "Go, sell what you own, and give the money to the poor . . . ; then come, follow me." But Mark tells us the man was unable to do so for he had many possessions. Jesus was inviting him to apostolic *communio*. Instead the man walked away, the almost-apostle.

In our next two chapters we will consider the relationship between the deacon and Jesus, the second person of the Trinity, the Word made flesh. Mark's story of the encounter between Jesus and this man helps us to understand that Jesus invites deacons to a type of "apostolic" relationship with him. As he did with that man, Jesus invites deacons to go, sell, and give to the poor. As such, deacons are invited to come to the possession of the kingdom of God.

> As he was setting out on a journey, a man ran up and knelt before him, and asked him, "Good Teacher, what must I do to inherit eternal life?" Jesus said to him, "Why do you call me good? No one is good but God alone. You know the commandments: 'You shall not murder; You shall not commit adultery; You shall not steal; You shall not bear false witness; You shall not defraud; Honor your father and mother.'" He said to him, "Teacher, I have kept all these since my

youth." Jesus, looking at him, loved him and said, "You lack one thing; go, sell what you own, and give the money to the poor, and you will have treasure in heaven; then come, follow me." When he heard this, he was shocked and went away grieving, for he had many possessions.

Then Jesus looked around and said to his disciples, "How hard it will be for those who have wealth to enter the kingdom of God!" And the disciples were perplexed at these words. But Jesus said to them again, "Children, how hard it is to enter the kingdom of God! It is easier for a camel to go through the eye of a needle than for someone who is rich to enter the kingdom of God." They were greatly astounded and said to one another, "Then who can be saved?" Jesus looked at them and said, "For mortals it is impossible, but not for God; for God all things are possible."

Peter began to say to him, "Look, we have left everything and followed you." Jesus said, "Truly I tell you, there is no one who has left house or brothers or sisters or mother or father or children or fields, for my sake and for the sake of the good news, who will not receive a hundredfold now in this age—houses, brothers and sisters, mothers and children, and fields, with persecutions—and in the age to come eternal life. But many who are first will be last, and the last will be first."

Our story opens simply enough. Having just blessed little children and taught that "whoever does not receive the kingdom of God as a little child will never enter it" (10:15), Jesus set out for Jerusalem. Suddenly a grown man runs up and, kneeling before him, begs, "What must I do to inherit eternal life?" (Remember, in Jesus' time adults didn't run; running was child's play.) Jesus obliges and simply enough answers his question, sharing the secret for possessing the kingdom. In so doing Jesus teaches him and his disciples what he means when he says that one must accept the kingdom of God like a little child.

It is striking to note that although Luke characterizes the man of our story as both young and rich, Mark never describes him as either. Mark tells us only that he had obeyed certain commandments from his youth and that he had many possessions. To have many possessions is not the same thing as being rich. Think of hoarders, for example. I once had an aunt who threw nothing away. Her house was filled with everything you can imagine, knickknacks and curios that were never dusted, all sorts of *objets d' art* and pseudo antiques she had purchased at garage sales year after year after year. Her weaknesses were newspapers and magazines. Someday, she promised herself and others, she was going to go through every single one of them. One day, though, she died. The day she died her house was bulging from floor to ceiling and wall to wall with the things she had been unable to discard throughout her lifetime. It was not a home but barely more than a series of constricted pathways connecting its rooms. She had many possessions, but she was certainly not rich. Regarding the man in our story, it seems plausible to suggest that something similar might be said. Having many possessions did not necessarily make him rich. But he put his faith in what he possessed, and so he squandered not a thing. He was going to get to it all someday.

Kneeling before Jesus the man asked, "Good Teacher, what must I do to inherit eternal life?" Before answering his question, Jesus had one of his own. "Why do you call me good? No one is good but God alone." We need to understand why Jesus asked this question of the man before answering the man's own opening question. It is the key to understanding Jesus' invitation to "go, sell what you own, and give the money to the poor . . . ; then come, follow me."

From ancient days, people have wanted and needed to seek God and to draw near to him. In many futile ways—spiritually, intellectually, emotionally, erotically—have people attempted to do so but failed. One way, though, seemed to hold out promise, that is, seemed to give people access and proximity to the deity: the offering of sacrifices. By offering a sacrifice—mineral, cereal, animal, even human, giving life for life—ancient pagans believed they were doing what most pleased and appeased the deity. And in pleasing the deity it seemed to them as if the deity might deign to allow them to draw near. In the end, though, the ancient pagans were forced to conclude that they themselves were little more than pawns for their deities' amusement and that sacrificing was futile and meaningless. False gods never love their creatures, and a pagan can never really please a false god.

The Lord, the God of Israel, however, was a different sort of God. He was the true God. In the Lord people discovered not simply a God to whom it was pleasing to draw near. People came to know that God wanted to draw near to them, that God wanted even to live with them. In other words, Israel discovered that God loved. God required the making of sacrificial offerings. But he responded to Israel's sacrifice differently. God was pleased with the sacrifices Israel was offering. Moreover, he didn't accept Israel's sacrifices for his own sake, that is, simply because it pleased him to do so. God accepted Israel's sacrifices for Israel's sake. God ratified his pleasure in covenants he established between Israel, who sought to draw near to God, and himself, who dwelt in unapproachable majesty.

The Lord's covenants were unique, defining a relationship between his people and himself that was unlike any relationship of any pagan god with any pagan people. The Lord's covenants did not simply acknowledge and represent Israel's desire to draw near to God. Even more so, they established the Lord's desire to be near to his creation and to Israel. After the flood God made a covenant with Noah and his descendants that never again would he destroy what he had created. With Abraham God established a covenant that Abraham's descendants would be his favored children. On Mount Sinai God made a covenant with Moses and Israel, the chosen people he had freed from slavery. Time and time again God renewed his covenants with his people after they sinned and when they were deported into exile. "I will make a covenant of peace with them; it shall be an everlasting covenant with them; and I will bless them and multiply them, and will set my sanctuary among them forevermore. My dwelling place shall be with them; and I will be their God, and they shall be my people" (Ezek 37:26-27).

For a Jew, the covenant with the Lord meant life. Life was the goods exchanged in the covenant. The Lord demanded his people live faithfully in compliance with the terms of the covenant and sacrifice life to him, the living Lord. As long as Israel was faithful to the covenant and sacrificed as the Lord commanded, then the Lord would remain close to Israel; they would have long life on the land he had given them.

In Hebrew the word for sacrifice is *korban*. In the Old Testament the word is not used in reference to a creature or object of material value, that is, something with a price on its head or something to which people had assigned a calculated value. Nor is the word *korban* used negatively to describe doing something or giving away something, even giving away oneself or one's services, so as to please or appease another. Jews offered *korban* to express gratitude to the Lord for having freed them from slavery and drawing near, and to express their hope, their desire that the Lord who had drawn near would remain near. *Korban* was offered not simply to secure God's favor in the future but to thank God for his love in the past.

In that context, Jewish sacrifice was carried out for one or the other of two motives. First, a Jew offered a sacrifice to fulfill the requirements of the law, living strictly in accord with its dictates or to atone for its violation, for sin. In this way a Jew grew in holiness. Mary and Joseph, for example, went to the temple on the eighth day of Jesus' birth and offered two turtledoves or pigeons in sacrifice, to purify Mary and to present their firstborn son to the Lord (Exod 13:2; Luke 2:22-24). Second, a Jew was motivated to offer *korban* to express gratitude or fulfill a promise made to the Lord. Upon arriving in Jerusalem on pilgrimage, for example, one might offer a sacrifice to render thanks to the Lord for a good harvest or abundant livestock, a child's healing, the safe return of a loved one from a long journey or war. To sacrifice was to act righteously, and to act righteously was to be good. In being good one drew near to God. "But for me it is good to be near God; I have made the Lord GOD my refuge," sang the psalmist (Ps 73:28).

When we speak of the Lord's drawing near to Israel, we must keep in mind, too, that God's presence was not solely spiritual; it was physical. The Lord dwelt in the law of the covenant written in stone. The covenant itself dwelt first in the meeting tent and then, with its construction, in the temple. The Lord commanded that there, at the place of his dwelling, Israel was constantly to be offering sacrifices, every day and throughout the day. Before the façade of the temple a perpetual offering of incense was made to the Lord. In the temple cereal offerings and wine libations were made. At the foot of the temple animals were sacrificed. Who among the Jews did not know that in Jerusalem, at the temple, each and every day sacrifices were being made to the Lord, who was dwelling with his people, so that they might draw near to him? Who did not look toward the temple and see, even from afar, the unending plume of burning incense and smell the aromatic smoke rising from earth to the sanctuary of God's throne in heaven?

Keeping this in mind, let's return to the encounter between Jesus and the man with many possessions. The man had run up to Jesus, knelt, and addressed him with the title "Good Teacher." In calling him "Good," the man was not simply paying Jesus a compliment. Like others, he must have been "astounded" at Jesus' teaching, "for [Jesus] taught as one having authority and not as the scribes" (Mark 1:22). This man was making a sort of profession of faith. He was saying, first of all, "Jesus, I know you to be one who is making sacrifices. You are one who has drawn near to God. You are one in whom God dwells." Second, he was saying, "Jesus, I know you to be a teacher. You can teach me how to do the same. You can teach me, too, how forever to draw near to God."

Jesus did not reject or shirk from being called "Good Teacher." He accepted the man's simple profession of faith, asking in return, "Why do you call me good? No one is good but God alone." Since goodness was drawing near to God, Jesus affirmed that God alone, being the Good One, could be near to, that is, present to, himself. (Being present to himself is what it means that God is one and that he is holy.) In accepting the greeting "Good Teacher," Jesus affirmed that, yes, he was good, yes, he was offering sacrifice, for "though he was in the form of God, [he] did not regard equality with God as something to be exploited, but emptied himself, taking the form of a slave" (Phil 2:6-7). Yes, indeed, it was true that he was near to God.

Although explicit trinitarian affirmation is lacking in his response, Jesus was implicitly affirming what elsewhere he proclaimed explicitly, namely, "The Father and I are one" (John 10:30). Furthermore, by responding to the man's question with another question, Jesus showed that he wanted to dialogue with the man and so reveal to him the secret to everlasting life, teaching this man with many possessions "the way, and the truth, and the life" (John 14:6) by which he too could sacrifice ("go, sell, give"), be good ("you will have treasure in heaven"), and draw near to God ("come, follow me").

Jesus went on to answer the man's inquiry, "What must I do to share everlasting life?" But he didn't do so straightforwardly. He didn't say, for example, "This and that is what you must do." Why not? For two reasons. First, in law and in fact there was nothing that this man, or anyone for that matter, could ever *do* to merit or gain the inheritance of another. How one disposes of one's inheritance should be entirely at the discretion of the giver, not a potential receiver. Unlike the younger son's inheritance in the parable of the Prodigal Son, it should be the giver's prerogative to give away and not the receiver's prerogative to take or to earn. One who wanted to inherit might scheme and arrange so as to be included in another's will. But how this man might manipulate God so as to live forever doesn't seem to be quite the point of the man's question.

The second reason why Jesus did not give a straightforward answer to his question was because no one can ever earn his or her own life. Who ever asked to be born or earned his or her conception and birth? What death-row criminal, whom a governor or president pardons, merits the pardon? Moreover, the man was seeking the secret not to *bios*, physical life, but to *zōē*, life to the full, eternal life. *Zōē* is the very life that Jesus himself, the Good Shepherd, came into the world to give (see John 10:10), and to give freely. In a very real sense, by the very fact that Jesus had already come into the world and was standing then and there on that road to Jerusalem, the man with many possessions could then and there come to possess what he himself was asking for, life to the full. All life, earthly and eternal, is given to one by another. When the giver is God, his gift of life is always an act of free, generous love. And so, by not answering the man's question directly, Jesus thereby showed that its premise was entirely mistaken.

Yet in fact, Jesus does respond to the man's inquiry. He says, quite simply, "You know the commandments." Then he listed, not all, but only some of them. Curiously, Jesus called his interlocutor's attention not to the first through the third commandments, that is, the commandments that order a person's right relationship with God. Rather, he listed the commandments that order one's right relationship with one's neighbor: Do not murder, let alone look lustfully upon another. One must neither steal nor lie. Honor your father and mother, and so on.

By recalling only these commandments, the idle listener might have mistakenly concluded Jesus was indeed teaching that the secret to earning eternal life was found in obeying these alone. But by recalling these commandments Jesus wasn't excluding the others. Rather, the Good Teacher was only beginning to teach the man with many possessions the first step on the way to eternal life. The *korban* God required to draw near eternally to God, the sacrifice the man was to make, the goodness Jesus elicited from him was first of all a right relationship with his fellow human beings. Jesus was trying to teach him, "If you want to draw near to God, then as God has commanded you must draw near, be in a right relationship, be in *communio* with your fellow human being." This was the first, but only the first, step toward the inheritance of eternal life.

The man assured Jesus—we can even detect a hint of pride in his voice as he responded to him—that he had obeyed those commandments from his youth; he had indeed taken the first step, and for a very long time. But that all seemed too easy. Was that all that it took? Surely it wasn't enough? Surely there must be more? Yes, Jesus went on to say, the man was correct; there was still one more thing he had to do. "Go, sell what you own, and give the money to the poor, and you will have treasure in heaven; then come, follow me."

Many translations of this text read that Jesus told the man there was one more thing he had to do. But the Greek, *husterei*, is literally "lacking" or "wanting." There was one more thing he was lacking. Even though he owned, perhaps hoarded many things, there was yet one more thing he still had to come to possess. Paradoxically, inheriting the kingdom of God is not the consequence of doing something, of right action, but truly coming to possess something. But what?

In Jesus' time, many had come to believe that God bestowed his favor on certain individuals by endowing them with wealth and riches. For example, we read in 1 Chronicles 29:12, "Riches and honor come from you." Likewise God favored Solomon, who had sacrificed a thousand sacrifices, and bestowed upon him riches galore (see 1 Kgs 3:4-14 and 2 Chr 1:11). Therefore, it might have seemed to this man that Jesus was going to tell him that to have it all—riches in this world and eternal life in the next—he needed to possess that one thing that would surely prove he had won God's eternal favor. Imagine his initial joy at hearing Jesus' response, at hearing there was yet one more thing he had to come to possess. He had proven himself adept at acquiring possessions. Surely, this last one too would be within his grasp.

Jesus was throwing the man what we would call a curveball, indeed one of God's great curveballs. In truth, the kingdom of God is not a thing to be possessed. Instead Jesus proceeded to teach the man that to own the kingdom of God he had to dispossess himself of everything, dispossess himself of everything he had come to own since his youth. "Go, sell what you own, and give the money to the poor, and you will have treasure in heaven; then come, follow me." Jesus was calling the man to enter into a true spiritual paradox. Having implied that the man had to possess one more thing to possess everlasting life, Jesus seemed to be reversing himself. To possess that one thing the man had to sell everything, give the money to the poor, and then follow him. St. John of the Cross put it this way: "If you want to come to the possession of all, come to the possession of nothing."

Moreover, it was not enough for the man simply to divest himself of his possessions, perhaps keeping the proceeds in trust or directing how they would be spent. Jesus required him to deposit the proceeds not with family members, nor in the temple treasury, nor anywhere else, but with the poor. Only after he had done so, taken up his life with Christ, and entered into communion with Christ's disciples, would he come to possess everlasting life. Only when he dispossessed himself of all earthly goods so as to possess Christ as his only good would he have true treasure. Only when he gave up his "buying power" and security and entrusted himself to Christ could Christ then give to him all that he desired. Only when he stopped promising himself that he would get to it all someday would he be able to possess it all that day.

What Jesus required of this man, in other words, was not that he do anything but that he become something, become someone new. This is why I believe that the man in the story was in fact older, not young. He had kept all the commandments from his youth. He had certainly acquired richness of age, status, and social security. But now Jesus was inviting this man of mature years to become like a little child, the little child whom he, Jesus, had sat in his lap, whom he had touched and blessed, and who was able to accept the kingdom of God from Christ.

Our story is coming to an end. Mark tells us the man went away *stugnazas*, which is often translated as "sad." (In Matthew's gospel the young man departs *lupoumenos*, which is used frequently in the New Testament to describe grieving [see Matt 19:22].) The only other use of the word *stugnazō* in the New Testament occurs in Matthew 16:3. There Jesus used it to describe the red skies that threaten or portend overcast conditions for the coming day. Using this word, Mark wants to do more than simply tell his readers about this man's emotional state. When one decides not to follow Jesus, the forecast—that day, tomorrow, forever—is to be under a certain "overcastness." Because the man was unwilling to divest himself of everything and become like a little child who possessed nothing, the "overcastness" that came upon him that day would dawn on him every day unto eternity.

This man, we can sense, must have been very afraid to die. Now, in addition to his fear of death, he had lost his hope for eternal life. The self-deluding promise that he would get to it all someday, the false hope he possessed when he shamed himself and ran up to Jesus seeking to purchase eternal life—he found all he had come to possess to be too little for its acquisition. He turned away alone, overcast, and in darkness.

In a postscript of sorts Mark tells us that Jesus, reflecting on what had just taken place, turned to teach his disciples: "How hard it is for those who have wealth to enter the kingdom of God!" The Greek word Jesus uses for "wealth" is rightly translated as "wealth." Elsewhere it is also translated as "money." But it has another meaning in Greek too. (It is used a total of six times in the New Testament.) It can refer to anything that one uses or needs. Jesus could have been saying to the disciples, and just as likely was, that it is hard for one who uses or needs *anything* other than Jesus to come to the possession of the kingdom of God. He alone is the wealth of the kingdom of God and he alone is what one needs, or needs to use, to come to its possession. How hard it is for one who uses or needs anything else to inherit eternal life.

At Jesus' teaching the disciples were completely taken aback. Surely the rich were getting into heaven before everyone else and much more quickly than the poor, weren't they? Perhaps down deep they too believed wealth and possessions to be a sign of God's favor. Now the very one who had come down from heaven was teaching that it wasn't true.

The Greek word Mark uses in verse 24 to describe the disciples' reaction to Jesus' teaching is *ethambounto*. They were astonished, frightened at what he was teaching. And it only got worse when Jesus repeated it. In verse 26, Luke tells us that they were *exeplēssonto*, that is, "greatly astounded," at what he taught. *Exeplēssō* means panicked, overwhelmed without measure. Like the man who had walked away, now they too were glum, overwhelmingly so, and darkened. But perhaps, after all, the story doesn't end tragically. Perhaps the threatening clouds of their gloom cleared when Jesus at that moment called them "sons" and affirmed, "For mortals it is impossible, but not for God; for God all things are possible" (10:27).

What the Almost-Apostle Can "Sell" to the Deacon

Let's now turn our attention to the deacon. What does this story of Jesus and the almost-apostle have to teach us about his life and ministry?

In this gospel story of the almost-apostle, we saw that the man departed Jesus' company, for he could not accept the Good Teacher's instructions regarding eternal life. In the Gospel of John, at the conclusion of the Bread of Life discourse, Jesus asked the apostles if they were going to depart, as had all the others. Peter responded, "Lord, to whom can we go? You have the words of eternal life" (John 6:68). This same question in some form Jesus asks of every disciple. Everyone who is of the company of Jesus, perhaps having obeyed the commandments of the Lord from his or her youth, at some point comes to this crisis moment where he or she understands that doing so is not enough. "Are you too going to leave?" Jesus asks us. "Are you going to go and sell even the pride you feel at having obeyed all of my commandments, give to the poor, and come and follow me?" How each of us responds to these questions means everything, even eternal life. Being in the company of Jesus, being of good will, being respectful and deferential to him, obeying all of his commandments, even being ordained in and of itself is not enough to inherit the kingdom of God.

In our gospel story, recall that Jesus divided his answer to the man's question—"What must I do to inherit everlasting life?"—into two parts. In the first part Jesus made reference to the commands that deal with one's relationship with others. The almost-apostle had obeyed these commands since childhood. In the second part, Jesus commanded the man to sell his possessions and follow him. These commands the almost-apostle was unable to do in his adult life. By dividing his question thus, Jesus is teaching, among other things, that to be good it is not enough simply to do good for others. As the almost-apostle was instructed to give the money earned from the sale of his goods to the poor, so to be good, to draw near to God, requires first that one have a different attitude toward the poor. It also requires at the same time that one follow Jesus, becoming a member of his band of disciples. If one's faith life is limited to doing good to others but not joining the *communio* of the Lord and his disciples, then one is yet far from the kingdom of God. In other words, to be perfect, which is what Christ calls us to be, it is necessary not simply to do good. We must give to the poor *and* follow Jesus in the company of the others who have accepted his invitation. In this way one accepts the kingdom of God as a little child, and comes "to maturity, to the full stature of Christ" (Eph 4:13).

Experience tells us that many people never really grow up; they remain juvenile even in adulthood. So too many even in adulthood remain immature in faith. For example, how many people, including many Christians, have deluded themselves into believing that it is enough to be "a good person" (often defined as simply tolerating others, letting others live their lives as they choose to, or not hurting others) to merit God's favor, even to merit eternal life? Who of us hasn't heard bad behavior excused with the (actually) unflattering excuse, "So what if he [insert behavior]? Deep down he's a good person." In Jesus' answer to the man in Mark's story, he teaches us that being a good person is only the first of several steps to drawing near to God. The vital next steps are to acquire a new attitude toward, a new relationship with the poor *and* to accompany Christ more closely in the company of his disciples.

This lesson stands as an admonition to a deacon. Any one of us can delude himself into believing that he is a good person because of all the good he does for others. Good for others, indeed, we are called to do. But what Jesus asks of us is not simply altruistic acts, even carried out in his name. Jesus asks us to have a new attitude to the poor *and* to give ourselves totally to them, that we may be in *communio* with them and they with us in Christ. One could not imagine a marriage to be good, for example, in which one of the spouses simply acts kindly toward the other but in which there is no loving and honoring of the other and thus no exchange of hearts, no *communio* between them. Just so in one's relationship to Christ and to the poor, what Christ expects of a deacon is not simply that he do good to others but that he give himself away, first to Christ himself *and* to the poor. As a deacon, the way one gives himself to Christ is by serving the poor, for Jesus identifies himself closely with them. ("Truly I tell you, just as you did it to one of the least of these who are members of my family, you did it to me" [Matt 25:40].) In our gospel story the almost-apostle's inability to follow Christ was evidenced by his unwillingness to sell all and give to the poor. So too a deacon's sincere following of Christ is measured not simply by his obedience to the bishop but by his loving service to the poor.

Being ordained an icon of Christ the Suffering Servant and serving the poor also challenges the deacon to consider the evangelical counsel of poverty and the place of material possessions and riches in his own life. Jesus may not call him to go and sell all his material goods. He may not be calling any individual deacon to live the same life of poverty to which he calls celibate bishops and priests. Nonetheless, Jesus does call deacons to dispossess themselves of anything and everything, material and relational, that they use or need and that causes them to hesitate in following Christ or seduces them to turn away from him. He indeed calls deacons to poverty, even if it is not abject poverty. After all, poverty, as the *Catechism* teaches, is an evangelical counsel that Christ "proposes" to every disciple (915). If this is true of every disciple, even more so does Christ propose it to deacons, who stand as his visible representation, that of Christ the Suffering Servant, in the church and to the world. Indeed, it must be admitted that there is a real incongruity in a deacon (or any cleric, for that matter) who in virtue of ordination, as an icon of Christ the Suffering Servant, seeks to share the lot of the poor but is materially wealthy in his lifestyle. While providing reasonably for the needs of his family, he is called not simply to do things for the poor but in his own poverty of spirit to become conformed to the One who was poor.

We should also consider why, in his initial response to the man, Jesus skipped over the Torah's first three commandments. Had he forgotten them? Are they no longer valid for Christ and the church? Had Mark deemed them not important to the main point of the story? Certainly the answer is no to each of these questions. To the contrary, in his very first sermon Jesus had affirmed, "I have come not to abolish [the law or the prophets] but to fulfill" (Matt 5:17). So why did Jesus not make mention of them here?

Recall that the first three commandments, those that order our relationship to God, are (1) you shall not worship false gods, (2) do not swear by or blaspheme the name of God, and (3) keep holy the Sabbath day. To obey these commandments was to acknowledge God's sovereignty over oneself, Israel, and all creation. Obeying these commands also expressed one's gratitude to God for having drawn near to humankind even while one sought to draw near to God.

But Israel had developed a wrong attitude toward these commandments. It was very tempting to believe, falsely, that all that was necessary in order to draw near to God was to keep the first three commandments of Torah. The fourth through the tenth commandments became regulations of secondary importance. One might even neglect the fourth through the tenth commandments all together, with the convenient justification that one was entirely dedicated to keeping the first through the third. (Isn't it just the opposite today, with people believing that as long as they tolerate, live and let live, and do no harm to their neighbor they can completely ignore their obligations to God—their obligations to worship him, respect his name, and keep holy his Sabbath day?) Jesus himself decried this practice. "Woe to you scribes and Pharisees, hypocrites! For you tithe mint, dill, and cummin [remember that tithes were owed to God], and have neglected the weightier matters of the law: justice and mercy and faith. It is these you ought to have practiced without neglecting the others" (Matt 23:23). And again, "But you say that if anyone tells father or mother, 'Whatever support you might have had from me is Corban' (that is, an offering to God)—then you no longer permit doing anything for a father or mother" (Mark 7:11-12). In many other condemnations besides, for example, condemning the neglect on the Sabbath of one's neighbor in need, Jesus confronted this mistaken belief.

In our present story, being as smart as he was, surely the almost-apostle wondered why the Good Teacher did not mention the first three commandments and spoke immediately of the fourth through the tenth. He could only have concluded that Jesus took them for granted as necessary to the inheritance of everlasting life. But Jesus was not simply taking them for granted. What he did by first recalling the commandments that order one's relationship to one's neighbor was actually to reunite all ten commandments, reunifying those that have to do with one's relationship with one's neighbor, the fourth through the tenth, back to their rightful place alongside of those that order a person's relationship with God, the first through the third. Jesus was teaching that obedience to all the commandments is necessary, not just obedience to some.

Jesus made clear to the almost-apostle that obeying the law and treating his neighbor according to its prescriptions was the first step to eternal happiness, but it wasn't the last. The man still lacked one more thing. What specifically did he lack? Mark gives us a clue when he tells us that Jesus "looking at him, loved him." Sometimes when one looks into another's eyes one can see exactly what the other person is thinking, what joy or sorrow they are experiencing; one knows instinctively what he or she

must do. This is what occurred between Jesus and this man to whom he
was extending an invitation to discipleship and to eternal life. Looking
at him, loving him, Jesus showed him what exactly it was that he lacked.
With his own eyes, what Jesus sought to elicit from the man was love. The
man had obeyed the commandments from his youth, but he did not love
God nor did he love his neighbor and the poor. Looking back into Jesus'
eyes, surely this is what the man saw reflected in them. Even before Jesus'
invitation to go, sell, and follow had left his lips and reached the almost-
apostle's ears, the almost-apostle knew simply by gazing into Jesus' eyes
what it was he lacked and what it was he needed to do.

There, on that road to Jerusalem, Jesus loved him. Because Jesus loved
him he sought to give him what he lacked, to give him even the very
kingdom of God. But the almost-apostle could not receive Jesus' love
because he could not make room for it in his life. To receive Jesus' love
he had to empty himself, for there can be no room in the same heart for
love of Jesus and love of possessions. But the almost-apostle had acquired
too many possessions. His soul was open only to possessions, not to the
person of Jesus, and certainly not to the poor. Perhaps no one had ever
before looked upon him with love. Perhaps he had never looked upon
another with love. Perhaps that is why he had acquired so many possessions, to fill up the bottomless pit that he had dug because he was lacking
in love, because, like the younger son in the parable of the Prodigal Son,
no one cared, until Jesus. Perhaps that is why the almost-apostle could
not recognize love even in Jesus' eyes.

You might object. From his childhood this man did everything the
law required of him. Surely that showed that he loved? It is true that
the man obeyed the law. It is also true that he wanted to draw near to
God, even to inherit everlasting life. But he obeyed the commandments
out of insecurity and fear, not out of love. Like many others, he thought
that maybe, just maybe, if he could possess absolutely everything there
was to possess, he could prove to himself and to others that he was lov-
able. By obeying from his youth absolutely everything God had ever
asked of him, down to the smallest detail of the law, he thought maybe
he could win God's favor, convince himself that God loved him. Like a
modern teenage girl who adorns herself with all sorts of makeup and
jewels and accessories to try to look pretty, and so win the attention of
a boy or inclusion in a clique, he adorned himself with the makeup and
accessories of obedience to the commands in order to win the approval
of God. He certainly held the mistaken belief that he could merit for
himself God's otherwise free gift of salvation.

Yet, even though from his youth into adulthood this almost-apostle had obeyed every single one of the commandments, it wasn't enough; now Jesus wanted him to do more. Jesus was calling him to move beyond the fame he received from obeying the commandments to the gain he would receive from the Lord of the commandments. Jesus wanted him to become like a little child and receive the kingdom as a free gift from God.

Jesus wanted to teach the man, then, that while the first commandment was to "love the Lord your God with all your heart, and with all your soul, and with all your mind, and with all your strength," the second was like it: to "love your neighbor as yourself" (Mark 12:30-31). The man had to obey the first three commands of the Torah, true. He had to obey all the commandments, indeed. But he had to obey them not out of fear, on one hand, or out of desire for security or gain, on the other, but out of love. In his answer to the almost-apostle, Jesus did not neglect the first three commandments, skip over them, or assume that everyone listening understood them. In teaching the man how to inherit everlasting life, Jesus was teaching him how to obey all the commandments out of love.

In actuality, Jesus presented the first through the third commandments of the Decalogue to this would-be apostle in such a way that they could be obeyed right there on the road and not solely in the temple or on the Sabbath. If this man obeyed the Good Teacher's command, he could possess eternal life at that very moment, he could share divine *communio* then and there, not even having to die to possess it. How? Because the first commandment teaches "you shall have no other gods before me" (Exod 20:2), then "go, sell what you own." Because the second commandment teaches "you shall not make wrongful use of the name of the LORD your God" (Exod 20:7), then "go . . . and give the money to the poor," for "[n]ot everyone who says to me, 'Lord, Lord,' will enter the kingdom of heaven, but only the one who does the will of my Father in heaven" (Matt 7:21) and "[t]ruly I tell you, just as you did it to one of the least of these who are members of my family, you did it to me" (Matt 25:40). Because God commanded that one "remember the sabbath day, and keep it holy" (Exod 20:8), then come and follow me, for "the Son of Man is lord even of the sabbath" (Mark 2:28).

Mark clues us in with one other little detail that helps us understand this important dynamic. When the man first ran up to Jesus, Mark tells us he knelt, assuming before Jesus a gesture of adoration. As the dialogue progressed, Jesus "looked at him with love." The Greek is in the present tense and is translated literally, "Jesus looking at him loves him." This must have been a very affectionate moment, even one of tender intimacy between the two. For the eyes are not only the windows, they are also the doors to one's soul, and to look with love is to get inside the heart of the other.

This little detail tells us that at some point Jesus himself either knelt on the ground before the man or brought the man to his feet; he had to do one or the other in order to look into his eyes. The psalmist prays, "Truly the eye of the Lord is on those who fear him, on those who hope in his steadfast love, to deliver their soul from death" (Ps 33:18-19). Jesus could have done either. He could have knelt down to the almost-apostle or simply have instructed him to stand up. I myself like to think that Jesus did both, that he first knelt down, descending to where the almost-apostle bent low, and from there raised him to his feet as he himself stood. In so doing, Jesus, looking at him and loving him, sought to raise him from death, to give him then and there eternal life.

But just as much as wanting to look into his eyes, Jesus wanted the man to gaze back into his. He wanted the man not only to hear his answer to his question regarding the gaining of eternal life. Jesus wanted the man to know that true adoration is not simply kneeling before the Good Teacher and complimenting him but following him. And Jesus wanted this almost-apostle to look into his own eyes and see that God loved him, that he was loved. He wanted the almost-apostle to see what love looked like—even more so, to see the face of love.

The story of the almost-apostle also teaches us that even on the road, that is, daily, we must develop this ever-new attitude toward God and God's commands. It is not enough for a deacon simply to kneel before Jesus, as before one's bishop at ordination, and believe that thereby he has come to the possession of eternal life, that he is saved. The true adoration Jesus desires is not only that we sit face-to-face with him but that we follow him back to front. Nor can one simply obey Jesus' commands out of fear of punishment or of loss or out of the desire for possession and for gain, for example, to earn a reputation, to gain standing, to acquire advancement in one's ministerial career, to be given a more prestigious or sought-after assignment, to be invited into a closer relationship with the bishop, to have security in this life because of a mistaken belief that once ordained the church "owes" one a living, or to gain eternal life solely because one is a deacon. Nor must a deacon allow his desire to draw near to God present barriers or obstacles in his relationship with others. Service to the sacramental Body of Christ is absolutely united to service to his Mystical Body. "[J]ust as you did for one of the least of these who are members of my family, you did it to me" (Matt 25:40).

Both are possible, and in diaconal ministry both are necessary—a deep intimate relationship with Christ found in following him and a life lived in loving service to others, especially the poor.

At the end of the story, when the man went away "overcast," note what Jesus did not do. Sullen as the man was, precisely because Jesus loved him he let him go. He did not run after him. He did not yell out, "Have a nice day." He did not wish him well, good luck, or even goodbye. Having extended to him an invitation to eternal life, what more could Jesus say or do? Yet Jesus' was an open invitation. On any given day the man might respond to grace, have a change of heart, do exactly what Jesus on the road to Jerusalem called him to do, and return. Not a single tomorrow awaited him that could not be the day the clouds of gloom would part and he could come back to claim his one true possession—the treasure held in store for him in heaven.

In essence, the almost-apostle asked Jesus what he had to pay, what price had been set for eternal life. Jesus didn't tell him that eternal life was priceless. Nor did he exactly tell him that it couldn't be bought. Eternal life is a loving relationship with the one who alone is good, not simply the carrying out of this or that command. The inheritance would cost nothing; it was free for those who sold everything, gave to the poor, and followed Jesus. Herein lies the true irony, and tragedy, of this story. Eternal life is "that they may know you, the only true God, and Jesus Christ whom you have sent" (John 17:3). Eternal life is simply a relationship with Jesus, which one cannot buy but only inherit. If the almost-apostle had sold his goods and given the proceeds to the poor, he would have acquired the funds necessary to "purchase" eternal life, even though eternal life is itself beyond price. That is why I believe it is not entirely accurate to call this man rich. True, he had many possessions, but possessions do not make one rich. To the contrary, ironically, the almost-apostle was so poor he did not have the "purchase price" for eternal life. The price was love, and, as we might say, he couldn't come up with the financing.

Finally, as we conclude this reflection, let's say a word or two about the disciples standing on the sidelines. They witnessed this encounter and heard the conversation between Jesus and the one invited to join their company. We can see them listening intently and cheering him on. "Come on. Say 'yes.' We did. We left everything and followed him." Indeed, in their panic at Jesus' teaching regarding the rich not entering the kingdom of God, Peter pointed to their own leaving everything behind as a plea lest they too, poor as they were, not come to inherit the kingdom of God (v. 28).

A command to follow Jesus is never an invitation to a private relationship with him, even if it is intensely personal. First, a relationship with Christ is always trinitarian, for Jesus and the Father are one in the Holy Spirit (John 10:30). But a relationship with Jesus is also always ecclesial, for Christ's identity is inextricably caught up with the disciples and in their *communio* with him *and* with one another. At the Last Supper he prayed to his Father, "[T]hese [men] know that you have sent me. I made your name known to them, and I will make it known, so that the love with which you have loved me may be in them, and I in them" (John 17:25-26). For the almost-apostle, selling his many possessions and giving the proceeds to the poor would have meant being inserted in the *communio* of Christ with his disciples. Calling the almost-apostle to this *communio*, Christ called him from slavery to his possessions to freedom for the sake of others, especially the poor, who are always with Jesus (Mark 14:7). Having kept the commandments since his childhood, the almost-apostle had acted in an ordered way toward all. But he had gazed on none with love. Now Christ, gazing upon him with love, offered him eternal life through eternal *communio* with the poor and with the disciples, that is, the church.

The deacon, a new friend of Christ, must ensure that his possessions, whatever he uses or needs, whatever they may be, never prevent him from entering into communion with the poor and sharing with them the communion of the Trinity and the church. This can be a perpetual temptation for a deacon, truly for all professional ministers. It is easy to do things on behalf of the poor, especially since so many are incapable of acting on their own behalf. But this is not what Christ wants of his deacons, whom he has called to be icons of his own suffering. Christ calls deacons to be with him and then, out of that *communio*, to serve his brothers and sisters, to serve sinners and the poor. He calls his deacons to love him before ministering to those whom he himself loves. Then, as Jesus gazed with love upon the almost-apostle, so the deacon is to gaze upon the poor. And this the deacon can do only when he first stands, looks into the eyes of the Lord, and sees love. Then go, sell, give, and follow Jesus. Finally, kneel before the poor and teach them how to inherit eternal life.

A deacon's being with the Lord must become his being for the Lord. His being for the Lord must become his being as the Suffering Servant for sinners and the poor. For this to occur, the deacon must first be emptied so as to receive and receive so as to give.

chapter four

The Deacon, Servant of the Word Made Flesh

The Father Feeds; the Son Is Food.
The Deacon Is Nourished by and Distributes the Bread of Life.
The Deacon's Munus Sanctificandi, *the Office of Sanctifying.*

"When a person is touched by the Word," Pope John Paul II wrote, "obedience is born, that is listening which changes life" (*Orientale lumen* 10). Touched by the Word spoken, the deacon has responded and at ordination voiced his own "Present" to the Lord's call. Before one is ordained he must kneel and place his hands in those of the bishop, promising to him and to his successors respect and obedience. With those same hands, that is, hands of obedient service, the deacon sets the altar for the eucharistic sacrifice, raises the chalice of the covenant to the glory of the Father, and ministers the Precious Body and Blood of the Lord to communicants, including the sick and dying.

In this reflection we will consider the deacon's participation in the *munus sanctificandi*, the office of sanctifying. First, we will consider the Eucharist as a sacrifice. Then we will focus on the deacon's role at the eucharistic sacrifice. Finally, we will attend to some ways in which Christ and the church spiritually nourish the deacon to live and exercise his diaconate.

The Sacrifice of the Eucharist

The Second Vatican Council teaches that the Eucharist is "the source and the summit" of the Christian life. Accordingly, the worshiping assembly has the right and duty to participate in it fully, actively, and consciously (*Sacrosanctum concilium* [The Constitution on the Sacred Liturgy] 14). This being true of the assembled congregation, it goes without saying that it is true of the deacon. The Eucharist is the source and summit of his life and ministry; he must carry out his role in its celebration fully, actively, and consciously. The liturgy, especially the Eucharist, sanctifies him and enables him to love and be faithful to what he promises at ordination. His ministry at the altar strengthens him in living a diaconal life and unifies his many ministries as diaconal.

Vatican II teaches, "At the Last Supper, on the night he was betrayed, our Savior instituted the eucharistic sacrifice of his Body and Blood. This he did in order to perpetuate the sacrifice of the Cross throughout the ages until he should come again, and so to entrust to his beloved spouse, the Church, a memorial of his death and resurrection: a sacrament of love, a sign of unity, a bond of charity, a paschal banquet in which Christ is consumed, the mind is filled with grace, and a pledge of future glory is given to us" (SC 47).

The Eucharist is first of all a sacrifice. Its celebration is the celebration not simply of the Word becoming flesh but of the Word's flesh being offered as expiation for sin and for salvation, as well as true spiritual food and drink for the life of those who partake of it. For this reason, when we say that a deacon is servant of the altar we are saying that at one and the same time he serves the person of the sacrificing Christ, the sacrificial act that takes place on the altar, as well as the sacrificial food distributed from it.

In the course of the eucharistic liturgy, the priest, having received the gifts brought forward by the faithful and prepared by the deacon, asks the assembled congregation (in the original Latin), "Pray, my brothers and sisters, that this, my sacrifice and yours, may be acceptable to God, the Father almighty." In his 1980 Letter to the Bishops on the Eucharist, Pope John Paul II taught, "These words are binding, since they express the character of the entire Eucharistic liturgy and the fullness of its divine and ecclesial content" (9). The *Catechism* teaches, "In the Eucharist the sacrifice of Christ becomes also the sacrifice of the members of his Body. The lives of the faithful, their praise, sufferings, prayer, and work, are united with those of Christ and with his total offering, and so acquire a new value" (1368). While there is only one sacrifice that the priest acting *in persona Christi* offers to the Father, that is, the sacrifice of Christ, that sacrifice is at the same time the sacrifice of the whole church and of each of its members assembled for worship. What the faithful in virtue of their baptismal priesthood offer, the priest-celebrant of the Eucharist accepts and unites with his sacrifice, the sacrifice of Christ, that the church might offer one sacrifice of praise to the Father.

An ordained deacon has a unique and important role to play in assisting *both* the lay faithful to offer their sacrifices *and* the sacred minister to accept them, to unite them into the one sacrifice of Christ and of the church, and to offer it to the Father. Therefore, as the *General Instruction of the Roman Missal* instructs, the deacon "serves the celebration of the Sacrifice" (94). His ministry "is intrinsic, fundamental, and distinct" (*Directory* 28).

Practically, this means that the first object of the deacon's ministry at Mass is *not* the presider-celebrant. To the contrary, it is the entire assembled faithful, presider-celebrant *and* baptized laity. In the *Directory*, in its section titled "*Diaconia* of the Liturgy," the church makes this point repeatedly. It specifies first that "in the Eucharistic Sacrifice the deacon does not celebrate the mystery: rather, he effectively represents on the one hand, *the people of God* and, specifically, helps them to unite their lives to the offering of Christ; while on the other, in the name of Christ himself, he helps the *Church* to participate in the fruits of that sacrifice" (28). It continues, "Deacons shall observe devoutly the liturgical norms proper to the sacred mysteries so as to bring *the faithful* to a conscious participation in the liturgy, to fortify their faith, give worship to God and sanctify the Church" (29). Because deacons in fact "'assist the bishop and priests in the celebration of the divine mysteries[,]' [t]hey should therefore work to promote liturgical celebrations which involve the *whole assembly*, fostering the interior participation of the faithful in the liturgy and the exercise of the various ministries" (30). Finally, "[t]he ministry of deacons also includes preparation of the faithful for reception of the sacraments and their pastoral care after having received them" (30; all emphases added).

The deacon therefore serves the celebration of the divine liturgy itself and assists the bishop or priest when, in the first order, he catechizes, prepares, and cares that the lay faithful themselves fully, actively, and consciously participate in its celebration. In the second order, he exercises specifically defined auxiliary tasks of liturgical ministry, for example, helping to receive the gifts, setting the altar, and distributing the Precious

Blood. In this way, like the deacons in Acts 6, he assists the faithful, and particularly the poor, to come to the table and to be seated so as to be fed. The deacon serves them at the table that they might receive the fullness of grace poured out in the Word made flesh and the Word's flesh sacrificed as food. Finally, he leads them from the table into the world, to "[g]o in peace to love and serve the Lord," that is, to feed others as they themselves have been fed.

In the sacred liturgy the deacon's every word, gesture, and action, his very presence should be inspired and evaluated from this one criterion: does it lead the assembled faithful and every member thereof—the presider and the congregants—to participate fully, consciously, and actively? If because of the deacon someone in the sanctuary or someone in the pews is not so participating, then he is not doing his job well, even if he has attended to every need of the presider and carried out every rubric of the liturgy exactingly.

For this reason it is important that a deacon be familiar not simply with the rites of liturgy, the *accoutrement* of sacramental worship, and the functions of each of the ministers, especially of his own and those of the presider. More than that, the deacon needs to be a liturgist. The full, conscious, and active participation of the worshipers demands that he understand the dynamics of liturgical worship, is sensitive to the mood and condition of those who gather to worship, and is able, together with the presider, to lead the worshiping assembly in its drawing near to God.

The Meaning of Sacrifice

Before turning to the deacon's specific functions at the eucharistic sacrifice, I want to reflect a bit on the institution of sacrifice in the Old Testament. My intent is not to enter into an extended, scholarly discussion of the meaning of Jewish temple worship, which would be beyond the scope of these reflections. Rather, I want simply to offer a few salient points on which to reflect, in light of a deacon's ordained service to the eucharistic sacrifice of Jesus and that of the church, because its meaning is rooted in the Torah, the covenant, and the temple.

Webster's dictionary defines sacrifice as either an act of sacrificing or the object sacrificed to a deity on one's own behalf or on behalf of others. In ancient times, as we saw in the last chapter, some pagans sacrificed to their gods in vain attempts to please them. They sacrificed because they stood servile, helpless, and pathetic before their gods, hoping to stifle their wrath from flaring up against them.

In the Old Testament, however, the act of sacrifice meant something wholly dissimilar from such Gentile notions. Sacrifice that simply pleased or appeased the Lord was foreign to the Jewish understanding of this act. The Hebrew words for sacrifice are *korban* and *lehakriv*. They have the same root as "to come near, to approach, to become closely involved in a relationship with someone." In the Old Testament they were used exclusively in the context of man's relationship to God, not to neighbor. To offer *korban* was the means by which Israel as a nation and her people individually became closely involved with and drew near to the Lord who, although holy, that is, set apart and unapproachable, nonetheless had chosen them to be a people peculiarly his own, a people to whom he wanted to draw near. *Korban* was the gratitude that was rendered so as to draw near to the Lord who had drawn near to Israel, liberating her from Egypt, leading her through the desert, and bringing her into a land flowing with milk and honey. The God of Abraham, Isaac, and Jacob did not need to be pleased or appeased. He was almighty. What the Lord God desired was to be approached; he desired Israel's remembering and her gratitude. When his anger blazed up against them it was because they had forgotten and turned away from him who had drawn near to them. Turning their faces away from him, they turned to the worship of false gods and to wickedness.

But how does one draw near to another who is unapproachable? What made it possible for Jewish sacrifice to effect a drawing near of human beings to God?

As we have said, the Lord had a different relationship with his people than pagan peoples believed their gods had with them. In creating Israel, the true God established between himself and his people bridges: responsible persons whom he would allow to stand with one foot on both sides of the relationship divide. In contemporary religious terminology we call such a person a vicarious representative. A vicarious representative makes it possible for two or more parties who, for whatever reason, are unable to otherwise have a personal relationship to do so. Being near to each, a vicarious representative is able to draw each to the other, bridging the distance between the two. A vicarious representative personally "represents" the one to the other and vice versa.

The Lord took the initiative in establishing his relationship with Israel, desiring to draw near to her. But the Israelites could not draw near unless there was someone on their side who trusted the one who was extending the invitation. In the 1997 movie *Contact*, Ellie, a young scientist, sends mathematical signals into space, convinced that somewhere out there intelligent life exists, that her signal will be received, that contact will be made between human beings and extraterrestrial life. Reverse the point from which the contact signal originates and you have the Lord. He was the other "out there." He knew humankind existed. Yet humankind had sinned and gone into hiding, and God, if you will, had lost contact with his creation. "Where are you?" the Lord God called out to Adam and Eve (Gen 3:9). Yet, even then, when humans sinned and hid themselves from God, the Lord did not abandon them but continued to seek them out and to love them.

What would enable humans to hear God's signal of love and respond and in freedom, bold confidence, to draw near to the unapproachable? Read Paul's exhortation to the Ephesians: "This was in accordance with the eternal purpose that he has carried out in Christ Jesus our Lord, in whom we have access to God in boldness and confidence through faith in him" (3:11-12). The answer is faith. This faith, though, is not the faith that assents to dogmatic or intellectual propositions about God, as vital as such faith is. No, the type of faith that was necessary so that the Lord could draw near to humankind and humankind to the Lord was a personal, never-ending giving of oneself to the person of God, a faith because of which one was willing to sacrifice oneself to the other, a trust so deep that at the command of God one was willing even to sacrifice one's own son. God anointed those men and women who demonstrated such faith and believed in him as his vicarious representatives to Israel. What is more, because of them God could designate Israel herself in turn to be his vicarious representative to all the nations of the earth. Conversely, being men and women of faith, they could be not only Israel's but all of creation's representatives before the throne of God.

God's nature is love; faithfulness is the virtue by which his vicarious representatives lived. God's love and the vicarious representative's fidelity allowed God to establish between the two of them an intimate relationship. For example, God said to Abraham, who had passed his test of fidelity, "For now I know that you fear God, since you have not withheld your son, your only son, from me" (Gen 22:12). Therefore, "By myself I have sworn, says the LORD: . . . I will indeed bless you" (Gen 22:15-17). God's intimacy with Moses was an archetype of the intimacy he extended to all whom he liberated from slavery and to their descendants. "[Moses] is entrusted with all my house. With him I speak face to face—clearly, not in riddles; and he beholds the form of the LORD" (Num 12:7-8; see Exod 33:11; Deut 34:10). God revealed his desire for intimacy with his chosen people in the establishment of the high priesthood, an office necessary to ensure the renewal of the covenant—not necessary, certainly, on the Lord's part but rather on Israel's. The Lord allowed Aaron alone to accompany Moses up Mount Sinai to receive the Ten Commandments (Exod 19:24), the law given to those who are the Lord's "treasured possession out of all the peoples . . . a priestly kingdom and a holy nation" (Exod 19:5-6). Throughout the history of Israel, time and time again the Lord manifested his intimacy with her representatives: for example, with David, his anointed one, and with his servants, the prophets. These latter, for their part, characterized the relationship between the Lord and Israel using the language of the most intimate of human relationships, of "drawings near," that of bridegroom and bride.

Each whom the Lord invited into intimacy with himself, he invited not simply for that person's sake but for the sakes of all the people, just as he invites the deacon into a new friendship with him not simply for his own sake but for the sakes of all the people. Abraham's devotion was counted in his favor on behalf of his descendants, Moses' and Aaron's on behalf of the chosen people, David's for the sake of the entire kingdom, unified under his rule and recalled to fidelity by the prophets. In their intimacy with God, all stood representing both the Lord and Israel to the other. The Lord's intimacy with each of them individually was his intimacy with all Israel. Their intimacy with the Lord was Israel's intimacy with its God.

Furthermore, the Lord's intimacy with Israel was not simply "spiritual." It was rational, emotional, corporeal, and covenantal. Abraham and his descendants wore the mark of intimacy in their circumcision. Moses' face was covered by a veil, lest his intimacy with the Lord frighten, even repulse the people. God dwelt with his people in the commandments, written by his own hand and "housed" in the ark and in the temple.

The Torah itself was an expression of the intimacy between the Lord and Israel. Israel had a different understanding of religion than did the pagans. They did not simply submit to unreasonable or irrational gods, obeying what they commanded and avoiding what they forbade so as to please them. Rather, on Mount Sinai the Lord by his own hand inscribed the Ten Commandments on stone and revealed the Torah to Israel for her own good—that Israel, not he, might be pleased. As Moses said, "For what other great nation has a god so near to it as the LORD our God is whenever we call to him? And what other great nation has statutes and ordinances as just as this entire law?" (Deut 4:7-8). The Torah was itself the vicarious representative between God and Israel. It was the means through which to draw near to the Lord.

We can see, then, why the Lord God commanded that sacrifices be offered and why it was necessary to offer sacrifice in order to know intimacy. The Lord was life ("I AM WHO I AM" [Exod 3:14]) and had given life to his people—creating them, liberating them from slavery, giving them the Torah by which and the Promised Land on which to live. To draw near to that life and to live intimately with the Lord on the land, it was necessary to sacrifice the life that the land produced. Sacrificing life showed that one was faithful—like Abraham and the patriarchs, Moses and Aaron—so deeply faithful that at God's command one was even willing to take the life of another being to represent the sacrifice of one's own. Jewish temple sacrifice, in fact, engaged all four elements of created life. The priest represented the human world; the animal sacrificed, the animal world; the cereal, wine, and oil libations, which required sun and water, the vegetative world; and frankincense and salt, the mineral world.

The Jew who offered a sacrifice understood life—whether his own or that of the animal, vegetable, or mineral being sacrificed—to bear the mysterious character of gift from God. Life was not a natural and autonomous possession of one's own; one's own life was not one's to possess. Rather, the Lord alone possessed life. Gratitude that he who alone possessed life shared it with creation and with Israel required that in return Israel and all creation share life with the Lord God and with others.

In their relationship with the Lord, as in any intimate relationship between persons, the exchanging of gifts was necessary. The Lord's gift of life demanded the gift of life in exchange. These premises, that no life is possessed autonomously and that all life is shared, "support the assumption that living beings can represent one another, stand in for one another: humans can represent all creatures before God, and one human being can represent other humans before God" (Luke Timothy Johnson, *Hebrews: A Commentary*, p. 26).

A Jew offering a sacrifice, then, believed that although one was bringing to an end the life of a being of a lower order, nonetheless through vicarious representation the sacrifice he or she was making was that of his or her own person, of his or her own life. In so sacrificing, the Jew would be allowed to approach, to draw near to the God of life. God, to whom the sacrifice was made, assigned vicarious meaning both to the act of sacrifice and to the matter being sacrificed. By God's own decree, that which was sacrificed took on, assumed vicariously, the life of the one who was making the sacrifice. The flesh and blood of the animal sacrificed or the pulp of the cereal offered, the wine or oil poured out, or the frankincense burned, represented the materiality and spirit, the body and blood, the soul and flesh of the one making the sacrifice. The turtledove, the goat, the heifer or bullock died, but by the decree of the Lord to whom it was sacrificed, the one who offered the sacrifice lived so as to draw near to the living God. This is what it meant that God accepted Israel's sacrifice. The one who offered it was given new life, was given a fuller share, if you will, in God's own life.

Historically, though, from Mount Sinai—that is, from the time of the revelation of the covenant and the institution of sacrifice by which it was ratified—through the Babylonian captivity, exile, and the subsequent return of God's people to the Promised Land, and until the coming of Christ, it appears that God himself underwent a sort of change of attitude regarding sacrifice and the "delight" he took in them. Yves Congar writes,

> Here, God wishes sacrifice; there, he does not wish it. Is this a contradiction? . . . No, not a contradiction, but a simultaneous affirmation in respect of the same thing, of a Yes and a No that expresses the dialectic of progress which is at the heart of the prophetic mission. The Yes and the No are concerned with the same reality; but the No is looking at an aspect of it that must be rejected and left behind, while the Yes is looking at a deeper aspect which must confirm a new state of things. . . . God desires sacrifices, but not such as are offered in a spirit of unrighteousness; he wants mercifulness and not outward observance, inward godliness and not the equivocal carrying out of a rite. He wants, indeed, the offering not of material things, animals and first-fruits, but of the living man himself. What God wants offered is nothing but the man himself: not irrational beasts but the spiritual, "rational," worship and sacrifices of his reasoning creation, who is made that he may as a son render up again to God the Image that he bears. (*Lay People in the Church*, pp. 125–26)

In the impassioned words of the prophet Micah: "'With what shall I come before the LORD, and bow myself before God on high? Shall I come before him with burnt offerings, with calves a year old? Will the LORD be pleased with thousands of rams, with ten thousands of rivers of oil? Shall I give my firstborn for my transgression, the fruit of my body for the sin of my soul?' He has told you, O mortal, what is good; and what does the LORD require of you but to do justice, and to love kindness, and to walk humbly with your God?" (6:6-8). Doing right, loving what is good, walking humbly with the Lord is the true sacrifice that God would accept and by which man could draw near to the Lord. In the Talmud

Berakhot 22:A, it was written that God required sacrifice to better man, but he would prefer that man not sin; if he did not sin, then no sacrifice would be necessary.

Now, Jesus was a good Jew. For example, we know that his family went up to Jerusalem every year for the feast of Passover. In fact, to emphasize the point Luke tells us that it was their custom to do so (see Luke 2:41-42). Jesus himself ate the sacrificial meal of Passover. There is no evidence that Jesus rejected temple sacrifice or that he was critical of ritual sacrifice if it was carried out not just with a purified body but especially with a pure heart. And Jesus was highly critical of the attitude with which rituals were often carried out, that is, perfunctorily, simply going through the motions in order to fulfill the law, without a right disposition and penitent heart, as required by the Torah. For example, he affirmed the scribe's insight into the greatest of the commandments, namely, that "'to love [the Lord your God] with all the heart, and with all the understanding, and with all the strength,' and 'to love one's neighbor as oneself,'—this is much more important than all whole burnt offerings and sacrifices," even telling the young man that he was not far from the kingdom of God (Mark 12:33-34).

That having been said, it is also true that in the gospels, although Jesus himself neither taught against nor forbade the offering of ritual temple sacrifice, there is no evidence that he himself offered a material sacrifice at the temple. Why not? First, if temple sacrifice was necessary so that man could approach and draw near to God, Jesus knew that in his own person the opposite had occurred: God had drawn near fully, completely, and intimately to man. Second, Jesus knew himself to be in the flesh the ultimate sacrifice of God on behalf of man but also of man on behalf of drawing near to God. He knew himself to be the "first born, one year old, unblemished" lamb, the sacrifice of which would fulfill all others and show all others to be forever superfluous. His sacrifice on the cross was to be the sacrifice "once for all" (Heb 7:27). Once he offered himself on the cross, the church understood that Jesus had fulfilled the prophecy of Psalm 40. "Consequently," as Hebrews teaches, "when Christ came into the world, he said, 'Sacrifices and offerings you have not desired, but a body you have prepared for me; in burnt offerings and sin offerings you have taken no pleasure. Then I said, 'See, God, I have come to do your will, O God.' . . . And it is by God's will that we have been sanctified through the offering of the body of Jesus Christ once for all" (10:5-10).

The church came to see, then, that Jesus was not only the sacrificial victim but also the temple, the altar, and the high priest. His sacrifice on the cross, the one sacrifice that fulfilled all others, from then on made the historical institutions of the old covenants superfluous. The Father, having accepted his Son's perfect sacrifice, would never again need or seek another vicarious representative to represent him to humans and humans to him. Jesus forever will be the perfect vicarious representative through whom God had drawn near to all creation and creation could forever draw near to God. Because God raised his Son from the dead, thereafter the sacrifices of all born of water and the Spirit could be joined with Christ's sacrifice on Calvary. In Christ and through his blood all could "approach the throne of grace with boldness, so that we may receive mercy and find grace to help in time of need" (Heb 4:16).

In Christ Jesus, the perfect sacrifice was accomplished, perfect because in the first place it attained not the drawing near of man to God but rather the drawing near of God to man. In Jesus' sacrifice of the cross God found Adam and Eve, who had been hiding in death. He forgave their sin, and so the right relationship between God and all humankind was restored. In Christ Jesus, then, as St. Augustine taught, "[T]rue sacrifice is every work done with the aim of uniting us with God in a holy fellowship, that is to say, every work that is referred as its end to the good which can make us truly blessed" (*City of God*, Bk. X, c. 5,6).

The Deacon and the Eucharist

With this background, what can we say now of diaconal ministry at the altar of sacrifice?

Having been ordained, the church assigns to the deacon various functions within the liturgy "distinct from that of the ordained priestly ministry" (*Directory* 28). At the Mass he serves the sacrifice itself and the assembled community, namely, the presider-celebrant *and no less*, as we have seen, the baptized lay faithful, for they too celebrate the Eucharist in virtue of their baptismal priesthood. The deacon assists all who celebrate the Mass to join their sacrifice to that of the ordained presider-celebrant, so that the drawing near of God to humans and humans to God that it effects is most fully brought about, its copious fruits most widely distributed. The deacon should understand—and this point bears repeating—that at Mass his ministry is not simply "to help Father," but equally and perhaps even more crucially to assist the baptized faithful to participate fully, consciously, and actively. If by the deacon's words and actions the faithful indeed so celebrate the liturgy, then the deacon will be his most effective, he will be most perceptibly and evidently imitating Christ the Suffering Servant, whose icon he has been ordained to be.

At the beginning of the eucharistic celebration and at its conclusion, accompanying the presider, the deacon venerates the altar of sacrifice with a kiss. This simple gesture of the liturgy is jam-packed with meaning, and the deacon should never take it for granted.

Christ ordains the deacon into a new intimacy, a new friendship. Kissing is a gesture of affection. The deacon expresses his new friendship with Christ when he, the deacon, venerates Christ's altar with a kiss. With this gesture he expresses his affectionate gratitude to Christ for his sacrifice on the cross, that very same sacrifice about to be represented in an unbloody fashion on the altar he kisses. With a kiss the deacon professes his ever-deepening love for his Beloved, who wrought the salvation of the church and his own salvation through suffering, sufferings he now assigns to his deacon.

Further, by kissing the altar the deacon communicates to the presider, with whom he kisses the altar, and to the assembled faithful, whom he assists to join their sacrifices to that of the Mass, first, that he himself loves the Eucharist and, second, that the presider can count on him and his collaboration, whether the presider is the pope or the pastor of the smallest parish in the furthest corner of the globe, to serve the faithful in serving the eucharistic sacrifice of Christ. Like a young lover who has fallen in love and isn't afraid to kiss his or her beloved in public, by kissing the altar the deacon wants everyone to know how much he himself loves the Blessed Eucharist, by which more than any other sacramental reality the Savior's saving sufferings are communicated to his people, and that in life and collaborative ministry with his bishop and the priests, he will serve it to sinners and to the poor.

Additionally, in regard to the specific assembly gathered for the celebration of the Eucharist, a deacon's kissing of the altar represents two things.

First, by kissing the altar the deacon signals to the assembled community, a community that in some way he has been responsible for gathering together, that he loves them, and so will make available to them what he himself will receive from the altar: the Eucharist. In other words, because the deacon loves, the gift he himself will receive from the altar he will in turn give from the altar as a gift. "'Worship' itself, Eucharistic communion," Pope Benedict XVI teaches in his encyclical *Deus caritas est*, "includes the reality both of being loved and of loving others in turn. A Eucharist which does not pass over into the concrete practice of love is intrinsically fragmented" (14).

Second, kissing the altar of sacrifice at the beginning and conclusion of every Eucharist is a kind of petition. As he kisses the altar the deacon should pray that the members of the ecclesial community, both while assembled for the eucharistic sacrifice and as they disperse from the meal, be faithful to the Lord: faithful as Mary, who kissed with a mother's kiss, and not as Judas, who with a kiss betrayed.

Finally, in his own regard, kissing the altar is for the deacon a prayer for the renewal of his life and ministry. The *Catechism* teaches that deacons are "more closely united to the altar so as to exercise their ministry more fruitfully through the sacramental grace of the diaconate" (1571). As from a lover's kiss, a deacon draws from the altar of sacrifice the strength needed to carry out his ministry with fidelity and zeal.

When the Eucharist begins and as the assembly becomes a united people, the deacon may (with option C) lead the congregation in its act of penance. In one of the earliest of the church's documents implementing the liturgical reforms of the Second Vatican Council, *Eucharisticum mysterium* (1967), it is written, "The Eucharist should . . . be presented to the faithful 'as a medicine, by which we are freed from our daily faults and preserved from mortal sin;' they should be shown how to make use of the penitential parts of the liturgy of the Mass" (35). In the penitential rite, this is the deacon's role, presenting the Eucharist to the faithful as medicine.

Additionally, according to the *GIRM*, the penitential rite is "very useful for expressing and fostering the faithful's active participation" (36). Here (and at the prayer of the faithful, together with other parts of the liturgy assigned to him) the deacon not only brings and welcomes sinners and the poor to the altar but contributes to making of the entire congregation one united body, a family conscious of the mercies of the Lord and open to the graces to be poured out when it fully, actively, and consciously participates in the eucharistic sacrifice.

For these reasons, leading the assembly in the penitential rite is something the deacon should undertake quite prayerfully. Christ the Suffering Servant came "to bring good news to the poor" (Luke 4:18). What greater poverty, what greater illness is there for which we need divine medicine than to be a sinner? The presider invites the members of the assembled congregation to recognize that all are sinners, to examine their consciences, and to ask God's mercy; he calls them to arise from the poverty of their sinful ways to the rich new life of holiness. The deacon then takes up the presider's invitation and in turn announces good news to the assembly, all of whom are poor because of sin. This good news is found in the form of the penitential praises he articulates in the name of the community. The deacon is to praise the Lord for who he is ("You are mighty God and Prince of Peace," "You are Son of God and Son of Mary," and so on) and for what he has accomplished in our salvation ("You came to call sinners," "You raise the dead to new life," etc.).

Each and every one of the petitions of penitential praise that the church proffers in option C is addressed directly to Christ in the second person singular—they all use the word "You"—recalling who he is and what he has done to forgive our sins. In not a single one of them is the priest or deacon to shine the spotlight on the community for what it has done or failed to do or for what it may need. If a deacon composes his own penitential invocations, therefore, he should always address them to Christ. He should never say, for example, "We are all sinners, Lord have mercy" or "We are all hurting, Christ have mercy." Why not? First, Christ's faithfulness should be proclaimed to us, not our sinfulness, need, or present circumstances to him. In this way, too, the deacon is announcing to sinners the good news that Christ is our Savior who rescues all of us from our greatest poverty, that of sin. Second, none of us approaches the eucharistic table as a saint, that is, as someone who has accepted Jesus as his or her personal Lord and Savior. To the contrary, we admit our sinfulness, that we have rejected and wandered far from him, and that we have forgotten him who remembered us when he took possession of his kingdom. Through the deacon's articulation of Christ's saving deeds he calls the presider and the people to remember Christ, "who is peace itself / and who has washed away our hatred with his blood" (prayer over the gifts for the Mass in Time of War or Civil Disturbance), and to do what we have assembled to do in memory of him. Finally, the penitential invocations of the Lord must always be exactly that: penitential. Examples of non-penitential invocations that should never be voiced might be: "Lord, you have given us this beautiful day," or "Lord, help us to finally win the Super Bowl" (both of which I have actually heard, and similar ones besides).

Following the Liturgy of the Word, the deacon approaches the altar for the Liturgy of the Eucharist. The church and the poor rely on the deacon to bring their sacrifices and gifts to that altar. How? First, even before the eucharistic celebration begins, it is the deacon's proper function, not the sacristan's, to ensure that everything necessary for its celebration has been provided and made ready—that the vessels and linens are prepared; the liturgical books have been marked; the offertory procession is assigned; the servers, lectors, and extraordinary ministers of Holy

Communion are prepared and in place (including ensuring that lectors are able to pronounce properly all of the words in that Mass' readings); the sound system and microphones are working; etc. Jesus entrusted this diaconal function to his apostles, who asked him where he wanted them to prepare for the Passover feast on the night of his Last Supper. The apostles' successors in turn entrust that function to deacons. To ensure the preparedness of the Eucharist is an apostolic function, and the deacon should not neglect it.

Then, as the Liturgy of the Eucharist unfolds, the deacon himself prepares the altar for the sacrifice and places upon it the sacred vessels necessary for its celebration and for the sacrifice that the presider and the baptized faithful will offer. Preparing the altar is the deacon's archetypal ministry; truly, it embodies all that he is about as a deacon. He serves sinners and the poor that they might be brought to the altar and fed from it; he now sets the altar so that Christ himself can serve his sacrificial meal to his people. The deacon assists the presider in receiving from the poor the gifts they themselves bring for the eucharistic meal; he sets those gifts on the altar. He dismisses sinners and the poor from that same altar to be as an altar for others; he himself kisses the altar as he takes his leave of it, for as Christ the Suffering Servant he makes himself a sacrifice to the poor for the sake of their salvation. According to the *GIRM*, at the conclusion of Mass only the presider and the deacons venerate the altar with a kiss, not the concelebrants (251).

At the offertory, the presider incenses the eucharistic gifts of bread and wine as well as the altar of sacrifice on which they have been placed. It pertains to the deacon to incense the presider *and* the assembled worshipers, for they too exercise their baptismal priesthood in offering their sacrifices, which are joined to the eucharistic sacrifice on the altar. If there are deacons present and vested, whether they are assisting the celebrant or not, they are incensed separately from the presider and any concelebrants, and should not stand next to him or with them, for they do not offer the eucharistic sacrifice as priests. (Generally, the *GIRM* instructs that deacons should not stand, function, or gesture in any way that seemingly equates them with priests or might confuse the assembly as to their own proper role and ministry.)

Next comes the doxology. The doxology is the word and gesture of both the presider and deacon that summarize the Eucharist in its entirety. The deacon (and not a priest) elevates the chalice as the presider elevates the consecrated host. This simple gesture of the Eucharist clearly shows forth to the assembled worshipers the unity of holy orders, that is, of the ministry of the ordained priest and deacon. The presider and the deacon elevate the sacred Body and Precious Blood of Jesus so that the assembled community might behold him who is the great "Amen" to the Father's love and in turn give all glory and honor to the Father. Too, elevating the chalice, "the one cup" filled with Precious Blood, the deacon anticipates distributing it to the congregation, who gaze upon what God is giving to his people, the community, for the salvation of all. Finally, in preparing the assembled worshipers to receive him who "is our peace" and who "in his flesh . . . has broken down the dividing wall . . . thus making peace" (Eph 2:14-15), the deacon invites them to exchange the sign of peace.

At the offertory the deacon hands to the presider the paten with unconsecrated bread and the chalice with unconsecrated wine. Then at Communion he receives from the presider the Body and Blood of Christ. Having received his own Communion, because he is ordained to ministry and not to the priesthood, the deacon receives from the hands of the presider or concelebrant the chalice he will hand to the faithful; he does not "grab" it for himself. As at the doxology the deacon elevated the chalice standing alongside the presider, at the distribution of Holy Communion he distributes the Precious Blood of Jesus alongside the presider who distributes his Body.

If Communion is being distributed under both species, even if extraordinary ministers of Holy Communion are helping, the deacon does not distribute the consecrated hosts to the faithful. His ministry is that of the chalice alongside the presider. Why? What the chalice is to the Blood of Christ, so the deacon is to the church's love and care for the poor. As the deacon extends the chalice to others so that they may drink of Christ's forgiving mercy, so the church "hands" the deacon to the poor so that they might have the Good News announced to them. As one must hold the chalice to drink from it, so the poor should be able to cling to the deacon in his love and ministry for them, and in so doing cling to Christ himself. By the grace of his ordination as icon of Christ the Suffering Servant, whose blood was "poured forth for the many," the deacon is graced to sacrifice his own body and blood for love of sinners and the poor, not simply to feed them with Christ's. It is no accident that the restoration of Communion under both species, a more perfect sign of participating in the passion and death of Christ, is accompanied by the restoration of the diaconate as a permanent ministry in the church.

At the conclusion of the Communion rite, the deacon attends to the sacred vessels. He serves Christ in purifying the sacred vessels as the friends of Jesus served him who removed his body from the cross, wrapped it in linen, and laid it in a tomb. In this act, the deacon is also like the women who kept vigil at the tomb of Christ and came on Easter morning to anoint him with perfumed oil and spices. Regrettably, the size of many Sunday eucharistic assemblies today, requiring as they do a large number of patens and chalices, being scheduled quite tightly, with congregants convinced that Mass always goes on too long as it is and that it ends the moment they themselves receive Communion and not a moment later, all too often turn the rite of purifying the sacred vessels into a task more akin to the washing of dishes, if it is even carried out at all. The deacon, however, should exercise this function with reverence, the same reverence he brings to the elevation of the chalice at the doxology and to the distribution of the Precious Blood itself.

Being Fed for Ministry

The deacon feeds others with the Body and Blood of Christ. How is he himself to be nourished for the sake of his diaconal life and ministry? In the sacraments of both orders and marriage the recipient receives what he is called to become and is called to become what he receives. Because of holy orders, then, a deacon should:

- Attend the Eucharist daily, or, if that is not possible given his work schedule, as frequently as possible. A deacon should also develop the habit of participating in the eucharistic sacrifice on the anniversaries of significant occasions in his life and in the lives of his family members, for example, birthdays, baptisms, first Holy Communions, confirmations, graduations, marriages, and deaths. It is also important for a deacon to participate in the Eucharist on the significant events and anniversaries in the life of his local church and Christian community and its leaders: anniversaries of the establishment of his diocese, the founding or feast day of his own parish or ecclesial community, the dedication of his cathedral and parish church, anniversaries of his ordained and professed colleagues (especially those of his bishop and coworkers in the parish), etc. It is not necessary that the deacon vest and function as a deacon at the daily celebration of the Eucharist (see *Directory* 54). Certainly there are times when it is more appropriate to do so, for example, on certain major solemnities, feast days, and memorials, or the anniversary of his ordination. But there are also days on which it may be more appropriate in living his sacrament of marriage and in family life that he participate in the eucharistic celebration alongside his spouse, children, and family. Attending Mass daily, at least frequently, may be precisely what he needs to counter the claims his secular employer makes on him and restore balance in his life and in that of his family.

- Daily, at least regularly and frequently, spend time in adoration before the Blessed Sacrament. When a deacon adores Jesus in the Blessed Sacrament he allows the Lord to be his Suffering Servant, receiving from him strength to suffer and to serve as his icon. In adoration the Lord satisfies a deacon's own hunger and thirst for justice. To the eucharistic Lord, too, the deacon is to bring the poverty and needs of all those whom he serves. He discovers in extended adoration that his life and ministry are clarified; the Lord makes sense of all that he, the deacon, is about in word and deed on behalf of the church and the poor. If his secular work requires that the deacon travel, he should not neglect daily adoration. Daily adoring the Lord, who is the same "yesterday and today and forever" (Heb. 13:8), will ground the *habitus vivendi et ministrandi* of his diaconate.

- Make regular and frequent use of the sacrament of reconciliation. Not baptism alone but also the sacrament of penance is the door to the Eucharist. If the deacon is not dependent on this sacrament and does not draw from it strength in living the Christian life and carrying out his diaconal responsibilities, others will see his ministry as the façade that it will have become; for example, he would simply pretend to lead the congregation in the eucharistic penitential rite rather than knowing himself to be among the first in need of God's cleansing mercy. He himself would earn the prophets' and Christ's wrath at Israel's empty sacrifices.

- Because he is an ordinary minister of Holy Communion, a deacon should regularly bring Communion to hospitals, nursing homes, the homebound, the sick, prisoners, and others who are not able to attend the Eucharist celebrated in community. No matter what else he may be assigned to do in the parish, this should be one of his duties. Psalm 23 announces that the Good Shepherd spreads the table of finest food in the sight of one's foes. Wherever the foe of the Lord and of his people lurks, there should the deacon be, setting up house and spreading the eucharistic table of the Lord.

- Live the spirituality of stewardship, regularly tithing a certain percentage of his time each day in prayer; his talent in service to the poor and the community, even outside the context of his formal ecclesial duties, for example, as a boy scout leader or athletic coach; and at a minimum 10 percent of his total family, pretax income to the church. By tithing, a deacon accepts the apostolic charge to be, as St. Paul said of himself, "servants of Christ and stewards of God's mysteries" (1 Cor 4:1), showing his life and that of his family to be truly eucharistic at the very foundational level of its security. He will demonstrate that his family and he recognize that the source of all they are and have is their heavenly Father, whose sacrificial love for them in Jesus Christ is given in the Eucharist. In stewardship a deacon bends his knees before his heavenly Father, for God himself has given the deacon's family its very name (see Eph 3:14). Living the spirituality of stewardship, a deacon gives evidence that he practices what he preaches, that he sacrifices so as to draw near to God and relies on God alone—on their new friendship—for his family's livelihood and well-being. Through stewardship a deacon lives in his own life and shows forth to other families the virtue of hope.

Married deacons, in some sense even more than celibate priests, are called to serve as eucharistic models of Christian living for other men. Many Catholic husbands and fathers sincerely want to love the Lord with all their strength and to teach their children how to draw near to God. But many are anxious about providing for their families, especially when the economy is in recession or has negatively impacted them, for example, through the loss of work. Offering himself to Christ for ordination and being presented to the church by his family, a deacon has professed his own family's total reliance on Christ. Because he serves the altar of Christ's sacrifice, he is in a unique position to mediate Christ's grace to husbands, fathers, and family men who find themselves being sacrificed at the pagan altar of the world's worship of power, profit, and greed.

chapter five

The Anointing Spirit

In these reflections on the diaconate we are considering the relationship of the deacon to each of the persons of the Blessed Trinity. We began by looking at the relationship of the deacon with the Father, the One speaking, and considered the deacon's *munus docendi*. Next we considered the Son, the Word spoken who became flesh, and thought through some elements of the deacon's *munus sanctificandi*. Our next two reflections have as their object the relationship between the deacon and the third person of the Trinity, the Holy Spirit. In these reflections I invite the reader to think of the Holy Spirit as both the Anointing Spirit and as the One who echoes the Word that has been spoken, deepening in the hearer the truth of God's Word.

In this chapter we will consider the Spirit's role in two episodes in Jesus' life, both of which occur at the beginning of his public ministry. First, Jesus is baptized by John and then anointed by the Father with the Holy Spirit (Mark 1:9-11; Matt 3:13-17; Luke 3:21-22; John 1:32-33). Second, in the Nazareth synagogue Jesus reads from the prophet Isaiah, "The Spirit of the Lord is upon me." He continues, proclaiming to the assembled worshipers, "Today this scripture has been fulfilled in your hearing" (Luke 4:18-21). Both in this chapter and in the next we will consider the deacon's participation in the church's *munus regendi* within the context of his relationship with the Anointing Spirit.

The Baptism of Jesus

It is inopportune for us to consider the vast theological meaning of Old Testament purification rituals, from which, undoubtedly, John's baptism, and therefore his baptism of Jesus, acquire some of its own meaning. Be that as it may, I want to put before the reader the image of the purification ritual Moses commanded for a person cured of leprosy, found in Leviticus 14:1-20.

Highly contagious, usually incurable, and most often deadly (at least until modern medicine discovered a way to contain if not to cure it), leprosy could wipe out an entire community. To protect themselves, communities banished lepers from their midst, exiling them to live (if one could call it that) outside the camp or city, beyond its walls and boundaries. In some instances, however, leprosy was cured and the leper healed. In that case, his or her reinsertion into the community was a highly ritualized affair.

> The LORD spoke to Moses, saying: This shall be the ritual for the leprous person at the time of his cleansing: He shall be brought to the priest; the priest shall go out of the camp, and the priest shall make an examination. If the disease is healed in the leprous person, the priest shall command that two living clean birds and cedarwood and crimson yarn and hyssop be brought for the one who is to be cleansed. The priest shall command that one of the birds be slaughtered over fresh water in an earthen vessel. He shall take the living bird with the cedarwood and the crimson yarn and the hyssop, and dip them and the living bird in the blood of the bird that was slaughtered over the fresh water. He shall sprinkle it seven times upon the one who is to be cleansed of the leprous disease; then he shall pronounce him clean, and he shall let the living bird go into the open field. The one who is to be cleansed shall wash his clothes, and shave off all his hair, and bathe himself in water, and he shall be clean. After that he shall come into the camp, but shall live outside his tent seven days. On the seventh day he shall shave all his hair: of head, beard, eyebrows; he shall shave all his hair. Then he shall wash his clothes, and bathe his body in water, and he shall be clean.
>
> On the eighth day he shall take two male lambs without blemish, and one ewe lamb in its first year without blemish, and a grain offering of three-tenths of an ephah of choice flour mixed with oil, and one log of oil. The priest who cleanses shall set the person to be cleansed, along with these things, before the LORD, at the entrance of the tent of meeting. The priest shall take one of the lambs, and offer

it as a guilt offering, along with the log of oil, and raise them as an elevation offering before the Lord. He shall slaughter the lamb in the place where the sin offering and the burnt offering are slaughtered in the holy place; for the guilt offering, like the sin offering, belongs to the priest: it is most holy. The priest shall take some of the blood of the guilt offering and put it on the lobe of the right ear of the one to be cleansed, and on the thumb of the right hand, and on the big toe of the right foot. The priest shall take some of the log of oil and pour it into the palm of his own left hand, and dip his right finger in the oil that is in his left hand and sprinkle some oil with his finger seven times before the Lord. Some of the oil that remains in his hand the priest shall put on the lobe of the right ear of the one to be cleansed, and on the thumb of the right hand, and on the big toe of the right foot, on top of the blood of the guilt offering. The rest of the oil that is in the priest's hand he shall put on the head of the one to be cleansed. Then the priest shall make atonement on his behalf before the Lord: the priest shall offer the sin offering, to make atonement for the one to be cleansed from his uncleanness. Afterward he shall slaughter the burnt offering; and the priest shall offer the burnt offering and the grain offering on the altar. Thus the priest shall make atonement on his behalf and he shall be clean.

What was the meaning of such a ritual? Its requirements seem strange, even silly to us. But its meaning contains the seeds of both John's and Jesus' understanding of baptism. Let's consider this ritual in light of John's baptism of Jesus.

One cured of leprosy was welcomed back into the camp only after the cure had been verified by a priest. The priest ventured outside the camp, putting himself at risk of contracting the disease through his contact with the leper. If the priest verified the cure, he ordered the leper to slaughter a bird and mix its blood with pure spring water. The priest, using a second bird, some scarlet yarn, and cedar, then sprinkled the leper with the mixture of blood and water. Sacrificing a bird and mixing its blood with pure spring water, then dipping another bird in that mixture before freeing it, symbolized the leper's having been saved from the deadly life and certain death that the disease would have wrought. The washing of garments and the shaving of body hair were not meant to cleanse the leper from the physical disease; he or she was already healed and the cure verified. These were rites of rebirth. Standing before the priest, naked, with no body hair, covered in blood and water, the leper was like a newborn baby just delivered from his or her mother's womb.

Having performed the ritual prescribed by the law, lepers were allowed back into the community, but could not yet enter their tent; they were to sit outside it for seven days. These seven days recalled for the leper the seven days of creation. Through ritual purification the leper was first reborn into and reunited with the community of faith. Then the community of faith, having allowed the leper to return, reintegrated him or her into the order of creation itself. Rebirth into the community, being allowed to come home but not to go home, was the first, necessary step of the healed person's total re-creation. (On a side note, we might draw the following implication from this prescribed ritual. A person's "natural state" is first of all to be a member of the faith community. Only from there does one draw membership in the created order. In other words, before one can understand oneself to be a son or daughter of creation, of mother nature, it is necessary first of all to be a son or daughter of the Father and of his covenant, or faith community. One has to "go God" before one can really "go green.")

After sitting for seven days, on the eighth day—that is, the first day of the new creation—cured lepers were required once again to offer a sacrifice, this time of cereal offerings and unblemished lambs. They stripped, again shaved off all their body hair, and bathed in the blood of the lamb they had sacrificed and in oil. After their first bathing eight days earlier, in the blood of birds and pure spring water, lepers were restored to the community of faith. Sitting outside their tent for seven days, they were restored to their place in creation. On this eighth day, through bathing in the blood of a lamb (lambs are otherwise sacrificed at Passover) and anointing with oil, cured lepers were reborn into the covenant the Lord established at Passover and ratified on Mount Sinai. Eight days previously they were covered with the sores of leprosy and death. Now, bathed in the blood of the covenant and anointed, they stood cured. In these rites, surely, we can see the prefiguration of our own sacrament of baptism.

Let's fast forward now to John the Baptist and the baptism he preached. Why did he baptize in the first place? In Matthew's gospel, John explains that he baptized with water for the sake of repentance, *metanoian* (3:11). He baptized so as to bring about reform and to prepare the people for the coming of the one much more powerful than he, one whose sandal he himself was not worthy to unfasten. In John's gospel (see 1:29-34), however, the Baptist's explanation of his mission is different. John the Evangelist tells us that it was God himself who sent John the Baptizer to baptize (1:6). The Baptist himself would then testify that he "came baptizing with water for this reason, that [the Lamb of God] might be revealed to Israel" (1:31). This being the case, it seems odd indeed then, as John himself intimates in verses 31 and 33, that when the Messiah came he failed to recognize him. He, the Lord's own cousin, failed to recognize Jesus to be the Lamb of God. How could that be?

The Scriptures reveal that God sent John the Baptist to baptize *that* the Messiah would be revealed, not *to* reveal him. John's role was not to be the agent who revealed the Messiah. That role and mission belonged to the Anointing Spirit. John was to prepare for the coming of the Lord. He was to baptize sinners for the sake of *metanoia*. Then, when all was prepared and all the characters in this divine drama of salvation had assembled, namely, Israel, John, Jesus, and the Anointing Spirit, the Messiah could be revealed. No doubt John's heart was open to and yearned for the Messiah. But even he only recognized Jesus to be the Lamb of God, the Christ, the Anointed One, when, after baptizing him, he witnessed the Spirit coming down upon him and anointing him.

That being the case, the question arises why in Matthew's gospel, when Jesus came forward to be baptized, John the Baptist actually did recognize him as the Messiah. John protested at that time, "I need to be baptized by you, and do you come to me?" and at first downright refused to do so (Matt 3:14).

That the other evangelists do not record John's protest is a very good clue that Matthew included it in his text in order to address a specific question that had arisen in his own community. Being predominantly of Jewish origin, Matthew's community undoubtedly understood the meaning of purification rituals in the Old Testament, including the one described above, as well as the purification rituals associated with the temple. For this reason they struggled to understand why it was necessary that Jesus, whom they believed to be sinless and therefore in no need of purification, be baptized. John the Baptist's protest to Jesus, then, is the question on the minds of Matthew's community. Jesus' answer to the Baptist's protest supplies the answer to their question. At the same time it reveals to us Jesus' own understanding of his baptism, the Spirit's anointing, and of his mission. "Let it be so now; for it is proper for us in this way to fulfill all righteousness" (Matt 3:15). Thus Matthew emphasizes that John's baptism of Jesus was not for the purification of sin, which in any case was not necessary with Christ, but rather to bring about the righteousness, that is, the *right relationship* between God and man, their drawing near about which we have spoken in earlier reflections.

What were God's demands, his righteousness that Jesus came to fulfill? Much has been written on this subject, and assuredly no attempt on my part could summarize it or do it justice. I do want, however, to draw your attention to two passages of the New Testament that seem to reveal to us something of the early church's reflection on the meaning of God's demands and righteousness. First, in the letter to the Hebrews we read that "[s]ince, therefore, the children share flesh and blood, [Jesus] himself likewise shared the same things" (2:14). Two verses later we read that it was necessary that Jesus become like his brothers and sisters "in every respect" in order to prove himself a high priest merciful and worthy of faith (2:17). Second, St. Paul taught of Christ that "[f]or our sake [God] made him to be sin who knew no sin, so that in him we might become the righteousness of God" (2 Cor 5:21).

What is the righteousness of God? It is this: that Jesus, whom St. Paul in the Areopagus preached to be the "appointed" one (Acts 17:31), should take upon himself the fullness of our humanity and become like us in every way. That full share even included being subjected to the devil's every temptation to sin (Heb 4:15). Presenting himself for baptism, Jesus showed that he was willing not simply to be counted among sinners; he was willing to be reckoned as a sinner. He was willing not simply to pass through the baptismal waters of reform. For the sake of sinners he was even willing to be baptized into the fires of Gehenna. Being baptized, Jesus was proclaiming to John, to Israel, to the cosmos, and even to Satan himself that he was willing to go wherever man had gone, wherever man was hiding from God. Jesus was proclaiming that he was willing to go, even to death itself and, finding man hiding there, bring him back to new life. Being baptized, Christ testified that he was willing to go anywhere and everywhere to find sinners, that sinners might again draw near, that sinners could "approach the throne of grace with boldness, so that we may receive mercy and find grace to help in time of need" (Heb 4:16). This was God's demand, God's righteousness, the restoration in Christ of the drawing near, of the right relationship of God and human beings that God himself was establishing in Christ.

(As an aside, don't we often minimize the revelation that Christ was tempted to sin as we are *in every way*—tempted to break the commandments, to break faith with life and with God—but never did? It seems easier for us to believe that Jesus obeyed God's will perfectly if we somehow lessen the devil's attempts to seduce him to sin. "Sure, Jesus never sinned. He wasn't tempted *as I am*," or, "It's impossible for *anyone* to resist the temptation to sin. Jesus never sinned because he was never really tempted." When we minimize Jesus' temptations we provide ourselves with both an easy excuse to sin and justification for our having sinned. Jesus' baptism and subsequent resistance of the temptation to sin implicate us. They teach us that the human person, washed clean from original sin in baptism and cooperating with God's grace, is able truly to resist temptation and to love God and one's neighbor even as Jesus loved. For this reason liturgically the church celebrates Christ's baptism as part of the celebration of Christmas, linking it to the mystery of his incarnation, the mystery of the Divinity assuming the nature of humanity in all things but sin. But the church links the mystery of Jesus' temptations and sufferings—the gospel of Jesus' temptations in the desert being read each year on the first Sunday of Lent—to the celebration of Easter.)

Now maybe we have a better idea of why John did not recognize Jesus at the moment he baptized him but only subsequently at his anointing. Sin obscures one's true identity and denigrates one's personhood. It causes one to be anonymous and unrecognized. Listen again to Genesis. After Adam and Eve sinned, "[they] hid themselves from the presence of the LORD God." He "called to the man, and said to him, 'Where are you?' He said, 'I heard the sound of you in the garden, and I was afraid, because I was naked; and I hid myself'" (3:8-10). For his part Christ, not because of personal sin, but, to the contrary, because of perfect love, assumed Adam's condition and so took upon himself even this nakedness and its shame, this hiding and anonymity, this original "unrecognizability," and the obscurity of personhood caused by Adam's sin. By assuming absolute anonymity among sinners, Christ assumed universal solidarity with them. So even John the Baptist failed to recognize him among sinners. Only when the Holy Spirit anointed Jesus did John too recognize him for who he was—God's chosen one (John 1:34, 33) and God's beloved Son on whom his favor rested (Matt 3:17; Mark 1:11; Luke 3:22). Only when John the Baptist saw that Jesus was like his brothers and sisters in every way and in this way understood God's absolute solidarity with sinners, only when he saw the Father anoint Christ with the Holy Spirit, could John the Baptist himself know, believe, and proclaim Jesus to be the spotless Lamb of God.

In the Sermon on the Mount, Jesus proclaimed that he had come not to abolish the law but to fulfill it (Matt 5:17). This being true, in being baptized by John and anointed by the Holy Spirit, Jesus brought to perfection the ancient Old Testament purification rites, making them henceforth obsolete and assigning them new meaning in himself. Look how the Levitical purification ritual of lepers, with which we began this chapter, acquired new meaning in light of Christ's own baptism and crucifixion.

In the old dispensation the community banished a leper so that the camp, village, or city might remain clean. By the time God sent John the Baptist, though, the whole community had become leprous. Rather than individual lepers being banished, the gospel tells us that all the people left their camps, towns, villages, and cities—from Jerusalem, all Judea, and the whole region of the Jordan—and went out to John in the wilderness, confessing their sins, and being baptized. For his part, John the Baptist was a member of the priestly class, his father being of the house of Abijah and his mother a descendant of Aaron. Living in the wilderness and baptizing at the Jordan River, does he not assume the figure of the priest who left the camp to verify a leper's cure? The Old Testament priest who left the camp to verify the leper's cure, did he not prefigure Jesus, who was crucified outside the city (Heb 13:12)? The scarlet yarn dipped in blood, the cedar wood, which does not decay, and the hyssop with which the priest sprinkled the sacrificial blood on the leper—are these not the wool of the innocent Lamb shorn, the wood of the cross of eternal life, and the sponge soaked with gall for Christ to drink? Does not the clean bird dipped in blood and pure spring water and released to freedom prefigure the Holy Spirit whom Christ, dying, breathing his last breathed forth (John 19:30)? A leper sat outside his or her tent for seven days before being reinserted into creation and being reborn into the covenant. Did not Christ lay three days in the darkness of the tomb before giving a new birth to all of creation felled by sin? Did Christ not constitute a new and eternal covenant? In the waters of the Jordan River, Jesus himself assumed priestly solidarity with all lepers, that is, with all who because of sin are divided from God and from one another and live outside the walls of *communio*. In unidentifiable anonymity before even his cousin, the Baptizer, Jesus stood shoulder to shoulder with all who have lost their identity, their personhood, in sin; although he was sinless, Jesus not only was counted among sinners but allowed himself to be thought of as a sinner. Anointed by the Holy Spirit, Jesus became the "the way, and the truth, and the life" (John 14:6) for all who sought to come home, be reborn into the faith community, the covenant, and creation, and live anew.

It is important, too, to note the order of this saving mystery. Jesus was baptized by John before he was anointed by God's Holy Spirit. In other words, the Anointing Spirit did not anoint Jesus so that he might be like his brothers and sisters in all things. Rather, Jesus, the favored Son, the chosen One of God, by receiving baptism showed himself to be like his brothers and sisters in all things. Thereupon the Spirit anointed him.

God favored Jesus not simply because he was his only begotten Son. God favored his only begotten Son because he was brother to all who, because of him, in him, and through him, would become God's own adopted sons and daughters. The Spirit anointed Jesus because Jesus was the servant who took upon himself the sufferings of all and in so doing became God's Suffering Servant.

In the Synagogue of Nazareth

Let's now move on with Jesus from the banks of the Jordan River to the synagogue of Nazareth, in Luke 4:14-30. Having united himself in baptism with all men and women in their sinfulness and suffering, having been anointed by the Holy Spirit as God's Suffering Servant, Jesus then presented himself in the Nazareth synagogue to begin his ministry publicly. There, as the *Basic Norms* affirm, Christ "recognized himself as the one announced in the servant of the first song of the *Book of Isaiah*" and so is the model par excellence of servanthood "lived totally at the service of God, for the good of men" (11).

Luke is the only evangelist to recount the story of Jesus' appearance in the Nazareth synagogue. He does so for three reasons. First, the story reveals to us how Jesus understood his relationship to his heavenly Father and his relationship to his earthly brothers and sisters. Second, it reveals to us Jesus' understanding of the mission for which the Holy Spirit had anointed him. The Spirit anointed Jesus to suffer so as to justify the many whose guilt he would bear (see Isa 53:11). Finally, this encounter teaches us the importance Jesus placed on Sacred Scripture in his ministry and in his relationships. In the Gospel of Luke, as Jesus took up his ministry publicly, the first words out of his mouth were a quotation from Sacred Scripture.

Luke begins: "Jesus, filled with the power of the Spirit, returned to Galilee" (4:14). The word he used to speak of this power is *dunamei*. (From this word we get our English words dynamism, dynamic, etc.) *Dunamei* refers to a natural, inherent power, a power existent within someone or something in virtue of that person's or thing's nature. It is the same word the archangel Gabriel used to explain to Mary how she would conceive God's Son even though she was a virgin. "The Holy Spirit will come upon you, and the power [*dunamis*] of the Most High will overshadow you" (Luke 1:35).

Using this word to reveal the cause of Christ's return to Nazareth, Luke teaches us that from the beginning of and throughout his ministry,

Jesus labored under no external force or compulsion. "In the power of the Spirit" means that Jesus came to his ministry freely and in absolute freedom carried it out, for indeed "where the Spirit of the Lord is, there is freedom" (2 Cor 3:17). The Anointing Spirit was the dynamism because of which Isaiah's prophecy was fulfilled in Jesus and Jesus understood himself to be the Suffering Servant. The same Spirit who anointed Jesus at his baptism was the dynamism of Jesus' preaching, miracle working, truly of his whole mission.

On that Sabbath, as was his habit on every Sabbath, Jesus went to the synagogue to hear the Word of God and worship with his people. In Jesus' time a traditional Sabbath service consisted of six readings from the Torah and one from the prophets. Just as God originally created the world in six days, on every Sabbath day he was re-creating his people through the reading and hearing of six passages from the Torah. The seventh reading, from the prophets, reflected God's rest. It called the people to fidelity to the Torah at the same time that it projected them to the tomorrow, to living the Torah as they again took up the new day, the first day of their being created anew. That the scroll of the prophet Isaiah was handed to Jesus tells us that at that service he was the seventh reader and that his passage was intended to call his co-worshipers to fidelity to the Torah even as it ushered them into God's rest.

Let me pause here briefly to reflect on what God's rest on the seventh day is all about. Remember that on the first six days of creation (except the second day) God blessed as good what he had created. But he did not create anything on the seventh day, so he had no new creatures to bless. Instead, Genesis tells us that God blessed the day itself. He had not blessed any of the first six days, only the creatures he had created on each of them. The seventh day was the only day in and of itself that he blessed. It alone he made holy precisely in its "dayness," for on it he himself rested "from all the work he had done in creation" (Gen 2:3). To enter into God's rest, then, is to enter into the one day that God has blessed. To honor the Sabbath is not simply a matter of not working so as to imitate God, who rested. To keep the Sabbath means that every seventh day one lives the only day that God blessed. In doing so one thereby opens oneself to receive fully the blessings of the creatures God created on each of the other days, creatures God judged to be good and very good. One who does not honor the Sabbath cannot live fully the other six days of the week, can never come to know God's blessing—the fullness of his gracious bounty in creation and especially in one's fellow human being. To not honor the Sabbath day is to not be living life to the full. To not honor the Sabbath day is to reject God's creation of each of the other days and therefore to reject God's blessings and goodness, to reject God's work, and so to reject God himself. To not honor the Sabbath is to refuse the grace of renewal and rebirth in the Spirit, who hovered over the waters at the very dawn of creation.

Back to the synagogue. We do not know what Torah passages were read before Jesus was handed the scroll of Isaiah. Being the seventh reader, though, Jesus read what he read so as in some way to bring forth the meaning of those earlier passages. As the seventh reader his job was to lead the people to the seventh day, the day of God's rest, so as to know fully God's blessings in time and creation. Seeing himself as the fulfillment of Isaiah's prophecy, Jesus understood himself as the one who would lead the poor, captives, the blind, prisoners, all of Israel and all God's children into the tomorrow of fidelity to God's law of love, into the "year" of God's favor, and into God's rest. He read,

> The Spirit of the Lord is upon me,
>   because he has anointed me
>   to bring good news to the poor.
> He has sent me to proclaim release to the captives
>   and recovery of sight to the blind,
>   to let the oppressed go free,
> to proclaim the year of the Lord's favor.

Finishing his reading, handing the scroll back to the attendant, Jesus sat down. With this gesture he expressed his authority as the Suffering Servant. He took charge and he commanded attention. Luke tells us that the eyes of all in the synagogue were "fixed on him." The translation "fixed on him" is a bit of an understatement. The Greek word is *atenizontes*, and it means stretched. Their eyes were stretched out to him. We might say their eyes were popping out of their heads. Clearly they wanted and waited to see more. But what? What were they hoping and expecting to see? Was hearing with their ears what Jesus proclaimed from the Sacred Scriptures not enough for them? Contrast the attitude of these synagogue worshipers with that of Simeon in the temple thirty years earlier, who, when he simply beheld the child Jesus in his mother's arms, exclaimed, "Master, now you are dismissing your servant in peace, according to your word; for my eyes have seen your salvation, which you have prepared in the presence of all peoples, a light for revelation to the Gentiles and for glory to your people Israel" (Luke 2:30-31). Simeon's eyes didn't pop out expecting more. Instead his heart jumped for joy. The synagogue assembly, upon seeing and hearing Jesus, the Anointed One, should have responded as Simeon did, but they did not.

Those assembled in the synagogue that Sabbath morning thought there would be much more to come. Jesus' reputation had spread throughout Galilee; everyone else was loud in his praise. Now it was their turn. They wanted to see for themselves, to be entertained by a show of wonders such as they had heard he had elsewhere "performed." But in fact there was nothing more to see, for Jesus was not there to oblige their fancy. He was not there to entertain popped-out eyes. He was there to announce the Good News to the poor, to convert the hearts of the children to their Father, and to bear the sufferings of the many. "Doubtless you will quote to me this proverb," Jesus challenged his hearers, "'Doctor, cure yourself!' And you will say, 'Do here also in your hometown the things that we have heard you did at Capernaum.' And he said, 'Truly I tell you, no prophet is accepted in the prophet's hometown.'" So, having said all he needed to say but performing no magic tricks to entertain their popped-out eyes, Jesus proved to be a huge disappointment to them. Their hearts were closed to what their ears were hearing and their eyes beholding. They "got up, drove him out of the town, and led him to the brow of the hill on which their town was built, so that they might hurl him off the cliff" (Luke 4:23-29).

Talk about words that were "living and active, sharper than any two-edged sword" (Heb 4:12). If only all priests and deacons could be so effective when they preach their first homily, or any homily for that matter, as to engender such passion in their hearers! Isn't it sad if preachers' homilies are so dull and uninspiring that they never stir up in the hearts of their hearers this same passion to respond, albeit positively, to Christ?

The synagogue encounter in Nazareth is painful to read. Yes, Isaiah's prophecy of the Suffering Servant was that day fulfilled in Christ. But so too was his prophecy of hearts hardened and eyes closed: "Keep listening, but do not comprehend; keep looking, but do not understand" (Isa 6:9). Psalm 95 too prophesied the coming of that day, only even more damningly. "O that today you would listen to his voice! Do not harden your hearts, as at Meribah, as on the day at Massah in the wilderness, when your ancestors tested me, and put me to the proof, though they had seen my work. For forty years I loathed that generation and said, 'They are a people whose hearts go astray, and they do not regard my ways.' Therefore in my anger I swore, 'They shall not enter my rest'" (7-11). Jesus' own kinsfolk and countrymen, even though they had heard of his works and now had seen the Promised One for themselves, even though they heard him proclaim Isaiah's prophecy of the coming of the Lord's Suffering Servant and saw it at that hour fulfilled, tested him and hardened their hearts. Jesus was inviting them, but they refused to enter into God's rest.

The Anointing Spirit and the Deacon

With these two inaugural events of Jesus' public ministry as background, let us now consider more specifically the role of the Holy Spirit—he who anoints and echoes the Word—in the life and ministry of a deacon.

First, as we have seen, Jesus did not make himself out to be the fulfillment of Isaiah's prophecy or undertake his mission on his own initiative. Neither was he appointed to his task from below, by others, for example, the high priest or the Sanhedrin. To the contrary, as Isaiah prophesied of him, "[H]e had no form or majesty that we should look at him, nothing in his appearance that we should desire him" (Isa 53:2). Jesus' obedience to Mary and Joseph in the home at Nazareth was the fertile ground out of which he "increased in wisdom and in years, and in divine and human favor" (Luke 2:51-52). From his twelfth year on Jesus said of himself that he had to be about his Father's business (see Luke 2:49); he received his mission from his Father. Then, having become anonymous, completely unrecognizable to men, counted among sinners, the Holy Spirit anointed Jesus as the one on whom God's favor rested, as God's Suffering Servant. Finally, Jesus always did the works his Father gave him, which testify to the Father's mandate (see John 5:36).

Like Jesus, the deacon too should be careful in attitude, word, or deed not to make too much of himself, make himself out to be the fulfillment of any great prophecy or anyone's long-awaited hope. As Christ himself, deacons should humbly present themselves for service and ministry, and as Christ's ministers perform their duties with no stately bearing. There should be in a deacon nothing to make others look at him, nothing of pride or arrogance. He should not believe himself to be holier than others because he is ordained a deacon. In other words, the deacon should be careful to avoid any clericalism and all clericalist attitudes. He should grow in wisdom and age and grace through his obedience to the bishop and his supervisor. He must be about his Father's business. At the Jordan River Jesus stood with sinners and in the wilderness he was tempted to sin. So the deacon must sincerely know himself to be like his brothers and sisters in every way. Because Jesus freely and willingly stood in solidarity with sinners, the Holy Spirit anointed him as the Suffering Servant. So too the Anointing Spirit ordains deacons to stand with sinners and to preach the Good News to them and to the poor.

Next, Jesus loved the Father in the Holy Spirit; he prayed to the Father through the Holy Spirit; he served the Father by the power of the Spirit's anointing. The Holy Spirit was the dynamism of Jesus' ministry and preaching, his power and force. Love, prayer, and obedience are the motives and dynamism of his (economic) salvific mission on earth.

Love and obedience must be the reasons underlying one's own desire to be ordained and the grounding of a deacon's life; through these the Spirit will continually renew his anointing of the deacon for ministry. When the bishop ordains one to the diaconate, he has judged "his son" to have been called and to be worthy. It must be acknowledged though, that although judged by the church to have been sincerely called, when anyone presents himself for holy orders, it is usually for a range of reasons and from a mixture of personal motives that he does so. For example, being of sincere religious sentiment, nonetheless perhaps one sees the diaconate as something to take up in retirement, just the thing to keep busy now that he has raised his family, finished out his career, and faces the big "what next." Maybe being ordained a deacon promises to fulfill an unrealized desire to be a priest. As a young man one might have heard Jesus' call to priesthood but because of celibacy, unexpected fatherhood, or some other reason did not respond. One might see the diaconate as a way to make up to the Lord for his personal failures in life or to repay the Lord for blessings received. With apologies to the psalmist who prayed, "What shall I return to the LORD for all his bounty to me?" (Ps 116:12), one thinking of the diaconate might be answering, "I will take up the diaconate and call upon the name of the Lord." Yet again, ordination to the diaconate might bring with it elevated status in the eyes of one's wife, family, colleagues, community, pastor, or fellow parishioners.

In any case, whatever one's motives, both positive and negative, one must continually purify them. The only motive for seeking diaconal ordination and the only force for serving in diaconal ministry must be the anointing and dynamism of the Holy Spirit. And the Spirit's anointing and his dynamism are love, prayer, compassion for sinners, attraction to the Lord and to the poor, service, obedience, desire to seek out what is lost and in hiding, and the like. Through these the deacon is renewed in the Spirit's anointing. Through them a deacon grows to be absolutely anonymous, to look for no recognition, glory, or reward, to seek no status save that of a servant. The less a deacon is recognized for his ministerial success, the more he serves as Christ himself, who at his baptism stood anonymous and unrecognizable even before John.

Third, Jesus promised his disciples: "When the Spirit of truth comes, he will guide you into all the truth; for he will not speak on his own, but will speak whatever he hears, and he will declare to you the things that are to come. He will glorify me, because he will take what is mine and declare it to you" (John 16:13-14). The Spirit's anointing of Jesus teaches the deacon that the effectiveness of his ministry is neither solely by his efforts nor the result alone of his own creativity. Nor is his ministry more effective by his doing more—by busyness, multiplying works, attending more programs, seminars, and meetings, etc. The effectiveness of diaconal ministry—of all ministry—is the result of grace at work in the minister; it is the accomplishment of the Holy Spirit. The deacon must allow the word of truth that the Spirit echoes in him to take root in his life so that out of the integrity of diaconal life and an integrated diaconal ministry he echoes the same word of truth to others. He will be successful, then, not simply if Christ is proclaimed and the Gospel furthered. The deacon shines forth more luminously as an icon of Christ the Suffering Servant if he is himself transformed by the word of the one to whom he has been conformed and echoes to others only what he hears from Jesus' Holy Spirit. As in Luke's gospel, Jesus' first public words were words of Scripture, the deacon, being a man of the Word of God, must make his every word and gesture a word and gesture of God.

The Synagogue Attendant Handed Him the Scroll

To conclude this reflection, let's return to the synagogue of Nazareth.

As we have seen, it was not simply providential nor was it accidental that Jesus was in the synagogue on that Sabbath day. Informing us that Jesus was in the habit of going to the synagogue on the Sabbath, Luke was telling us that Jesus' ministry was squarely rooted in the life, prayer, and worship of the covenant people. There is no reason to doubt that Jesus attended synagogue every Sabbath of his life and ministry. Neither was it accidental nor a simple coincidence that on that day the attendant handed to him the scroll of the prophet Isaiah. Jesus did not grab for the Word of God or pick and choose what he would read, believe, and proclaim. He, the seventh reader, read what he received from the representative of the community at worship.

In this simple gesture, the handing of the scroll of the Scriptures to Jesus, the synagogue attendant has much to teach the deacon. Let's look first at the gesture and then at the attendant himself.

We do not know, of course, nor can we guess the attendant's motive for handing the scroll of Isaiah to Jesus. We must accept that he did so under the inspiration of the Holy Spirit, who echoes God's Word. This simple gesture of the servant of the synagogue, handing the scroll of the Scriptures to Jesus, gives us a key insight into the relationship of the deacon to the Holy Spirit. The scroll was the material parchment on which was written Isaiah's prophecy of the anointing of the Lord's Suffering Servant, from which Jesus himself proclaimed its fulfillment. The deacon is like that parchment, and in his person that parchment is still being handed to the Lord, so that the Lord's mission of redemption through suffering can be fulfilled. The deacon is the parchment on which is written and from which Jesus and the church announce the Good News to the poor, liberty to captives, sight for the blind, and a year of favor from the Lord. By the dynamism of the Holy Spirit, the deacon allows the words of redemption to be written on him so that, in his "being read" to sinners and the poor, that is, through his ministry, sinners and the poor might hear the Good News and know of God's favor.

The synagogue attendant himself is of interest to us, as well. He was not Jesus' assistant. He was that of the synagogue, and in that capacity he handed the Scriptures to the Lord. Precisely because he was functioning in his role as the assistant of the synagogue, the Spirit used him, enabling Jesus that day, in that place, and in the hearing of those people to proclaim that he was the Suffering Servant whose coming Isaiah had foretold, that he was the fulfillment of those very Scriptures and of all Scripture.

The word Luke uses for assistant is *hupēretē*. In the New Testament it is used generally to describe officers of the Roman army, assistants of magistrates and other public officials, assistants in synagogues, and the like. But its original meaning in Greek was "under-rower." Under-rowers were slaves who sat in the bowels of a ship and powered it forward. (The image of Charlton Heston as Judah Ben Hur, in the movie *Ben Hur*, enslaved and rowing in the bowels of a Roman galley, comes immediately to my mind.) Under-rowers were not, however, simply the force that propelled ships through water when no winds bellowed in their sails. In other circumstances, especially in turbulence and battle, under-rowers were the force necessary to maneuver safely, efficiently, and effectively.

The deacon as under-rower is the image I want to leave with the reader and on which I invite him or her to reflect. In antiquity an under-rower was possessed in slavery and chained to his oar. He served a master whom he never met. In a ship's bowels, in utterly inhumane conditions, at the waterline (he sat literally between the devil and the deep blue sea), he rowed. Packed alongside his fellow slaves, backward facing, his back breaking as he forced every ounce of his body's energy into the wood of the oar, he rowed forward to a destination he could not see.

The under-rower is a most apt image of the deacon anointed by the Spirit for the service of the Word echoed. A deacon serves a master he has never seen but whose icon he is and sacrifices for a destination he is not able to glimpse but that he has been promised. In the bowels of Peter's barque, a deacon, the under-rower of the church, together with his fellow deacons, rows on so that the Word spoken, made flesh, and echoed can be heard and so that those on deck might arrive safely at their destination. The sweat of his labors is as the anointing of the Spirit, that the Spirit himself might sweep over the waters (Gen 1:2) and blow where he will (see John 3:8).

chapter six

The Deacon, Servant of the Word Being Echoed

The Father Loves; the Son is Love Incarnate.
The Deacon is Loved by the Father and he Loves.
The Deacon's Munus Regendi, *the Office of Serving.*

We have considered how trinitarian life and Christian living entail giving and receiving, loving and honoring, dying and rising. Being true of the baptized Christian, this is all the more true of the deacon. Presenting himself to Christ and to the church for ordination and prostrating before the altar, he gives, loves, and dies. With the laying on of hands he receives, honors, and rises, conformed to Christ. Filled with the Holy Spirit he is marked with the character that identifies him as an icon of Christ who "emptied himself, taking the form of a slave, being born in human likeness," and who "humbled himself and became obedient to the point of death—even death on a cross" (Phil 2:8).

In the church's liturgies there are only two in which a deacon prostrates before the altar, namely, at his ordination and on Good Friday. Prostrations recall the words of Christ, "[W]hoever wishes to be first among you must be your slave; just as the Son of Man came not to be served but to serve, and to give his life as a ransom for many" (Matt 20:27-28). With

Christ the deacon willingly accepts "employment" in such a downwardly mobile career. Prostrating at the foot of the altar at his ordination and again each year on Good Friday, the deacon gives evidence that he is willing not simply to prepare the altar so that on it Christ may be sacrificed and from it his Body and Blood fed to sinners and the poor. Lying prostrate before the altar the deacon testifies that he himself is willing to lay down his own life in service to sinners and the poor, even to die for them. Such is the witness of St. Lawrence the Deacon, who gave his life as a holocaust offering for Christ and the poor of Rome.

In the prayer of diaconal ordination the bishop says, "Lord, send forth upon him the Holy Spirit, that he may be strengthened by the gift of the sevenfold grace to carry out faithfully the work of the ministry." The deacon is ordained not to priesthood but to ministry. A bishop's ministry is full: he teaches, sanctifies, governs, and serves. A priest's ministry is essentially at the service of the church's sacramental and liturgical worship. The deacon's ministry, although it has teaching and cultic dimensions, is essentially that of service. In this chapter, then, we will contemplate the Holy Spirit as the foundation and dynamism of diaconal service, especially the deacon's service in justice and charity to the poor.

The Role of the Holy Spirit in the Ordination of the Deacon

In the great mysteries of human redemption, from the very beginning of what Pope John Paul II called "God's salvific self-communication to the things he creates" (*Dominum et vivificantem* 12), the Spirit of God has been present and active. At creation's beginning, the Spirit of God hovered over the waters (Gen 1:2). Jesus, because he himself was filled with the Holy Spirit, accepted his Father's will and emptied himself, taking the form of a slave and being born in the likeness of human beings; it was the Spirit who came upon Mary and overshadowed her with the power of the Most High, incarnating the Son in her virginal womb and inaugurating the redemption of humankind. The Spirit anointed Jesus at his baptism and was the dynamism of his mission and ministry, as we saw in the previous reflection. From the cross and again in the upper room at Pentecost, Jesus breathed forth the Spirit on the church.

We know that the first effect of sacramental ordination to the diaconate is not to designate the deacon to be an employee of the church. He is not ordained simply to do something or to carry out some task or work, to be a functionary. Nor is a deacon simply an "addetto," one "attached" to the bishop, to an office, or to a staff. (Remember how the Prodigal Son was "attached" to the Gentile property owner.) Instead, he is ordained to be someone and, because he is that someone, to carry out certain ministries in the church. The sacrament of holy orders, the *Catechism of the Catholic Church* teaches, "configures the recipient to Christ by a special grace of the Holy Spirit, so that he may serve as Christ's instrument for the Church. By ordination he is enabled to act as a representative of Christ, Head of the Church, in his triple office of priest, prophet, and king" (1581).

As at Jesus' baptism the Holy Spirit anointed him to be the Suffering Servant, so the same Anointing Spirit imprints on the deacon's soul the sacramental character that conforms him to Christ and makes him an icon of his suffering servanthood. Jesus lived and ministered in virtue of the dynamism of the Spirit; the deacon, too, conformed to Christ, lives and ministers by the Spirit's power. When Christ died on the cross he breathed forth the Spirit upon the church; the deacon, dying to himself in ministry, breathes the Spirit of Christ on the poor. Christ was raised from the dead in the Spirit (see 1 Pet 3:18). Like St. Paul, by the power of the Holy Spirit the deacon is able to proclaim, "I have been crucified with Christ; and it is no longer I who live, but it is Christ who lives in me. And the life I now live in the flesh I live by faith in the Son of God, who loved me and gave himself for me" (Gal 2:20). Indeed, so conformed is the deacon to Christ the Suffering Servant that he is to accompany Christ even to hell and from there, from whatever hell in which he finds sinners and the poor, to bring them back to the altar, to the banquet table of the Lord and the church.

The Deacon's Ministry of Charity

Let's now consider the deacon's *diaconia* of charity, his participation in Christ's and the church's *munus regendi*, the office of serving.

Keep in mind what we considered in our last chapter, namely, that Jesus understood himself to be the one whom the Spirit anointed as the Suffering Servant, specifically "to bring good news to the poor. . . . [T]o proclaim release to the captives and recovery of sight to the blind, to let the oppressed go free, to proclaim the year of the Lord's favor" (Luke 4:18). In a nutshell, this too sums up the deacon's mission and ministry. It is for the sake of sinners and the poor that Christ and the church ordain a deacon. They commission the deacon to bring the Good News to sinners and to the poor, to be light to the hearts of those who dwell in darkness, to lead others to freedom in faith and love, and make known to all the love and care of God.

At diaconal ordination, the bishop in his exhortation teaches that "[o]nce he is consecrated by the laying on of hands that comes to us from the apostles and is bound more closely to the altar . . . he will perform works of charity in the name of the bishop or the pastor." Then, after the deacon is ordained and vested in the stole and dalmatic that symbolize his office and ministry, the bishop hands on to him his mission. Handing to the deacon the Book of the Gospels the bishop says, "Receive the gospel of Christ, whose herald you now are." From these, that is, from the bishop's exhortation to and commissioning of the deacon, we understand that deacons receive a threefold mandate for ministry. First, the deacon is mandated by the *laying on of hands*. Second, precisely because he is now more closely bound to the *altar*, he goes forth from it. Third, the *Gospel* of Christ sends him forth; he is now a bearer of the Good News to the poor. This threefold mandate—service, altar, and Word—unifies a deacon's ministry. From this threefold mandate his ministry is always to be exercised. This mandate is what makes his ministry diaconal and ecclesial and not simply humanitarian and social. These three, the church teaches, "represent a unity in service at the level of divine Revelation" (*Directory* 39).

Let us consider each of these three, that is, the laying on of hands, the altar, and the Gospel, as the specific mandates of diaconal life and ministry.

The Laying on of Hands for the Works of Charity

The first mandate a deacon receives is that of the laying on of hands for the works of charity. True, all Christians in virtue of baptism are called to serve others. Deacons, however, from the laying on of hands and their insertion into the threefold sacrament of orders, receive an ecclesial mandate to do so. "Deacons," the *Catechism* teaches, "are ministers ordained for tasks of service of the Church" (1596). When he serves, he does so "as a representative of Christ, Head of the Church, in this triple office of priest, prophet, and king" (1581). Specifically, although Christ is one and undivided and his saving ministry already accomplished, the deacon, because he is ordained to ministry and not to priesthood, acts not in the person of Christ who serves by preaching and sanctifying, but more particularly in the person of Christ who preaches and sanctifies by serving.

Acts 6 teaches us that the Lord and the church instituted the diaconal function and the apostles laid hands on seven men to maintain good order and, doing so, to ensure the distribution of bread to the poor. Good order could only be maintained when the apostles dedicated themselves to prayer and to the ministry of the Word *and* when the poor were served. The poor having been served, the unity and order of the church preserved, the preaching of the gospel could be more vigorously carried out.

Moreover, the church teaches that the *munus regendi* of the deacon "is exercised in *dedication* to works of charity and assistance and in the direction of communities or sectors of church life, *especially as regards charitable activities*." "This is the ministry," it affirms, "most characteristic of the deacon" (*Basic Norms*, Introduction 9; emphases added). I cannot emphasize this point enough. The bishop lays hands on the deacon to assist him in serving the poor; assisting the bishop and the church's pastors to serve the poor is what deacons do as deacons. A deacon is ordained for the sake of the poor and they, the poor, not the bishop or the priest as such, are the object of his ministry. Because the deacon receives the laying on of hands, whatever he does as a servant of the Word of God and at the liturgy, he does so that the poor might hear the Good News of their salvation and that they might be fed from her eucharistic and charitable bounty, that they too might "participate in the fruits of that sacrifice" (*Directory* 28).

A deacon's ministry is neither fully diaconal nor unified if he is only a servant of the Word or the altar, a liturgical minister, but does not serve the poor directly. His words will ring hollow if they do not come from a heart that has been touched by and united to the poor. Elevating the chalice of Christ's Precious Blood and handing it to the members of a worshiping community, baptizing newborn infants, blessing rings for newlyweds to exchange, burying the dead are indeed important ministries, and when he so ministers, a deacon does so as Christ the Suffering Servant. But in view of the laying on of hands, it is the deacon whom Christ and the church put forth as icon of his suffering servanthood and whom they hand to sinners and the poor as saving servant. To the poor the church sends deacons to preach the Good News. Having taken up the attitude of Christ, as at his ordination and on Good Friday, he then prostrates himself before the lonely, the noisome, sick persons, prisoners, juvenile offenders, the handicapped, addicts, the lost, the troubled, the difficult, the contentious and argumentative, unbelievers, atheists and agnostics, sinners—in short, all who live in darkness, the blind, the poor.

Moreover, diaconal functions exist in their own right, and in a deacon's own right he is responsible to serve the poor. He is not ordained to be a sort of executive assistant or pastoral aide for priests or simply to supply for their shortage. For example, in how many parishes do priests work hard, minister in busy circumstances, and find themselves overloaded with their responsibilities? A parishioner of goodwill takes notice of how busy his parish priest is. He thinks to himself, "If only I were ordained a deacon, I could do more. I could be of some help to poor Father and relieve him of some of his duties." As sincere as this motive may be to seek holy orders, it is contrary to both the nature of the diaconate and the church's intentions in restoring it as a permanent order. Cardinal Walter Kasper comments, "The council explicitly affirms that it intends to facilitate the introduction of the permanent diaconate because it would otherwise be difficult to ensure the exercise of those tasks that belong to the theological essence of the diaconal ministry" (*Leadership in the Church*, p. 15).

Note that the cardinal spoke of the "theological essence of the diaconal ministry." Diaconal ministry is not priestly ministry; it is of a different theological essence than and not simply a lesser degree of priesthood. Continuing, the cardinal added (and he is worth quoting at length), "The gradations in participation in the bishop's ministry thus denote two different structures: the bishop is aided by two separate arms (so to speak), which have differing tasks but must collaborate with one another" (p. 18). Then again, "The deacon is not a 'mini-priest' who fills gaps left where no priests are available, nor is his ministry a mere transitional stage on the path to the priesthood. It is an autonomous ministry, a specific articulation of the ministerial service entrusted to the church by Jesus Christ" (p. 20). Finally, "This situation makes an urgent appeal to the communion-diaconia. It is here that its task lies, for it is the deacon's special call to be on the front line, an attentive listener and a pioneer who leads the church's response to these challenges. . . . This is why deacons should not seek to take over as large a slice as possible of the specifically priestly ministry of leadership: their task is different and it is important and urgent enough" (p. 36).

The bishop does not ordain deacons so that priests may be relieved of their duties, their loads lightened. To the contrary, the bishop ordains men to the diaconate to aid him in his ministry of preserving the unity of the church and extending Christ's and the church's service to the poor. Through the ministry of *diaconia*, the deacon widens the church's embrace of the poor, who might even be unknown to her, and builds up the community. If anything, by carrying out his ministry faithfully and zealously he will be adding to his bishop's and pastor's many concerns, although for that reason not adding to their burdens. To the contrary, because the deacon's is a ministry of *communio-diaconia* exercised in hierarchical communion, and because charity overcomes slavery to duty and function, when he is successful in ministry, no matter how much "work" he may add, he nonetheless gladdens a bishop's and priest's heart and lightens their load of care. Pastors of souls should rejoice that by the ministry of deacons the Gospel is being preached and the poor being served wherever and whenever they themselves are unable to be, to communicate it, and to serve.

Bound More Closely to the Altar

Second, the altar, that is, the liturgy, the church's public act, and especially the eucharistic meal mandate the deacon to serve the poor and needy. "It is never enough simply to eat and drink the body and blood of Jesus," Robert Barron writes. "One must become a bearer of the power that one has received. The meal always conduces to the mission" (*Eucharist*, p. 48).

All ordained ministry in the church is for the sake of the eucharistic Lord, indeed. Yet the deacon is not ordained to the priesthood of the altar but to the altar of the priesthood. That is, the altar itself mandates the deacon to serve sinners and the poor. The *Directory* teaches that a deacon's ministry of the Word leads to ministry at the altar. Ministry at the altar in turn "prompts transformation of life . . . resulting in charity" (39). In other words, a deacon does not serve the poor that he might be a better preacher or so as to improve his ministry at the altar. It is the reverse. He proclaims the Word and serves the altar that he himself might be transformed (assuming his cooperation with grace) and so better serve the poor.

The very outline of the Mass, especially those liturgical functions that a deacon carries out, shows this to be true. As Mass begins, the deacon accompanies the priest into the assembly that he, in some way through his ministry of charity, has been instrumental in gathering. Next he leads that assembly in the penitential rite, by which those gathered recognize themselves to be sinners and begin their eucharistic reconciliation to the Lord and to one another. In the hearing of the Word of God and especially of the gospel, which the deacon proclaims, he is renewed for service. He is then nourished with the Bread of Life and Cup of Salvation poured out for him and for the many. The Mass strengthens him that, just as much as those he sends forth (the deacon dismisses *both* the presider *and* the assembled worshipers), he himself will go in peace to love and serve the Lord. Then together with the presider he leads the assembly out of the church and into the world.

The altar mandates the deacon to two tasks. First, it mandates him to gather the poor into community and, second, once gathered, to foster the community's worship. At Mass the deacon's acceptance of this mandate is symbolized by his standing with the priest or near him. In his person the poor themselves are placed at the right hand of Jesus: priest, prophet, and king.

We read in the book of Proverbs that Wisdom has built her house. She then invites "you that are simple," "those without sense," to come and "eat of my bread and drink of the wine I have mixed" (9:4-5). Isaiah too invited to the Lord's mountain all those who had no money. "[C]ome, buy and eat! Come, buy wine and milk without money and without price. Why do you spend your money for that which is not bread, and your labor for that which does not satisfy? Listen carefully to me, and eat what is good, and delight yourselves in rich food. Incline your ear, and come to me; listen, so that you may live" (55:1-3). Jesus appropriated Isaiah's image to himself when he proclaimed, "I myself am the bread of life. Whoever comes to me will never be hungry, and whoever believes in me will never be thirsty" (John 6:35).

Before the Eucharist can be celebrated the church must be gathered. That is the deacon's role. Deacons are the king's servants dispatched to the byroads, the margins, and the edges to bring in any who would come to the king's son's wedding banquet. Having set the banquet, the deacon seats at table those who accepted the king's invitation, filling the banquet hall with banqueters (see Matt 22:1-10).

Again the image of St. Lawrence the Deacon comes immediately to mind. Having been ordered by the prefect to bring him the treasures of the church, he gathered together the poor. The image is all the more striking when we remember that pagan gods rejected the poor. And pagan peoples, Romans in particular, despised the poor, who to them were revolting and despicable. Yet the poor were and are the church's supreme treasure. Reflecting on the ministry of St. Lawrence the Deacon, Jean Vanier wrote, "His voice continues to speak through the centuries: the poor and the lame are the riches of the Church because they are the presence of Jesus. In their vulnerability they, like Jesus, are begging for our hearts, our love and our friendship" (*The Gospel of John*, p. 239). As such, the church historically entrusted the poor, and entrusts them now to the deacon. Cardinal Kasper wrote, "[B]efore a community can be guided and before the Eucharist can be celebrated in it and with it, it must first be gathered together and built up." Therefore, "the deacon's place is in these marginal areas of church and society, where breakthroughs can occur. He is not to think only of those who 'still' belong to the church and to accompany them, but also to invite those who perhaps may belong to the church tomorrow. His communio-diaconia means that he builds up the church in view of the future. This is an absolutely essential contribution to the 'new evangelization' about which we hear so much today" (*Leadership in the Church*, p. 36).

Jesus taught his disciples, "My food is to do the will of him who sent me and to complete his work" (John 4:34). Serving the poor, building them into community, gathering them at the altar, and feeding them there with the Lord's Word, Body, and Blood, the deacon discovers that he himself is fed for ministry, his food is his ministry, he is strengthened for ministry. In a wonderfully insightful reflection on the resurrection story of Jesus on the shore of the Sea of Galilee, Cardinal Ratzinger noted that the disciples first had to feed Jesus before he in turn could feed them. "When Jesus asks the disciples if they have any fish they do not yet recognize him. They must give to the unknown person who is hungry. It is only when they themselves learn this giving that there ripens in them the love that makes them capable of accepting the new food, the quite different bread, that God himself becomes for us in Christ. The social dimension is not something stuck on the Eucharist from the outside; it is rather the context without which the Eucharist cannot take shape" (*Ministers of Your Joy*, p. 59).

"Proclaim the Gospel, Whose Herald You Now Are"

Third, God's Word itself mandates the deacon to serve the poor. The Father speaks his Word and commands that it be echoed. Jesus, the Word made flesh, came that the poor might have the Good News preached to them, and until the cross he knew that his mission had not been accomplished. For example, after having spent the night in prayerful communion with his Father, he called his disciples and said, "Let us go on to the neighboring towns, so that I may proclaim the message there also; for that is what I came out to do" (Mark 1:38). John the Baptist, knowing that the poor had the Good News proclaimed to them, knew that Christ was the one who was to come, that there was no other to expect (see Luke 7:22). Christ at his Ascension entrusted his Good News to the apostles to be announced "to the ends of the earth" (Acts 1:8). To this day, the fact that the Gospel is preached to the poor in every corner of the globe still witnesses to the world that Christ is the fulfillment of Isaiah's prophecy, the Suffering Servant.

At a deacon's ordination the bishop exhorts him, "Now you must not only listen to God's word but also preach it." Where does listening take place? In the heart. For this reason a deacon's preaching must be not simply *from* the heart but, even more, *of* his heart. He is not simply to speak words to the poor. The deacon must share his heart with them, something he cannot do if he is never personally present to them. His model must be God the Father himself, who chose to save us not with a snap of his fingers. Rather, God chose to send us his own heart. Jesus, "the only Son, who is close to the Father's heart . . . has made him known" (John 1:18). The word that Saint John uses for "at the Father's side" is *kolpon.* It means literally the front of the body between the arms. This is how the Father chose to reveal himself to us, by sending to us the front of his own body between his arms—his heart, Jesus. This is what a deacon is ordained to do: to echo the Word of the Father he hears in his heart; he opens his arms and embraces sinners and the poor and gives to them his heart.

The word the deacon is called to echo is not simply a word voiced and spoken but the very Word made flesh. Therefore, while he has an important function to carry out in preaching as well as in evangelization, catechesis, and devoting attention to the problems of our time, in some sense the word that the church and the world most thirst to hear from deacons is the word they echo when they personally serve the poor. While the saving Word is the subject of his ministry, his service of the poor is its most effective means of transmission. Because he represents Christ and the church as a deacon, when he serves the poor he is in that act preaching the Good News to them.

This is an important point, so let us pause and consider it more deeply. The unity of altar, Word, and service in diaconal ministry is rooted in Trinitarian *communio*: the Trinity's reciprocal loving and honoring, giving and receiving. The Father serves the Son by pronouncing him as Word. The Son hears the Father and becomes flesh, so serving him. The Spirit echoes the Word, so serving the Father who speaks and the Son who is spoken.

The ground in which this trinitarian unity of Word and service can take root in the deacon is his faith, but not a faith that is simply intellectual assent to dogmatic or theological propositions. The unity of Word and service is rooted in faith-in-action, his cheerful courage, showing that as a deacon he really does believe the Word he reads, is teaching what he believes, *and* is practicing what he teaches. It is the faith-in-action by which the deacon will show that he is not deceiving himself, let alone the church and others, deluded that he is being a deacon simply because he has been ordained a deacon. "Be doers of the word, and not merely hearers who deceive themselves," St. James teaches. "For if any are hearers of the word and not doers, they are like those who look at themselves in a mirror; for they look at themselves and, on going away, immediately forget what they were like. But those who look into the perfect law, the law of liberty, and persevere, being not hearers who forget but doers who act—they will be blessed in their doing" (Jas 1:22-25).

This faith-in-action is the same faith about which we spoke in chapter four, that bold confidence that God found in Noah, Abraham and the patriarchs, Moses and Aaron, and Mary, because of which God designated them as his vicarious representatives and used them to build bridges between himself and human beings. Cardinal Kasper writes, "Faith without diaconia is not Christian faith; preaching without diaconia is not Christian preaching" (*Leadership in the Church*, p. 27). The words of St. James in regard to Abraham, our father in faith, speak eloquently of the deacon: "You see that faith was active along with his works, and faith was brought to completion by the works. Thus the scripture was fulfilled that says, 'Abraham believed God, and it was reckoned to him as righteousness,' and he was called the friend of God" (Jas 2:22-23).

That is why the most important preaching a deacon does is not giving the homily at the celebration of the Eucharist (which in any case belongs more properly to the presider and to a priest). His service to sinners, the poor, the rejected, the marginalized, those denied their human rights, or they who otherwise are made to sit on the floors and in the corners of the dining rooms of the rich and eat the scraps of life that the rich might deign to throw them or waste as leftovers—it is this service by which the deacon practices what he teaches and believes. This diaconal service is the most eloquent and effective sermon he will ever preach, even if only one little old lonely lady, or suffering sick person, or broken prisoner, or terrified addict, or depressed unemployed husband and father, hears it.

A Unity of Service

That these three—Word, altar, and service—are united is also the criterion by which the credibility of a deacon's ministry is judged. If a deacon assists at the altar or preaches the Word but does not actively serve the poor, his ministry is lacking an essential element. It would be "intrinsically fragmented," analogous to how Pope Benedict described Eucharist that does not become concrete in the practice of love (see *Deus caritas est* 14). Nor on the other hand is a deacon credible if he serves the poor but does not proclaim God's Word, teach what the church teaches, and live by those teachings himself. Since the unity of Word, altar, and service is the source of the integration of diaconal ministry, without exercising all three functions he would lack integrity, and therefore credibility, in diaconal life. In such a case, although he would be a deacon by ordination, in functioning he would be, on one hand, hardly more than a social worker, utilitarian humanitarian, administrator, bookkeeper, a fundraiser who happened to be ordained, or, on the other hand, one who did not practice the virtue of love, "which binds everything together in perfect harmony" (Col 3:14), and, in that case, nothing more than "a noisy gong or a clanging cymbal" (1 Cor 13:1).

A deacon should not stand before the people of God, vested for liturgical service, proclaiming the gospel and preaching, setting the altar and serving the chalice, especially on the Lord's Day, if he does not exercise a specific concrete, hands-on and arms-embracing service to the poor on any of or throughout the other six days of the week. Likewise, his service to the poor is not complete if he is not bringing to sinners and the poor the Gospel, the Eucharist, and the *communio* of the church. In this context it is important to note that when deacons are "hired" for employment in diocesan, parochial, or other ecclesiastical communities, they should not be hired to carry out functions that are not proper to the diaconal office. "Those deacons who are called to exercise [judicial, administrative, and organizational] offices should be placed so as to discharge duties which are proper to the diaconate, in order to preserve the integrity of diaconal ministry" (*Directory* 42).

It is not accidental that the Holy Spirit inspired the church to renew its service to the poor through the permanent ministry of deacons just as over the other two holy orders the dark shadows of shame and scandal began to gather and threaten. As we see in the experience of the early church, service to the poor is necessary for the church's unity and good order. From those days to our own, whenever the church's unity is threatened and she is otherwise weakened, the Lord strengthens her through the poor and through diaconal service to them. As Christ the Lord himself, and as his church has done throughout the millennia, the church, whenever doubted, challenged, and accused, must be able in its own defense to bring the poor before her accusers and point to its ministry on their behalf.

Be Genuinely Concerned

In this context, we must pause and consider what Jesus meant when, quoting Isaiah, he proclaimed that he had been anointed by the Spirit "to bring good news to the poor." What is the content of this good news?

The Greek word that Jesus uses in Luke 4 to speak of his mission is *euaggelisasthai*. It is the same word, *euaggelion*, that Mark uses as a noun at the beginning of his gospel to introduce the very person of Jesus, the Son of God (1:1). We can conclude first of all, therefore, that the person of Jesus is himself the Good News preached to the poor; he is both the subject and object of preaching. Second, all that is contained in the Gospel, both scripturally and as it is taught to us by the church, is good news for the poor. The poor do not receive a different gospel than the one preached by Christ and that the church has handed down to all generations.

That having been said, though, there is a little detail in one of St. Paul's letters that, I submit, gives us a very specific indication of the content of the Good News preached to the poor, of what it can be summarized to be.

In his letter to the Philippians (2:19-23) St. Paul holds up Timothy as a genuine model of *diaconia*. Timothy, he wrote, was to him as a "son with a father," who with him served the Gospel. Paul reminded the Philippians that they knew Timothy's character from personal experience. Then, in an admission at once sad (in view of what it said of Paul's collaborators) and uplifting (in view of what it says in Timothy's regard), Paul confessed that "all of them are seeking their own interests, not those of Jesus Christ." In other words, since love does not insist on its own way (see 1 Cor 13:5), Paul was admitting that except for Timothy the virtue of love was not to be found among his coworkers. Of Timothy, to the contrary, he wrote, "I have no one like him who will be genuinely concerned for your welfare." Timothy alone was "genuinely concerned" for Paul's beloved Philippians.

Paul taught Timothy, his "son," that God cared. From his own side he would send him to proclaim this Good News to the Philippians. For his part, Timothy would proclaim it to the Philippians not only with words but by his own person and presence to them. Timothy's own attitude toward the Philippians revealed God's. And God's attitude toward his children is precisely the content of the Good News announced to the poor. What is God's attitude? What is that content? It is nothing less than that God cares. God is genuinely solicitous and anxious for the poor. Paul's attitude and Timothy's behavior toward the Philippians teach us that God's caring is not simply something he does. God *is* care.

In his letter to the Galatians, too, St. Paul used another word to describe this attitude of care. There, in 2:9, Paul reported that those who were the pillars of the church, namely, James, Peter, and John, gave to Barnabas and him "the right hand of fellowship." Together with the handclasp of fellowship (*communio*) and essential to it, however, the "acknowledged pillars" of the church exhorted Paul and Barnabas to "remember the poor," something Paul was "actually . . . eager to do." "This," Cardinal Ratzinger wrote, "is an injunction of a totally different kind. First of all, we must stress the social character of this injunction: fellowship in and with the Body of Christ means fellowship with one another. Of its very essence, it implies mutual acceptance, give and take and the readiness to share. . . . Fellowship in the Church is always 'table fellowship' in the fullest sense; the Church's members are pledged to give 'life' to one another, spiritual *and* physical life. In this sense, the social question is at the theological core of the Christian concept of communio" (*Behold the Pierced One*, p. 80).

This remembering and caring, I contend, is the heart of the Good News deacons are ordained to proclaim. Unlike everyone else, who is busy insisting on his or her own way rather than that of Christ Jesus, the deacon is to be mindful of the poor, care for the poor, and preach the Good News to the poor. He does so with his words, certainly. But he must do so especially by his person and presence to them, proclaiming to sinners and to the poor that God cares. The deacon "enfleshes" God's care of the poor, that God hears their cry (see Ps 34). The deacon is God's caring for the poor. In the deacon, who remembers, is genuinely mindful of, anxious on behalf of and in his care for the poor, the poor will come to know that God himself is mindful of them. The poor will come to know that God cares.

Remember the parable of the Prodigal Son. The younger son was on the verge of losing his humanity because he believed that no one cared—that people cared more for the pigs than for him. Then he remembered that his father cared. His father even cared for the poorest of the poor, day laborers. And so to his father and to home the Prodigal Son arose to return. Wherever sinners and the poor have lost their humanity because everyone else is busy seeking his own self-interests rather than Christ's, because no one cares, the deacon is to care and, in caring, to restore sinners and the poor to their Father and to their Father's house.

The deacon, then, is the ordained minister whose commission it is to ensure, not simply "table fellowship," but, as the future Pope Benedict XVI wrote, table fellowship "in the fullest sense of the word." There are not two tables, namely, the altar in a church sanctuary, from which the faithful are fed spiritually, and a separate table of service to the poor. There is only one table, the table of Christ's eucharistic love, from which is served both spiritual food for the life of the faithful and physical food for the life of the world. For example, the ancient meaning of the offering that was taken up at the Eucharist was not to secure income for the payment of the church's bills but rather to provide physical sustenance for the poor. The deacon serves this one table by being mindful of, remembering, and extending both spiritual *and* physical care to sinners and the poor. Doing so he receives from the acknowledged pillars of the church "the right hand of fellowship" and in his ministry exercises from an undivided heart, with integrity and even eagerly, the suffering servanthood of Christ.

Indeed, I would even suggest that if a bishop or pastor and his deacon(s) are experiencing miscommunication, misunderstanding, and tension in their relationship, that is, tension in their *communio*, then one of the places they should look to heal their relationship is right here. Do they both know and understand that the deacon's *communio* with the church's leadership is expressed in large part through the latter's remembrance, his eager "mindfulness," of the poor? Does the bishop in fact assign his deacons, and are their pastors engaging them to serve the poor? Is the deacon in his life and day-to-day ministry serving sinners and the poor at one table of fellowship, a table integrally eucharistic and charitable?

The Deacon's Functions at Mass

We turn next to a more practical consideration of those functions at Mass that express a deacon's service to the poor, his participation therein in Christ's and the church's *munus regendi*. How specifically does he gather sinners and the poor to the altar and lead them in the public work that is liturgy?

The Prayer of the Faithful

First, at Mass, it is the deacon who leads the prayers of the faithful. The church calls upon him to be "the cry of the poor," giving voice to the prayers of the poor for the poor. "In a sense," the American bishops wrote in their *Study Text* on the diaconate, "the general intercessions are the prototype of diaconal prayer" (p. 40). But it should go without saying that a deacon cannot bring the needs of the poor before the Lord and the assembly of the faithful if he personally does not know the poor and is ignorant of their needs. How will he bring the poor to the house of the Lord if he has not first sought them out wherever they are to be found? How could he bring the needs of the poor to the attention of the gathered assembly unless he himself has been in solidarity with the poor where they are in their need? Can he place the poor at the heart of God and the community if he has not set them in his own heart first?

Of their very nature the prayers of the faithful are communal, and therefore general. The deacon begins each petition with, "Let *us* pray . . ." and concludes it with, "*We* pray to the Lord," inviting the entire community to be united in concern for the poor. In the prayers of the faithful the deacon becomes the advocate of the poor before God and the church. For this reason he himself should compose the prayers of the faithful; since "the general intercessions are the prototype of diaconal prayer," he should understand this duty to be one of his most important liturgical functions. Even if there is more than one deacon assigned to a single parish, each deacon should compose the prayers of the faithful for those Masses at which he himself functions as the Deacon of the Word. Additionally, as the assembled community at each Mass is different, so too may be its needs, and so too, therefore, should be the prayers of the faithful that they pray. In no instance should a deacon ever simply repeat prayers of the faithful that others have composed, or, especially, purchase prayers of the faithful from commercial sources that sell generic prayers.

In order to compose and pray the prayers of the faithful, the deacon must know what is happening to the poor and in their lives in his community and in the world. Among other things, he should be aware of celebrations and commemorations in the life of the universal, particular, and local churches he serves. He must be attentive to history and knowledgeable of both local and global current events. In whatever way his ecclesial and civic community is grieving and hurting, he should bring that hurt to prayer, his and the assembly's. Is Christ the Suffering Servant doing any less? He should inquire of his collaborators for news and information regarding those whom they serve in their ministries and of the poor of their community. Because of the liturgy, therefore, outside of the sacred celebration he should be an advocate for the poor on diocesan and parish pastoral councils, willing to serve on community boards, and undertake community service.

Because he is a deacon, he is dedicated to the common good and must labor for justice and righteousness for all. It is most fitting for a deacon to be involved in community organizing. With the permission of his bishop, he should run for public office and accept appointments to public service. Deacons are exempted from the canon law that prohibits bishops and priests from assuming public office (see canons 288 and 285, §3). The *Directory* permits active involvement in political parties or trade unions "for the defense of the rights of the Church and to promote the common good" (13). In the United States a deacon may present his name for election, accept nomination to a public office, and actively participate in another's political campaign with the prior written permission of his bishop (*National Directory* 91).

Deacons are to write and pray the prayers of the faithful as often as the church gathers to celebrate the Lord's resurrection and the great mysteries of his life, that is, every Sunday and holy day, except for one: Good Friday. On Good Friday, at the Celebration of the Lord's Passion, deacons echo words the universal church herself articulates at the foot of her bridegroom's cross, prayers of the faithful that priests and deacons pray in every Catholic community gathered for worship that day. Good Friday's petitions serve as an extended pilgrimage of the faithful. Instead of the presider preaching a homily (which on Good Friday is optional), that day the deacon himself leads the faithful to the cross of Jesus in pilgrimage prayer, the cross that immediately thereafter they will venerate. Introducing each prayer of the Good Friday petitions and inviting the faithful to kneel and stand, the pilgrimage starts and stops, and starts up again on its way. With each petition the deacon gathers to the cross of Jesus the holy church itself, then the pope and all the church's ministers, followed by catechumens, all Christians, and Jews. Then to the cross of Christ he even gathers those who do not believe in Christ or in God, those who govern and serve in public office, and finally the poor in trouble and in need.

Moreover, the deacon not only gives voice to the church's needs. Even as each petition is placed before the crucified Lord, he invites the faithful to kneel and stand, in this way exhorting them to know in the carriage of their own bodies the dying and rising of Christ.

The Kiss of Peace

In the Sermon on the Mount, Jesus taught that before one may approach the altar he must be reconciled and at peace with his neighbor (Matt 5:23-24). In obedience to this command, following the consecration of the Eucharist and before its distribution to the faithful, the presider prays repeatedly for peace, six times in fact. In the embolism that bridges the Lord's Prayer with its doxology, he prays, "Lord . . . grant us peace in our day." Then he recalls that at the Last Supper Jesus gave his farewell gift of peace to the apostles: "Peace I leave with you; my peace I give to you" (John 14:27). Again the presider begs the Lord to look not on our sins but to "grant us the peace and unity of [his] kingdom." The presider then prays that the community will know the peace of Christ; they pray the same for him. Finally, the deacon invites the individual members of the congregation to extend the sign of peace to one another. Peace, it can be seen, is a central motif of the Communion Rite.

In virtue of his ordination the deacon must be an advocate for justice and righteousness and a tireless worker for peace. It is to be hoped, therefore, that through his ministry justice is secured where injustice has been perpetuated, so that there may be peace. Inviting the faithful to extend to one another the sign of peace before they approach the altar to receive Communion, the deacon is urging them to be reconciled where injustices may have constructed walls in their relationships and to extend to one another the forgiveness they themselves receive from the Lord. He is inviting individuals who approach the Communion table to know full and right relationship, to know friendship, with Jesus and with one another. He is inviting families who will soon approach the altar to return to their homes in respect and reverence, accepting and caring for one another, to converse and communicate. St. Cyril of Jerusalem taught, "This kiss expresses a union of souls and is a plea for complete reconciliation. This kiss then is a sign that our souls are united and all grudges banished" (*Mystagogic Catechesis* 5).

It is regrettable that the meaning of this exchange of the sign of peace is perhaps altogether lost to modern congregations. The renewal of the ancient meaning of so valuable a gesture in the life of the early church is necessary so as to recover the sacred sense of the eucharistic celebration in general, as well as the reception of Holy Communion by the faithful, if not also their belief in the real presence of Christ in the Eucharist.

The Distribution of the Precious Blood

In the distribution of Communion, it belongs to the deacon to distribute the chalice of the Lord's Blood, not to distribute his Body. In pagan life and ritual, the cup spoke of power, luxury, and debauchery. Not so for Christ, who gave the chalice, and specifically the chalice of his own blood, a wholly different meaning. For Christians the cup is a symbol of Christ's high priesthood, of him who became like his brothers and sisters in all things except sin, including suffering, shedding his blood, and death. The chalice therefore is a symbol of service. Jesus taught, for example, that whoever hands a cup of cold water to another welcomes him (Matt 10:42). When Zebedee's sons' mother asked Jesus to assign her boys seats of honor at his right hand and left when he should enter into his kingdom, he challenged them directly, "Are you able to drink the cup that I am about to drink?" Then, calling the disciples together, he admonished them. "You know that the rulers of the Gentiles lord it over them, and their great ones are tyrants over them. It will not be so among you; but whoever wishes to be great among you must be your servant, and whoever wishes to be first among you must be your slave" (Matt 20:22-28). Fittingly, then, the chalice is a symbol of service, and when the deacon hands it to a communicant and proclaims, "The Blood of Christ," he proclaims to the communicant Christ's forgiveness of sins, his service of the poor, as well as his own eager mindfulness of their plight. By ministering the cup alongside the presider, the deacon affirms that he himself has accepted the chalice of the Lord and does not aspire to greatness but, rather, to the service of the lowest.

The Dismissal

At the end of Mass, having gathered the poor at the altar of the Lord, the deacon dismisses the congregation from it: he gives them their "marching orders." In each of the three options of the Mass's dismissal rite, the deacon says, "Go in peace." With these words he reminds the departing assembly that they too, as the apostles at the Last Supper, have received Christ's farewell gift of peace. The deacon exhorts them that what they have received from the Lord they must now give to others and to the world. In so dismissing them, he instructs the dispersing assembly that the gathering of the poor takes place not simply in the church, in a sanctuary, and around an altar. As the deacon gathered sinners and the poor into the community of the church, so too in imitation of his ministry must the members of the community serve the poor in their homes and communities. The word they have heard and that saves them they must now proclaim. The food of which they have eaten they must feed to others through service. Having received Christ's farewell gift of peace they in turn must be at and work for peace with others, and be agents of justice and righteousness for all.

I want to emphasize this point. Whereas the Eucharist is Christ's charity to us, it is our justice to others. Charity is that virtue by which we give ourselves to others, as Christ gave himself to us. Justice is that by which we give to others their due, which we are called to do in virtue of our baptism, and, especially for those who are ordained deacons, as icons of Christ the Suffering Servant. Accordingly, the Second Vatican Council calls all people, laity and the ordained, to not confuse the two, and especially to ensure that the demands of justice are met before the charitable gift is extended. "The demands of justice should first be satisfied," it teaches in its decree *Apostolicam actuositatem* (On the Apostolate of the Laity), "lest the giving of what is due in justice be represented as the offering of a charitable gift" (8). These two, namely, giving to the other what he or she is due *and* giving to the other one's own self, satisfying the demands of justice *and* serving the other in charity, together constitute authentic *diaconia* and therefore authentic diaconal ministry. As symbolized by the dismissal, it pertains to the deacon not only to act justly and charitably, but to teach and lead the baptized laity in doing so. Thus does he serve the unity and good order of the church and ensure the distribution of the Lord's bounty to sinners and the poor.

For this reason, I highly urge deacons to read and familiarize themselves with two extraordinary documents of the church that speak of the relationship between justice and charity, namely, the council's decree On the Apostolate of the Laity, especially its second chapter, "The Goals to be Achieved," and Pope Benedict XVI's first encyclical, *Deus caritas est*. Both of these documents are masterpieces in helping the laity and ordained ministers to love as Christ has loved us.

At the conclusion of Mass, the deacon accompanies the presider and together they leave the sanctuary and the church. How fitting it is that the deacon, being the first to leave the church's sanctuary, is the first on the front lines in service to the poor in the world. If he is not, his diaconal life and ministry would be "intrinsically fragmented." He would be failing in the carrying out of the threefold mandate of the laying on of hands, altar, and service. All he had been about in the sanctuary and in the liturgy would have been like looking in a mirror, and then "on going away," immediately forgetting what he looked like (see Jas 1:24).

Spiritual Aids

Finally, let's turn our attention to the deacon's spirituality. "The element which most characterizes diaconal spirituality," the church teaches, "is the discovery of and sharing in the love of Christ the servant, who came not to be served but to serve" (*Basic Norms* 72). How does a deacon discover and rediscover ever anew Christ's love so as to share it in service to others? In virtue of the threefold mandate to serve the poor and in the exercise of his *munus regendi*, there are two specific practices and habits of daily living that should mark his spirituality so as to grow stronger each day in bearing Christ to the poor and the poor to Christ.

This is an important distinction. The deacon is called not simply to bear the burden of the poor, but to bear the poor to Christ.

- The rosary of the Blessed Virgin Mary. A deacon is to have a special filial relationship with Mary. He must therefore be a man of the rosary. Mary was the first who loved God with all her heart, soul, mind, and strength, for God was her Father, Spouse, and Son. We can even say that in his incarnation Jesus is the icon of Mary: in assuming her sinless humanity Jesus became like her in every respect, merciful and faithful (see Heb 2:17-18). Mary taught the disciples what it meant to be a disciple when, at the wedding at Cana, they overheard her urging the waiters, "Do whatever he tells you" (John 2:5). Her Immaculate Heart was the first broken for her Son; even before her son's Sacred Heart was pierced by a Roman soldier's lance, her heart knew a double piercing, of both motherhood and discipleship. At Calvary, she stood faithfully at Jesus' cross, received his broken body in the center of her body between her arms, and then placed it in the tomb. She is the Lord's disciple par excellence, of one mind and one heart with her Lord. She is therefore archetype of the church and the model of a deacon's ministry carried out in its name.

  The rosary is a special prayer of diaconal ministry. In praying the rosary, the deacon accompanies Mary as she witnessed and shared in each of the great acts of salvation carried out by the Suffering Servant and in service to the poor. The Hail Mary itself is the prayer of Elizabeth, Mary's kinswoman, at the visitation (see Luke 1:42). In praying the Hail Mary the deacon joins with Elizabeth in holy wondering: "Why has this happened to me, that the mother of my Lord comes to me?" (Luke 1:43). The deacon prays that as Mary visited Elizabeth, so sinners and the poor might be visited with the knowledge that God cares. Only now it is the deacon who is ordained to be the "visitor" to bring the Lord to the poor. And in the rosary a deacon prays repeatedly for the poor, among whom he acknowledges himself to be, "sinner, now and at the hour of our death."

- "Situational awareness." Because "[t]he deacon is ordained precisely for service in both the sanctuary and the marketplace" (*National Directory* 59), he must be knowledgeable of and in touch with the contemporary conditions and daily circumstances of the world and of those he serves. As airplane pilots say, the deacon must never lose situational awareness. He must not be oblivious to what is happening around him, but aware particularly of the political and economic realities of his people and the community. History, sociology, and the other social sciences offer important insights into the world in which he lives. Culture, the arts, entertainment, sports, etc., should not be foreign to him. He should be able to evaluate them in the light of the Gospel and reasonably speak about them so as lead in their evangelization. Admittedly, one cannot be an expert in all things; there is always something or other of this life that is of little interest to a person. Nonetheless, the deacon must not insist on his own ways but be genuinely interested in others, like St. Timothy, and like St. Paul he must eagerly make himself "all things to all people" that he "might by all means save some" (1 Cor 9:22).

To this end the deacon must avail himself of those resources that will help him to know the social conditions of his brothers and sisters. Cardinal Stafford, the archbishop emeritus of Denver, used to instruct us priests that we should spend at least an hour a day praying, an hour a day doing theological reading, and an hour a day reading the newspaper. It seems to me that a similar principle of prayer and study is good advice for a deacon too.

Conclusion

In summary, the deacon works out his salvation and most radiantly shines as the icon of Christ the Suffering Servant when he is in hands-on and arms-embracing service to sinners and the poor. Serving at the altar he serves the poor, whom he has gathered there and whose thirst for care and life he quenches from there. The word he preaches in the liturgy and in catechesis is good news to the poor. The deacon is to kiss not only altars in the church and the gospel text he proclaims. Because he does so, because he kisses the altar of sacrifice and the Good News of salvation, he is the church's bow and embrace, the church's affection and care for the prodigal and the proud, the dispossessed and those unable to disposses themselves of their many possessions, and those who only see with popped-out eyes. The deacon is the church's kiss of sinners and the poor. The deacon is to slobber the poor with his kisses.

What the deacon does in the liturgy does not, as the commercial advertises, stay in the liturgy. The church needs him to proclaim the Good News not only to those who have assembled, but especially to those who have not yet been embraced. She needs the deacon to lead the faithful not only in voicing prayers and intentions on behalf of the poor. Rather, because "the LORD is near to the brokenhearted" (Ps 34:18), the church commissions deacons to go out to the poor and to lead others to where the cry of the poor can be heard. The church entrusts to the deacon the chalice of the Lord's Precious Blood, to be elevated to the glory and honor of God the Father, but also to be distributed to communicants. Therefore the church also entrusts to deacons the chalice of the Lord's suffering, from which those who have been excluded from the bounty of the world, made to sit on floors and in corners of the dining rooms and the halls of power of the rich, may drink and have their thirst quenched.

It may be time for a whole new consideration of the ordering of diaconal ministry. Does the deacon serve the poor in the world because he serves Word and sacrament at the altar? Or does he serve Word and sacrament at the altar because he serves the poor in the world? The bishops of the United States instruct, and it is worth quoting their instruction at length:

> The ancient tradition appears to indicate that *because* [emphasis added] the deacon was the servant at the table of the poor, he had his distinctive liturgical roles at the Table of the Lord. Similarly, there is a reciprocal correspondence between his role as a herald of the Gospel and his role as an articulator of the needs of the Church in the General Intercessions. In his formal liturgical roles, the deacon brings the poor to the Church and the Church to the poor. Likewise, he articulates the Church's concern for justice by being a driving force in addressing the injustices among God's people. He thus symbolizes in his roles the grounding of the Church's life in the Eucharist and the mission of the Church in her loving service of the needy. In the deacon, in a unique way, is represented the integral relationship between the worship of God in the liturgy that recalls Jesus Christ's redemptive sacrifice sacramentally and the worship of God in everyday life where Jesus Christ is encountered in the needy. The deacon's service begins at the altar and returns there. The sacrificial love of Christ celebrated in the Eucharist nourishes him and motivates him to lay down his life on behalf of God's People. (*National Directory* 37)

One is fully, integrally, and credibly a deacon not simply when he vests in a stole and a dalmatic and serves in the sanctuary. A deacon in some sense is more luminously the icon of Christ the Suffering Servant when in obedience to the example of Christ he arises from table, robes himself with a towel, and washes the feet of the poor in the sanctuaries of prisons and youth detention centers, nursing homes, hospitals, homeless shelters, detox centers, and the like. One is not completely exercising his diaconal ministry if all he does is preach from church pulpits, as important as this may be. It is just as important and just as necessary that deacons challenge the unjust words and deeds of those who preach from pulpits of worldly power and riches, those who deny the right to life of the unborn, who exploit or neglect or forget the poor. This is particularly pressing if the poor feel themselves to be unwelcome at the church's table because of their poverty, their status as immigrants or migrants, race, color, language, creed, nationality, or way of life. Indeed the deacon's words from church pulpits are credible only to the extent that they echo the words of justice and charity that he has preached, both with his lips and hands, from the pulpits of suffering and service.

Because the deacon will be reflecting Christ the Suffering Servant whenever he looks with love into the eyes of sinners, the hungry and thirsty, the stranger, the naked, the jobless or homeless, the ill of mind and body, the troubled and addicted, prisoners, the lonely, and heard the cry of them all, then he will more and more be seen to be the icon of Christ the Suffering Servant when, vested, he takes up the chalice of salvation and calls upon the name of the Lord (see Ps 116:13). Sinners and the poor are the mirror into which the deacon is called to look and not forget, to not forget and so to act, to act so as to bless and be blessed in all he does (see Jas 1:25).

chapter seven

"*Do Whatever He Tells You*"

The story of the wedding feast of Cana (John 2:1-12) has much to teach us about diaconal friendship with the Lord. In this reflection, therefore, we will study the relationships both of Jesus and Mary and of Jesus and the waiters.

> On the third day there was a wedding in Cana of Galilee, and the mother of Jesus was there. Jesus and his disciples had also been invited to the wedding. When the wine gave out, the mother of Jesus said to him, "They have no wine." And Jesus said to her, "Woman, what concern is that to you and to me? My hour has not yet come." His mother said to the servants, "Do whatever he tells you." Now standing there were six stone water jars for the Jewish rites of purification, each holding twenty or thirty gallons. Jesus said to them, "Fill the jars with water." And they filled them up to the brim. He said to them, "Now draw some out, and take it to the chief steward." So they took it. When the steward tasted the water that had become wine, and did not know where it came from (though the servants who had drawn the water knew), the steward called the bridegroom and said to him, "Everyone serves the good wine first, and then the inferior wine after the guests have become drunk. But you have kept the good wine until now." Jesus did this, the first of his signs, in Cana of Galilee, and revealed his glory; and his disciples believed in him.
>
> After this he went down to Capernaum with his mother, his brothers, and his disciples; and they remained there a few days.

On the Third Day

John tells us that the wedding in Cana took place "on the third day." On the third day of what? The context of the story provides two answers. First, literally, the wedding took place on the third day since Jesus departed Bethany across the Jordan, in whose waters he had been baptized. From there to Galilee was a three days' journey.

A closer reading of the first chapter of the gospel, beginning in verse 19, reveals, however, that Jesus left Bethany across the Jordan four days after John the Baptist had begun to proclaim the coming of the Messiah. The wedding in Cana, therefore, occurred seven days after John began to preach and baptize. Day one (v. 19): John appeared announcing the presence among the people of the one who was to come after him. Day two (v. 29): John saw Jesus and declared him to be the Lamb of God. Day three (v. 36): the disciples stayed with the Lord, and Andrew called Peter. Day four (v. 43): Jesus set out for Galilee and happened upon Philip and Nathaniel, who followed him. Three days later Jesus and the disciples arrived at Cana.

That Jesus performed his first miracle on the seventh day since John began to preach and to baptize, that is, since the advent of the Gospel, is not coincidental. In Genesis we read that "on the seventh day God finished the work that he had done, and he rested on the seventh day from all the work that he had done" (Gen 2:2). Jesus' appearance at the wedding on the seventh day recalls this seventh day of creation, the day on which God rested. By performing his first miracle seven days since John first heralded his coming, Jesus was revealing that in his person God was bringing to completion the work of creation and redemption, work God had been about "in the beginning" (Gen 1:1).

Additionally, by performing the miracle of changing water into wine on the day of the Lord's rest, Jesus "reversed" God's judgment against Moses and against the Jews. Moses broke faith with the Lord God and failed to manifest his sanctity to the Israelites, and so was forbidden to enter the Promised Land. The Jews in the desert refused to believe in the miracle of the water (see Deut 32:31). Because they contended with God at Massah and Meribah, God swore in anger, "They shall not enter my rest" (Ps 95:11; see Exod 17:7 and Num 20:13). At Cana, however, Jesus manifested his glory and the disciples believed in him—they believed in the miracle of the water turned into wine and they entered into God's rest, the rest of the seventh day, the rest of the eschatological wedding banquet of the kingdom of God.

Rabbi, Where Do You Stay?

The gospel narrative leading up to the events in Cana reveals another level of meaning to its wedding feast. Six days earlier, in Bethany across the Jordan, John the Baptist had pointed to Jesus and proclaimed him to be the Lamb of God. Two of John's disciples heeded his pointing, left his company, and followed the Lord. As they did so, Jesus, turning to face them, asked, "What are you looking for?" They responded, "Rabbi, where are you staying?" Jesus didn't answer them. Instead he invited them to "come and see." Jesus extended his invitation to John's disciples on the water's edge of the Jordan River, that is, at the very place from which Joshua and the Israelites first entered into the Promised Land. Later, as we will see, it is at a water's edge where Jesus will invite his disciples to stay and eat.

John the Evangelist records that the Baptist's two disciples stayed with the Lord that entire day. When the sun set, one of them, Andrew, left to find his brother, Simon, and brought him to Jesus. Three days later when Jesus set out for Galilee all three of these accompanied him. Then, on the first day of their journey, Jesus came upon Philip and called him. Philip in turn sought out Nathaniel. All five of these men "stayed" with Jesus. In fact, we know that they stayed with him at length, following him up and down the countryside until, six chapters later, they came a third time to the Sea of Galilee and to Capernaum. It is important for us to know of this journey of Jesus from the banks of the Jordan River to the Sea of Galilee, and especially the people he met and the places he visited, in order fully to understand the significance of the disciples "staying" with him.

The Fourth Gospel opens, in chapter one, across the Jordan. We have already considered that Jesus' baptism in the Jordan River marks Christ's new exodus into and "conquering" of the Promised Land and reveals God's absolute solidarity with sinners. After having been baptized Jesus undertook the first of three journeys northward to Galilee. On this first journey, at Cana, he turned water into wine at a wedding feast.

Jesus' second visit to Galilee is found in John 4:43. In the course of that visit he performed his second sign: he cured the royal official's son.

Jesus' third visit to Galilee then occurs in chapter 6. The all-important sixth chapter opens on "the other side of the Sea of Galilee," that is, on its eastern shore. There Jesus multiplied five loaves and two fish, feeding thousands of people. Following this miracle, at night, he withdrew and returned back across the sea to its northwestern shore. He did so, however, not as one otherwise is required by the laws of human nature to do, that is, taking a boat, swimming, or hiking its shoreline. Rather, he walked straight across on the water. When he came upon his disciples in the middle of the lake, they feared they were seeing a ghost and cried out. But Jesus reassured them, "It is I [*Egō eimi*]; do not be afraid" (6:20). Immediately thereafter Jesus and the disciples arrived at the sea's northwestern shore, at Capernaum, his own town. There too a crowd seeking bread was searching for him; however, Jesus attended to this crowd's need for bread not by multiplying loaves and fishes, as he had done on the eastern shore. Instead, he taught them that he himself was the bread after which they sought, that he himself was the Bread of Life.

Let's recap. By going down into the Jordan River, on its eastern bank, Jesus, whom God "made . . . to be sin who knew no sin" (2 Cor 5:21), allowed the waters to "conquer" him. Being conquered by the Jordan River's waters, "the death he died, he died to sin, once for all" (Rom 6:10). In rising from those waters, on the river's western bank, Jesus teaches sinners how to conquer sin and death itself, and enter forever into the Promised Land. Then later Jesus conquered the waters of the Sea of Galilee, walking on them from its eastern shore to its northwestern, and proclaiming along the way, "It is I." Thus did Jesus reveal himself in the flesh to be one with the Spirit of God that had hovered over the waters in the beginning (see Gen 1:1) and the Lord of all creation. Before conquering the waters of the Sea of Galilee, Jesus fed thousands of people with a mere five loaves of bread from the earth and two fish from the sea—a miracle indeed, but limited in its physical scope. After conquering the waters, he who at Cana had turned water into wine for the celebration of nuptials and who had multiplied physical bread for the feeding of thousands, then turned earthly bread into the Bread of Angels and the Bread of Angels into flesh, his own flesh for the life of the world (6:33, 51).

What has taken place between the eastern bank of the Jordan River and the northwestern bank of the Sea of Galilee? At the banks of the Jordan River the first two disciples to follow Jesus asked, "Where are you staying?" He responded, "Come and see." But then where did he take them? The answer is found not only on that first day of their encounter, or even on those first three days of their journey to Cana. The answer is found throughout the first six chapters of the gospel.

Where did Jesus go and where did he stay? First, Jesus went to a wedding, in Cana, where he encountered his mother. Following the wedding he went home with her and with his family and disciples (2:12). He then returned to Jerusalem, specifically to the temple, and, cleansing it, showed his zeal for his Father's house (2:17). He received Nicodemus at night and proclaimed baptism to be the way to see God's reign (3:3). He returned to Judea and "spent some time there . . . and baptized" (3:22; see also 4:2). Then in Samaria he healed a broken woman, desperate for acceptance and intimacy. As a result the Samaritans begged him to stay, and he spent two days among them. Returning again to Cana in Galilee he performed a miracle, "the second sign" (4:54): A Roman centurion, a pagan, begged the Lord to cure his son, who was dying, and Jesus did so. Having put his trust in the word Jesus spoke, the centurion and his whole family became believers. Then it was back to Jerusalem where on the Sabbath, at the pool of Bethesda, he healed a sick man (5:1-9). Jesus returned again to the Sea of Galilee, where, as we have just seen, he walked on water and revealed himself to be the Lord of creation. All of this before finally returning a third time to Galilee, and specifically to Capernaum, his home, where he revealed that he was the Bread of Life.

At the conclusion of this all-important Bread of Life discourse, we are told that many of Jesus' disciples abandoned him. As they turned their backs on him, Jesus turned to face the Twelve—Peter and Andrew, Philip and Nathaniel, and the others he had called along the way—and asked them, "Do you also wish to go away?" (6:67). He put it all on the line. At his home in Capernaum Jesus challenged them: "There you have it. You asked where I stay; now you have seen. I stay with sinners, in solidarity with them, so as to conquer sin and death. I stay in my relationship with my mother. I stay in baptism, healing, reconciliation, and in marriage. I stay in my zeal for my Father's house. I stay in the sick and the dying. I stay in foreigners who are broken and have lost faith, like the Samaritans. I stay in pagans, like the royal official, who, because faith has never been proclaimed to them are near death, and they find life in my word. Being the Lord of creation I stay in the conquering of the waters. I stay in the boat with the disciples, but not as a ghost; truly 'It is I.' And above all, I stay in the Eucharist, in the changing of water into wine and bread into flesh. That is where I stay, where I am at home. Now you know. You have seen it all. You have heard it all. You have walked it all. You must decide if you are going to stay with me. Do you too want to leave me?" Peter answered for all when he said, "Lord, to whom can we go? You have the words of eternal life. We have come to believe and know that you are the Holy One of God" (6:68-69). Jesus' invitation to "come and see," extended on the banks of the baptismal waters of the Jordan River, now at the shore of the conquered waters of the Sea of Galilee became the invitation to "stay and eat." Jesus stays in the eating of the Bread of

Life. Peter answered that there was no one else to whom and nowhere else they could go. They had seen where he stayed. They were not leaving. They would sit at his table. They were home.

And the Mother of Jesus Was There

We have wandered a bit far from the wedding at Cana. Let's return there now and take a look at the relationship of Jesus with Mary, his mother, she who *is* the first place where Jesus "stayed." Then we will study Jesus' encounter with the waiters.

Mary appears only twice in the Fourth Gospel, namely, at the wedding at Cana and again at the crucifixion at Calvary. At Cana, at this wedding, Jesus turned water into wine and his disciples began to believe in him. At Calvary, at the crucifixion, Jesus shed his blood and sealed the new and everlasting covenant that is the marriage of the Lamb of God with the church. Her appearance at both of these "weddings" unifies the two stories as prophecy (Cana) and prophecy fulfilled (Calvary).

In neither appearance is Mary named. John introduces her at the wedding simply as "the mother of Jesus" and at the cross as "his mother" (19:25). Mary's identity in the mission and ministry of her Son was her maternity, and her maternity was her discipleship. At the wedding in Cana Mary gave birth to her Son's hour. At the eternal nuptials of the Lamb at Calvary she gave him away as a spouse to his bride; she gave him away to the church.

Mary's presence at the wedding at Cana was a welcome one; she herself had been invited. In fact, the evangelist gives us the impression that she had been invited in her own right. We might even imagine that Jesus had been invited because his mother was to be there (as, for example, when an invitation is extended to Mr. and Mrs. So-and-So and family.) She, then, was a cause of the coming of Jesus to the wedding; her presence was the possibility of a miracle.

Let's look at the conversation between Jesus and Mary—a mere two lines—when she informs him that the couple had run out of wine. "They have no wine," Mary matter-of-factly stated. Jesus responded to her, "Woman, what concern is that to you and to me?" We'll look first at Jesus' questioning response, and then turn our attention to why he called his mother "Woman."

In the book of Ecclesiastes we read, "Go, eat your bread with enjoyment, and drink your wine with a merry heart; for God has long ago approved what you do" (9:7). Wine was a symbol of divine favor: that

God was pleased with what one was about, that he favored what one was doing. In our gospel story, then, we can interpret the presence or absence of wine as a sign that God favored or, conversely, was displeased with this couple who had wed. At least that's how the wedding guests themselves might have interpreted the unfortunate turn of events.

In Jesus' time it pertained to the groom and to his family to host a wedding and see to its celebration. Celebrating was not possible if there was not enough wine to last the length of the reveling. For their part, the groom and his family depended on the generosity of others—patrons, for example, and the guests themselves—to ensure that an adequate supply of wine was at hand for the eight-day celebration. (It is much the same in our own day and age when guests bring a hospitality gift of wine or food when invited to a dinner or party.) To bring a gift of wine or food to a nuptial banquet expressed bonds of affection and friendship with the newlyweds' families. It was a sign of one's favor for the couple. And it expressed more than a shared responsibility for hosting an eight-day wedding celebration. The community itself, through the bringing of food and wine to a wedding banquet, expressed its approval of the nuptials arranged between two families as well as its commitment to help this couple as it took up the lifelong covenant of marriage and beginning a family.

For the Cana couple to run out of wine, therefore, was disastrous. The text suggests that the groom's family was of some means, for they had six large stone water jars available for ritual purifications and they could afford a headwaiter and waiters to serve at table. Still the groom and his family were unable to meet the demands of the celebration. John doesn't tell us why they ran out of wine; we can only speculate. Perhaps the guests had been unable or unwilling to share the communion of the event and meal. For his part, Jesus, having just arrived from a three days' journey from Bethany across the Jordan, being poor and accompanied by at least five unexpected disciples, may not have done his part to provide for the celebration. Jesus himself and his disciples, Archbishop Fulton Sheen suggested, consumed all the wine. Or just maybe God did not bless this couple. Whatever the cause, it was potentially a matter of great shame to the couple and to their families to have been unable to provide for the celebration of the nuptials.

Demonstrating her extraordinary maternal sensitivity, and attentive as she always was to other's needs, Mary noticed the couple's plight. She did not dramatize the situation. She did not try to work it out for herself. Nor did she go about trying to minimize its impact and make everyone feel better about themselves. She simply took note. Then, interestingly, she turned first neither to the groom, nor to his father, nor to the head-waiter, any of whom might have been expected to be able to solve the problem. Instead she turned to her son, informing him simply, "They have no wine." No demands did she make upon him, nor anything of him did she ask. Mary simply informed him of the "facts on the ground" and allowed him to draw his own conclusions.

Jesus responded, "[W]hat concern is that to you and to me [*ti emoi kai soi*]." This question was frequently asked in the Old Testament (see, for example, 2 Sam 16:10 or 1 Kgs 17:18). It was not meant to disagree with one who was making an assertion or asking something of another, or to establish a defense against the request. Rather, one who responded with "What is that to you and to me" was trying to get at what or, more accurately, who stood behind the request. Asking "What is that to you and to me" was like saying, as we might today, "By whose authority do you speak or act?" "Where are you coming from?" or even "What's gotten into you?" By asking it of his own mother, Jesus too was asking of her, "Who stands behind you that you bring this concern to my attention?" "Who is behind all this?" Jesus knew who stood behind him, namely, his heavenly Father. In fact, that is the meaning of "My hour has not yet come." Now he needed to know that his heavenly Father stood behind his mother, that the Father was behind all this. He needed to hear her say that it was God's glory that she sought and not her own.

Surprisingly, Mary did not answer Jesus. Having informed him of the lack of wine, she dropped the matter, asking nothing further of him. In this way she witnessed to him that indeed it was the Father who stood behind her, that it would be his glory to be revealed, not hers. Neither from a position of weakness (an insecure ego, for example, or fear of being embarrassed), nor from some inappropriate expression of maternal care (trying to solve everyone's problems for them so that everyone will just get along and feel good about themselves), nor from false superior authority ("I am your mother and you'd better do what I tell you to do") did she force Jesus' hand. She had no idea how the situation would be resolved; she had no idea what, if anything, he would do. Remember, to that day Jesus had not exercised miraculous powers, had not performed, for example, even just an itsy-bitsy, teeny-weenie secret miracle for his mom! His hour had not yet come. No, Mary gave her son complete freedom to act or not to act as he himself saw fit. She knew simply that whatever he did he would do for God's glory. In this way she showed that it was the glory of his heavenly Father that stood behind her, and so behind them both. When in fact she didn't respond to Jesus' query, "What is that to you and to me?" Mary showed it was nothing to her. It was all to God and to his son.

Jesus then called his mother, "Woman." Both here and from the cross this is the only appellative with which he referred to her in this gospel. Such a greeting catches us off guard, is perhaps even offensive to our ears. In our own day, a child might refer to his or her father as "my old man." But it is (generally) socially unacceptable for a child to refer to one's mother as anything, for example, but "Mother," "Mom," or "Mama."

When Jesus called her "Woman" he was showing his mother no disrespect. But he was sending her a message. Having been baptized and anointed, having taken up publicly his ministry, having begun the gathering of disciples into what will become the new Israel, indeed having intimated that the hour of his glory had come, Jesus' relationship with his mother had to change. He could no longer relate to her simply on the level of intimate mother-son familiarity. If the hour to reveal his Father's glory had come, then too had her hour to become publicly his disciple, indeed the first of disciples, the first who from Cana would follow him to Calvary.

Jesus would "exalt" his mother as the first of his disciples, holding her up to everyone in his household of faith as the model of discipleship. In a different setting he asked, "'Who is my mother, and who are my brothers?' And pointing to his disciples, he said, 'Here are my mother and my brothers! For whoever does the will of my Father in heaven is my brother and sister and mother'" (Matt 12:48-50). And again: "My mother and my brothers are those who hear the word of God and do it" (Luke 8:21).

In this Fourth Gospel Jesus addresses Mary as "Woman." As woman, she becomes bride. As bride, she was now disciple. Mary, the woman, bride, and disciple who heard the word of God and kept it, at Cana is appointed by her son to be the mother of a new household, of his household of faith and of all the living. Thus did he reveal to his disciples that his mother, Mary, was the new Eve. She was the woman God promised would one day tread on the serpent's head (see Gen 3:15).

After Jesus performed his first miracle and departed the wedding, he led his mother, his family, and his disciples down from Cana to Capernaum. From the day of his conception until the day of his first miracle, she had made a home for the Lord in her heart, her womb, and at Nazareth. Now, from that day of the revelation of his glory at Cana he, the Son, would make a home for his mother. Like a bride waiting for her groom, Mary had preceded her Son to the wedding at Cana; he came to the wedding because she had been invited. But by his invitation she will now depart Cana to celebrate her Son's own wedding, the nuptials of the Lamb. After he had served the wine for the Cana nuptials, Jesus the Divine Bridegroom, claimed his own bride (Mary as the archetype of the church) and took her into his home. The prophet Jeremiah longed to see this day when he would hear "the voice of mirth and the voice of gladness, the voice of the bridegroom and the voice of the bride, the voices of those who sing, as they bring thank offerings to the house of the LORD: 'Give thanks to the LORD of hosts, for the LORD is good, for his steadfast love endures forever'" (Jer 33:11). Jeremiah's prophecy is now fulfilled in Christ and Mary, in Christ and his disciples, in Christ and the church.

At the end of the story, in verse 12, John tells us that Jesus went down to Capernaum. John leaves us with the impression that the wedding celebration continued; after all, the guests had 720 to 1,200 more gallons of vintage wine to drink! Yet even as Jesus departed the banquet, at the same time Christ did "stay" at the nuptials. His continued presence was now to be found in the choice wine he himself had "brought" and that the guests were privileged to drink for up to eight days more. After all was said and done, he had done his part.

What Jesus revealed at the wedding, through his mother, and especially through her "staying" with him in Capernaum, he sought to teach his disciples who had come to believe in him. Having departed from the wedding table of an earthly groom and bride, Jesus invited his disciples to sit at his own table, the banquet table of his, the heavenly bridegroom's, own nuptials. In chapter 2 of the gospel Jesus provided a choice wine at the earthly nuptials, from which he departed. Four chapters later, in chapter 6, he invited his disciples to "a feast of rich food, a feast of well-aged wines, of rich food filled with marrow, of well-aged wines strained clear" (Isa 25:6), that is, the rich food of his own body and the choice wine of his own blood. Having eaten he invited them to stay with him. "Those who eat my flesh and drink my blood abide in me, and I in them," Jesus declared in the Capernaum synagogue (John 6:56). Indeed, the word in Greek for stay, *meneis*, which the Baptist's disciples used to question Jesus when they asked "Rabbi, where do you stay?" is the same word the Evangelist used in chapter 2 to refer to the staying of Mary, the family, and the disciples with Jesus in Capernaum. Jesus himself also, in John 6, used this word to describe the "remaining" of the disciples in him who is the Bread of Life.

Those Waiting on Table

Let's turn our attention now to the waiters at the Cana wedding and see from how they related to both Mary and to Christ what they can teach deacons.

As from the banks of the Jordan River John the Baptist directed his disciples to follow Jesus, so too Mary, at Cana's water's edge (for "standing there were six stone water jars"), directed the waiters to do whatever Jesus instructed them to do. As John's two disciples "heard [John] say this, and . . . followed Jesus" (1:37), the waiters too heeded Mary's instruction and did what Jesus told them. John the Baptist directed his disciples to follow the Lamb of God. The Mother of Jesus exhorted the waiters to be servants of her son. Because they obeyed, John the Baptist's disciples and the Cana wedding waiters were the first to see the Father's glory revealed in Christ.

In the New Revised Standard Version, these servers are simply referred to as "the servants." The original text uses the word *diakonois*. From this Greek word, as we well know, we acquire our Latin word *deaconus* and the English word "deacon." Furthermore, the evangelist never actually tells us that they waited on tables. Nor does he even tell us that they served the wine at the meal. In fact, in the gospel narrative they did nothing more than fill six stone jars with water and, withdrawing it, serve wine to the headwaiter.

Of course on the literal level they were simple table waiters. But unquestionably at the spiritual level they were more. Mary instructed them, "Do whatever he tells you." They did; they did everything Jesus told them to do. Because they did, they were the first to whom Jesus revealed his glory and the first to behold him who was the divine bridegroom. Therefore, we understand them to be not simply waiters at a wedding banquet, but *diakonois* of the divine bridegroom. Remember, it was the responsibility of the groom and his family to furnish and serve the wine at a wedding feast. Who in fact supplied the wine at this wedding? Jesus. Who served it? The *diakonois*. Having supplied the wine at Cana, Jesus revealed himself to be the true bridegroom who had come into the world. The waiters, having obeyed his instructions and assisting him, doing whatever he told them, showed themselves to be his first "deacons."

What specifically did Jesus command these *diakonois* to do? First, he commanded them to fill six stone jars to the brim with water. It is important to note that there were six water jars on the scene and that they were stone. Recall that the wedding at Cana took place on the seventh day since John the Baptist began to preach the Gospel and the sixth day of Jesus' own public ministry. In Genesis, in the first week of creation, God created Adam and Eve from the clay of the earth and breathed his spirit into them on the sixth day. Yet, even as God brought them into being and set them at the threshold of life, this first husband and his wife lost it all, they ran out of wine. Adam and Eve sinned and brought death upon themselves and their descendants.

Now this couple of Cana, having been created anew in marriage and standing at the threshold of their new life, was running out of wine. They were about to lose it all. By changing the water of six ceramic jars into wine on the seventh day since the beginning of the proclamation of the Gospel, Jesus revealed that he himself was reuniting God with God's creation in marriage, the Creator with all that the Creator had created "in the beginning." At the wedding of Cana Jesus declared Adam and Eve's divorce from God to be null and void.

In addition, John tells us that these six jars were normally used "for the Jewish rites of purification." At the hour of Jesus' miracle they were empty. True, at a literal level the water might simply have been expended for the ritual purification of the guests. But at the spiritual level, the emptiness of these stone jars symbolizes two things. First the emptiness of these six *stone* jars symbolizes the meaninglessness, the futility into which creation sank as a result of Adam and Eve's sin. St. Paul wrote, "For the creation was subjected to futility, not of its own will but by the will of the one who subjected it, in hope that the creation itself will be set free from its bondage to decay and will obtain the freedom of the glory of the children of God. We know that the whole creation has been groaning in labor pains until now" (Rom 8:20-22). Second, the emptiness of these jars used for *Jewish* ceremonial washings symbolizes that the rituals of the Jews were incapable of attaining the purification they symbolized. Ritual purification of the outside of the body could not achieve the forgiveness of sins and cleansing of the heart, the genuine purity that would allow true communion with God. With Jesus' miracle, however, the water otherwise used for the ritual bathing of the outside of one's body will instead become suitable for drinking.

Moreover, those who drink of the water of Cana, water made wine, will not simply be purified on the inside. Jesus changed the water that Jews used to purify ritually their bodies into the choice wine that when drunk washes clean one's soul. And as the disciples that day saw Christ's glory and began to believe in him, those who drink this wine shall see God (see Matt 5:8). The letter to the Hebrews teaches, "For if the blood of goats and bulls, with the sprinkling of the ashes of a heifer, sanctifies those who have been defiled so that their flesh is purified, how much more will the blood of Christ, who through the eternal Spirit offered himself without blemish to God, purify our conscience from dead works to worship the living God" (9:13-14).

Jesus then instructed the waiters, having filled the water jars, to draw from them and to take some to the headwaiter. Note that he did not command them to draw out wine, simply to draw out what they had put in. In fact, John tells us that only the waiters who had drawn out the water knew where the wine had come from (2:9), implying that what they drew out of the jars still had the appearance and quality of water. Did it become wine when they poured water into the jars or as they drew it out? Did it become wine when the headwaiter tasted it? We do not know. In any case, the waiters did not have any idea that a miracle had taken place until after the headwaiter tasted the wine.

Furthermore, we have no idea who these waiters were. Perhaps they were servant-members of the groom's father's household. Perhaps they were day laborers hired for the occasion. Perhaps they were friends of the groom who had volunteered to serve. But we do know that to them Jesus was just another guest at the wedding. They did not know that he was the Messiah. Nor, of course, did they have any idea that Jesus could perform miracles or that he was in fact at that moment in the process of performing one; he hadn't yet, after all. So we can only imagine their dismay when Jesus commanded them to draw out and serve to their boss what they must have believed to be no more than water used to wash guests' feet. Imagine the faith in Jesus they had to muster to obey this command.

Doing as Mary exhorted them and whatever Jesus instructed them to do was a great risk on their part. If they were servants of the master, they risked their standing in their patron's house. If they were "professional" waiters or day laborers, they risked their livelihood, perhaps forever. Who would ever hire a server who had been dumb enough to serve unpurified water otherwise used for the purification of feet to his boss? Perchance they risked their own friendship with the groom and bride and with their families. They risked making a bad situation worse. But whatever risk they faced to their own standing and livelihood, they placed faith in Mary and Jesus and did what he instructed them to do. Doing so, they not only helped Jesus save the nuptial banquet but also helped him save the couple's nuptials. They not only helped save the couple's nuptials but also helped Jesus reveal God's new covenant with

Israel. They not only helped Jesus reveal God's new covenant with Israel but also served Jesus in restoring creation to communion with God. They were "deacons" of the nuptials of the divine bridegroom and the church. They were "deacons" of the hour of the glory of the Lord.

Cana and the Deacon

Let's take a look now at what this story of the wedding feast at Cana can teach deacons. What might deacons learn about their life and ministry from this story, from Mary, and from Jesus' question of his mother: "Woman, what concern is that to you and to me?" What do the "deacons" at the Cana wedding have to teach us about being a deacon in the church today?

First, Mary, having been invited, attended the wedding. We do not know whose wedding it was, perhaps of family or of friends. Deacons too, for their part, will be invited to participate in the lives and share in the living of many, some of whom may be anonymous to them. At Cana, Mary's acceptance of the invitation to attend was likely the cause for Christ to attend as well. Likewise in ministry a deacon's presence to the poor is the cause for Christ himself to be invited to come and to be welcomed. At the wedding Mary showed extraordinary sensitivity and took the initiative to meet the needs of the newly married couple and of their families. She took charge and presented their needs to her son. Deacons too are to be sensitive, tasked to take the initiative, and bring to the Lord the needs and longings of their people, of the poor, of the vulnerable whom they should love as family and friend.

What is more, Jesus held even Mary, his mother, accountable to the glory of God, asking her, "What is this to you and to me?" Jesus also holds deacons accountable, challenging them no less than his own mother, "Who stands behind you?" "Who stands behind your ministry?" "Whose glory are you seeking, your own or my Father's?" All that a deacon is about and all that he does he must do for the greater honor and glory of Christ, the Suffering Servant, whose "serving icon" he has been ordained to be.

The waiters at the Cana wedding who served Jesus also have much to teach deacons in service of the Divine Bridegroom. First, the waiters were men of blind faith. Something in Mary—in the way she related to Jesus, in her voice, in her eyes, in the way she loved the newly married couple, perhaps in the way she looked upon and addressed the waiters themselves, that is, most surely, with respect—assured them that they would be okay if they obeyed Christ's commands. So when she exhorted them to do whatever Jesus instructed them to do, they did exactly that. They did not hesitate or place limits on or exceptions to their obedience to Christ. To their boss they even served as drink what they had to believe was unpurified water. Because of their faith, which Mary elicited from them, they took great risks to their livelihood, their social standing, and their relationships with others.

To obey another is to give ear to, to listen attentively, to heed what is being said. Obedience is not simply the submission of one's will to the dictates of another. Rather, obedience is attentive listening and a sincere acceptance of another's will for the sake of a greater good. Hans Urs von Balthasar wrote that obedience in the church is "nothing other than love" (*Razing the Bastions*, p. 40). In this light, what the waiters showed in obeying both Mary's and Jesus' commands is that they had somehow in short order come to love her and her Son, as well as the newly married couple, and, above all, the good that, although unknown, even unfathomable to them, Jesus was to bring about.

Regarding the deacon, obedience establishes a loving partnership between the bishop, who is the overseer, and the deacon, who is the under-rower, for the sake of Christ, the church, and sinners and the poor, all of whom they both love. Through obedience the good that the bishop sees can be attained by the deacon who serves. Thomas Merton wrote, "We do not first see, then act: we act, then see" (*The Ascent to Truth*, p. 36). The waiters served and then saw; the headwaiter tasted and then believed. Even though a deacon as an under-rower in the church might not see the good to be achieved—it may be unknown to him, not yet revealed—nonetheless he hears, heeds, and obeys, whether it be his bishop or pastor, and so enters into a loving partnership with them that Christ, sinners, and the poor may be served.

Deacons will often be called upon by the Lord to muster blind faith and to serve to others what they will surely believe to be nothing more than unpurified water. How can this act make a difference? What difference has it made in the past? What difference will it make this time? Perhaps none. Perhaps a deacon's ministry to the poor will make no difference whatsoever in the life of the one he serves, because the one being served is closed to grace. Perhaps it will even put the deacon at risk. How often, for example, are those who pursue truth and seek justice marginalized by family or friends? How often do those who serve the poor whom society rejects find themselves rejected by society in turn? How often do those who defend life, especially life at conception or in embryonic form or life that is guilty of heinous crime, find themselves ridiculed? So what? If one learns the lessons of the waiters at the wedding at Cana, if one is obedient to Christ and to the church as the waiters were to Mary and to Christ, then as a deacon one lovingly does whatever Jesus tells him out of love for Jesus who tells him to do so, confident that the Lord is bringing about a great good. The deacon's ministerial objective is not success but fidelity; not acceptance but service; not a place alongside men of power but a place among the powerless. A deacon who is a man of faith, like the waiters at Cana, might risk much, even all, to do whatever Jesus tells him. But then like the Cana waiters, he will be the first to see the glory of the Lord.

Additionally, the waiters at Cana teach us something about the importance of community in diaconal ministry. Recall that there was more than one servant in the house of the father of the Prodigal Son. Likewise, at the wedding in Cana, there was more than one server whom Mary exhorted to heed Jesus' commands. More than one waiter was required to fill the stone jars with water and to serve the water made wine to the guests. (Remember, they didn't have running water and hoses. They had to draw water from a well, which might have been some distance from the site of the banquet, and transport it to where the six jars were located at the house.) In ministry, too, a deacon must neither be a loner nor minister alone. A deacon serves the Lord not privately or individually, but publicly and in community. He does so, therefore, under the instruction of the Lord, whose icon he is. He does so under the instruction of the church, in whose name he ministers. He does so under the direction of and in hierarchical communion with others, often pastors and other priests, who, like the headwaiter in our gospel story, are the ones who decide which foods and wines are served to the guests.

It is not the deacon's choice to command others to their service or to command others to serve where they themselves might prefer not to. A deacon has no choice but to serve. That is what a deacon does. At times, though, when appropriate, a deacon should step back so that others can exercise the functions the church has entrusted to them, for example, lectors and altar servers at liturgy. In this way too he serves, calling forth and engaging the service of others. And, when appropriate, a deacon steps forward to help others to exercise their baptismal priesthood or simply to do what needs to be done.

Finally, as surely as waiting on tables, a deacon's ministry can be mundane and tedious. A deacon may find himself bored with the oft-repeated stories of the elderly or the nonsensical gibbering of one suffering from

Alzheimer's. He may be repulsed by the physical stench of the poor, naked, or homeless or put off by their lack of social skills. He may be confused and feel lost when he must minister to those whose language he does not speak, nor they his. He may find himself judging those whom he serves; it is, after all, easier to judge than to join, isn't it? He may find that his service is never enough and that he never seems to please his bishop or pastor. He may sense that those whom he is serving are just taking advantage of his service; perhaps he has even been "burned" in ministry and made to suffer emotional, physical, material, or financial loss. He may believe that he has talents and gifts to give that are not exactly what the church or the poor are needing or asking of him. He may be hesitant, even frightened to enter prisons where criminals are incarcerated, into commitments with addicts, into relationships with the mentally ill, perhaps even into simple conversations with the tedious, needy, or difficult. Especially if he himself has been materially successful in life and become comfortable in his lifestyle, he may be tempted to impatience with those who lack basic life skills, who just don't get it. He may not see it as his responsibility to keep on looking for a job for the chronically unemployed or underemployed, who keep betraying his goodwill and that of the Christian community. He may simply tire of providing for, helping, visiting, serving the one who never seems to be satisfied and always seems to need more. He may question why it is always his job to open or close the church, to empty the trash, to shovel the walks, to clean up after meetings or gatherings—all simple and ordinary tasks but nonetheless extraordinary expressions of Christ's and the church's welcome and service of others.

How a deacon responds to the poor and in his ministry is the measure of his willingness to give his heart to Mary, his obedience to the church, and his body to Christ, the Divine Bridegroom. "Just as you did it to one of the least of those who are members of my family, you do it to me" (see Matt 25:40). If the deacon is open to what Mary wants to teach him at Cana and to giving his life to her son at Capernaum, he will see himself invited to the nuptial banquet of the Lamb of God and the church. There he will see, taste, and believe. He will discover that Jesus, who departed the wedding at Cana and led Mary, his brothers, and his disciples to Capernaum, invites him as well to stay with him. Jesus' invitation to the deacon to "come and see" will become the invitation to "stay and eat."

chapter eight

The Education of Suffering and Creative Fidelity

In his apostolic letter on the diaconate, *Sacrum Diaconatus Ordinem*, Pope Paul VI decrees that what is required of those who seek admission to the diaconate is "a natural inclination of service" (II, 8). Expounding on his predecessor's teaching, Pope John Paul II further specifies that this natural inclination should not be understood "in the sense of a simple spontaneity of natural disposition [but] rather an inclination of nature inspired by grace, with a spirit of service that conforms human behavior to Christ's." He continues, "The sacrament of the diaconate develops this inclination: it makes the subject to share more closely in Christ's spirit of service and imbues the will with a special grace so that in all his actions he will be motivated by a *new inclination* to serve his brothers and sisters" (General Audience Catechesis of October 20, 1993). In this reflection I want to consider how it is that Christ develops this "inclination of nature inspired by grace" into "a *new inclination* to serve [one's] brothers and sisters." Allegorically, we might ask how Christ continually turns the water of one's desire to serve into the choice wine of diaconal life and ministry.

Owen Vyner, my pastoral assistant for marriage and family life, wrote in an unpublished essay: "The recent form of *diaconia* has a tendency toward social activism which is almost indistinct from its secular counterpart or the reduction of service to mere function. When Christ came to definitively reveal the form that Christian service is to take, he chose the form of the suffering of love—he came as the suffering servant. Love, suffering, and service are all indispensable for the Christian because they are at the heart of the life of Christ" ("The Mystery of the Deacon in the Mission of the Trinity and the Church," p. 1).

Throughout these reflections, I have referred to the deacon not simply as an icon of Christ the Servant. I have invited the reader to consider the deacon as the icon of Christ the Suffering Servant, that is, as the icon of the revelation of "the form of the suffering of love." Since a deacon is the icon of Christ the Suffering Servant, this suffering of love is what distinguishes his service as specifically diaconal and prevents it from collapsing into humanism, simple community service, or mere functionalism. This form of the suffering of love is at the heart of a deacon's "new inclination" to serve. St. Paul himself connected suffering with service when he wrote, "I am now rejoicing in my sufferings for your sake, and in my flesh I am completing what is lacking in Christ's afflictions for the sake of his body, that is, the church. I became its servant [*diakonos*, deacon] according to God's commission that was given to me for you, to make the word of God fully known" (Col 1:24-25).

In this chapter we will consider three things: first, the image of the Suffering Servant in the book of Isaiah; second, how Christ the Suffering Servant is illuminated through a deacon's suffering; and, third, how in his life and ministry a deacon remains creatively faithful to Christ the Suffering Servant and to the church.

The Image of the Suffering Servant

The prophet Isaiah gives us four so-called Songs of the Servant or Servant Songs. In the first, Isaiah 42:1-9, God has set his spirit on his servant; therefore, his servant shall establish justice on the earth. The second song, Isaiah 49:1-6, sings of the servant whom the Lord called from his mother's womb to gather the dispersed, to restore the fortunes of Israel, and to be a light to all the nations. In the third song, Isaiah 50:4-11, the tone changes dramatically. Instead of being exalted for the work of justice, God's servant is now opposed, beaten, spat upon, disgraced before others. Still he trusts in the Lord. Because he trusts, he is the light in the darkness for all who fear the Lord. Those who likewise trust in the Lord heed the servant's voice and walk in his ways.

The fourth servant song, found in Isaiah 52:13–53:12, is the longest. Its tone is dramatically different from that of the first two and echoes that of the third. Strength and hope, characteristic of the first two songs, are missing. Instead, as the tension and opposition introduced in the third song are played out, condemnation and death draw near. Pope John Paul II writes of this song, "The prophet presents in this song an image of the sufferings of the servant with a realism as acute as if he were seeing them with his own eyes: the eyes of the body and of the spirit" (*Salvifici Doloris* [On the Christian Meaning of Suffering] 17).

This fourth song takes the form of alternating choruses between the Lord and Israel. In the first of these (52:13-15), the Lord proclaims that despite all outward appearances his servant shall be victorious; his victory will amaze, astound, "shock and awe" those who witness it. (For another example of such astonishment read the final judgment scene in Matt 25:31-46. Those condemned for their failure to serve the Lord because they failed to serve the least of their brothers and sisters are so "shocked" at their consequent fate.) In the second chorus (53:1-10a) Israel acknowledges and repents of her sins and the wounds she inflicted on the Lord's servant. In the third chorus (53:10b-12) the Lord restores hope. What he proclaimed in the first chorus he echoes here. The Lord will accept the sufferings of his servant, an acceptable sacrifice, and exalt him on high; his servant shall be numbered not among the dead but among the great. Despite Israel's rejection of his servant, the Lord has not rejected her, for "he bore the sin of many, and made intercession for the transgressors."

As we saw in chapter 6, Jesus understood himself to be the fulfillment of Isaiah's prophecy. On the part of the church, though, it required greater reflection to understand precisely how Christ fulfilled this prophecy, that is, how it was that Christ's sufferings justified the many and bore their transgressions and guilt, and forgave sins. What was it about his sufferings and his sacrifice that pleased the Father so that he accounted them as mercy on behalf of sinners?

The answer wasn't found in suffering itself. It wasn't simply that Christ suffered; everyone suffers, after all. But not everyone's sufferings gain for them the forgiveness of their sins, let alone the forgiveness of another's. Nor was the answer found in how Christ suffered, as horrific as the infliction and experience of his sufferings were. He was neither the first nor the last to be condemned unjustly and crucified. Others were too, but their crucifixions did not result in the salvation of the world. Upon reflection, the church had three insights into Christ's sufferings in which it came to understand why God accepted them and accounted them as the payment of the debt owed for the forgiveness of sins.

First, Christ's sufferings were borne from a different place than the sufferings of others. His sufferings were sufferings of trinitarian *communio*. Because Jesus, the only begotten Son of the Father, is at one and the same time true God and true man, his sufferings are both the sufferings of God for humanity and humanity for God. They are at one and the same time both the suffering of God borne for love of his sinful and prodigal children, and the suffering of humanity borne of the sin of Adam and Eve.

Second, Jesus knew full well that his sufferings were willed by the Father, not for their own sake but as the price to be paid for the redemption of Adam and Eve. As St. Paul taught, "for our sake [God] made him to be sin who knew no sin, so that in him we might become the righteousness of God" (1 Cor 5:21). And so Christ emptied himself and suffered for love of them. In other words, whereas Adam and Eve chose death through their failure to love and so suffered, Christ loved and so chose to suffer, and even accepted death on a cross.

Because of his divine *communio* with the Father, Jesus knew his Father's grieving over Adam and Eve's sin, their choice to break *communio* with the Father, their loss to the Father and their hiding in death from him. From the moment Adam and Eve sinned, Christ knew that his own descent into their suffering and death would be required so as to find them, to ransom them from death, and to restore his Father's joy. Jesus knew full well that, being the "older" brother, he had to leave his Father's estate and venture out to a foreign land where his Father could not go in search of his "younger" brother and sister, who were created in his very image and likeness. (Contrast Jesus with the older brother in the parable of the Prodigal Son. That brother stayed home, would not go and search out his little brother, and at the latter's return even refused to share his father's joy.)

Third, Jesus freely paid the price of love and bore his sufferings "to the end" (see John 13:1), even though there was no way that he could have known what that "end," namely, death and hell, were like. Before Jesus' cross, God had no taste of death. And before Jesus' descent into hell God's loss and absence to himself (hell being the loss and absence of God) was inconceivable. But on Holy Saturday Christ was truly "lost," "absent" from and "abandoned," by the Father. Into Adam and Eve's hellish hiding he had gone, to rescue them from death, from being lost and absent to God. For having experienced his Father's pain and suffering at the loss of Adam and Eve, Christ could only have imagined the suffering he was to experience on the earthly side of his cross, let alone that in which Adam and Eve were suffering on the hellish side. He shared his Father's grief and he loved. And so out of both divine and human freedom he chose to go where Adam and Eve had gone and his Father could not.

In summary, what marked Christ's sufferings as different, gaining the Father's mercy and winning the forgiveness of sins and the restoration of life, was, first, the *communio* with the Father and the Holy Spirit out of which he undertook them; second, the *meaning* the Father assigned to them in assigning them to the Son; and, third, the *freedom* with which Christ accepted them. If Christ had not intended his sufferings to be a sin offering, man could not be restored to communion with God. Without Christ choosing freely to lay down his life, that life would simply have been taken from him and the Father would not have accepted it as a sin offering on behalf of sinners.

"It was fitting," the letter to the Hebrews teaches, "that God, for whom and through whom all things exist, in bringing many children to glory, should make the pioneer of their salvation perfect through sufferings" (Heb 2:10). Then, regarding the high priesthood, the letter continues:

> And one does not presume to take this honor, but takes it only when called by God, just as Aaron was.
>
> So also Christ did not glorify himself in becoming a high priest, but was appointed by the one who said to him, "You are my Son, today I have begotten you"; as he says also in another place, "You are a priest forever, according to the order of Melchizedek."
>
> In the days of his flesh, Jesus offered up prayers and supplications, with loud cries and tears, to the one who was able to save him from death, and he was heard because of his reverent submission. Although he was a Son, he learned obedience through what he suffered; and having been made perfect, he became the source of eternal salvation for all who obey him. (Heb 5:4-9)

Through his suffering and by the sacrifice of his life Christ proved himself to be like his brothers and sisters in every way. Therefore, the Father consecrated him high priest and decreed that forever his sufferings and sacrifice would lead to the forgiveness of sins. Those same sufferings, the very sufferings because of which the Father appointed him high priest, Christ continues to bear in the person of the deacon, whom he ordains as his icon of suffering servanthood.

A deacon can find in the singing of each of the four servant songs a reflection or, better yet, a standard against which to measure his own life and ministry; he does well to make the servant songs a regular object of his scriptural reading, meditation, and prayer. Like the servant in the first song, the deacon knows the Lord has poured out his Spirit upon him that he might speak, even sing, justice to the people. Like the servant in the second song, a deacon's mission and ministry are universal: the Suffering Servant sends him to the margins and edges and from there gathers sinners and the poor to himself. The servant in the third servant song relies on the Lord God; the deacon must be boldly confident and of cheerful courage so that he is a bright light for those in darkness. The fourth song sings of the servant whose appearance held no attraction to others, yet giving his life as an offering for sin the Lord's will is accomplished through him. Deacons too bear neither title nor entitlement, no "majesty"; nor must they seek or expect reward, standing, or honor for their service other than that Christ is proclaimed to the poor.

Christ through a Deacon's Suffering Illuminated

Having considered how Christ was made high priest in virtue of his sacrificial suffering, we now shift our focus and consider how suffering itself is the *diaconia*, the discipleship of the deacon. How does Christ shine forth as Suffering Servant through a deacon's suffering of love? How does a deacon, like St. Paul, complete what is lacking in Christ's afflictions for the sake of the church?

First, it is the deacon's ministry to be the sharer of others' sufferings. This sharing of suffering is the first step of moving from the natural to the new inclination to service. Diaconal service is not simply helping other people out. Rather, on one hand it pertains to the deacon to share the sufferings *of the Lord*, and in doing so to bear the suffering Lord, the compassionate Lord, the merciful Lord to the poor. On the other hand, it is his ministry to share the suffering *of the sinner and the poor* and in so doing to bring them to the Lord and to the church. As a deacon and in ministry, one cannot give what he himself has not received; one cannot offer on behalf of others what he has not first offered in his own regard. A deacon cannot share the sufferings of the poor and bear them to the Lord if he has not first joined his own sufferings and, if he is married, the sufferings of his wife and family to the sufferings of the Lord. This he does through his open willingness to share himself—his life, his history, his questions and the answers he has come to, his own story of suffering with those who suffer. Then we see how, as Pope John Paul II taught, he begins to "share more closely" in Christ's own spirit of service.

To move from the natural to the new inclination to serve, a deacon must develop Christ's own attitude toward suffering. Once ordained, he is called to "intend" his sufferings as a vehicle for grace and therefore to offer them to Christ not only on his own behalf but on behalf of the poor. This is true in whatever he may suffer and from whatever source his sufferings may arise, but especially when he suffers simply as an effect of being a human being or if his sufferings, like Christ's, are the consequence of another's sin. Accordingly, he understands his own sufferings to be borne out of and as an expression of *communio*, both that of the Trinity and that of the church.

The first words of the Second Vatican Council's Pastoral Constitution on the Church in the Modern World (*Gaudium et spes*) are a sort of mission statement for a deacon. "The joy and hope, the grief and anguish of the men of our time, especially of those who are poor or afflicted in any way, are the joy and hope, the grief and anguish of the followers of Christ as well." We can see, then, that a deacon's suffering undertaken out of love for Christ and the church, intended and offered up for love of others, and freely assumed, *is* his discipleship, his ministry. And who of us, proclaiming Christ and ministering to the poor, witnessing to and seeking to ease their sufferings and improve their social conditions, does not naturally suffer for them? Does not our heart go out to them, even break for love of them?

But suffering with and for others is not simply a deacon's discipleship. The second movement from the natural to the new inclination to serve entails developing suffering as the very discipline of his life. Indeed we can say that as life precedes ministry, the discipline of suffering must precede the discipleship of suffering. What do I mean by that?

The letter to the Hebrews teaches us:

> Therefore, since we are surrounded by so great a cloud of witnesses, let us also lay aside every weight and the sin that clings so closely, and let us run with perseverance the race that is set before us, look- ing to Jesus the pioneer and perfecter of our faith, who for the sake of the joy that was set before him endured the cross, disregarding its shame, and has taken his seat at the right hand of the throne of God.
>
> Consider him who endured such hostility against himself from sinners, so that you may not grow weary or lose heart. In your struggle against sin you have not yet resisted to the point of shed- ding your blood. And you have forgotten the exhortation that addresses you as children—"My child, do not regard lightly the discipline of the Lord, or lose heart when you are punished by him; for the Lord disciplines those whom he loves, and chastises every child whom he accepts." Endure trials for the sake of discipline. God is treating you as children; for what child is there whom a parent does not discipline? (Heb 12:1-7)

This passage requires a bit of exegesis. The author of the letter to the Hebrews invites us to "look to Jesus, the pioneer and perfecter of our faith." In Greek the word the author uses for "look" is *aphorōntes*. This is the only place in Scripture where it is used. It means both and simultaneously to look away from one thing and to peer into another. Quite a feat. Yet we do have experiences of such a phenomenon. For example, consider athletes who, as St. Paul said, deny themselves all sorts of things in the hope of winning a crown of leaves that will wither and die (see 1 Cor 9:25). They turn their gaze from whatever it is that causes them to slow down, trip, or fall on their way to victory even as they look toward the crown of victory itself. Candidates for public office will subject themselves and their families to extraordinary hardship in order to win an election. Even as they are laden with the burdens of campaigning, the media scrutiny, the public criticism and opposition, the loss of family time, etc., they keep focused on what awaits in office should they prove victorious. And what about discipleship? Christ never turned away from the suffering and shame of the cross; he never lost sight of but considered intently the joy he believed awaited him when he returned to the Father with Adam and Eve in tow. For our part, we too are called to turn away from sin and from every burden with which our suffering lades us, even as we simultaneously keep our eyes fixed on Christ, and him alone. We accept our own sufferings, the sufferings that accompany our resistance to temptation and sin or brought about as a consequence of it, and even more so join the sufferings of others to our own, convinced of what lies on the other side of our own suffering, pain, and darkness, and theirs.

Look now specifically at verse 7 of our passage, which reads, "Endure trials for the sake of discipline. God is treating you as children." Unfortunately, this translation (the New Revised Standard Version) might give the impression that God inflicts suffering on us as a form of punishment and that we are commanded simply to accept and endure it. In the original Greek, however, the word here translated as "discipline" is *paideuō*, which means more properly education or rearing. When *paideia* was used in regard to children it meant the entirety of their formation—mind, morals, and body. When it was used in regard to adults, however, *paideia* more specifically meant not the cultivation of one's body but rather the cultivation of one's soul through the correction of mistakes, the curbing of the passions, and instruction in the virtues. Moreover, although our English translation is in the imperative case, in the Greek text it is written in the indicative. The verse correctly reads, "You are enduring for the sake of an education by God, who treats you as sons."

Suffering is not punishment but education and formation, rearing and cultivation. Suffering is how God rears us in his own fatherhood. Here, then, we find the second movement leading from a natural inclination to serve into grace-inspired diaconal service that conforms one to Christ. A deacon's sufferings and the sufferings of the poor that he bears become the means through which God the Father is himself educating both the deacon as well as those whom the deacon serves. Through suffering the Father is forming his deacon and his children in his own divine fatherhood, teaching them, that is, that he is the source of their life and that he cares. By bearing the sufferings of others, the deacon and those he serves are led by God into the knowledge and experience of God not simply as a father but truly as *their* Father. "You have one Father—the one in heaven" (Matt 23:9). When a deacon bears the sufferings of others, he educates them, that is, he "leads them out" from their sufferings, caused by creatureliness and sin, into the eternal care of God. As an older brother, the deacon leads sinners and the poor from the foreign land of their sufferings back to the fatherhood of God. This is what St. Paul means when he professes that in suffering he became the church's servant (*diakonos*, deacon) according to God's commission, "to make the word of God fully known . . . so that we may present everyone mature in Christ" (Col 1:25-28).

Truth be told, this is not how most people look upon suffering. Don't most people view suffering in the way the New Revised Standard Version of the Hebrew's text implies, namely, that God inflicts suffering to punish and correct us? But our divine and heavenly Father neither causes his children to suffer nor inflicts suffering upon them as punishment. Rather, suffering is "caused" by being human. Indeed suffering is uniquely a condition of humanity. We humans suffer because we sin. And because we sin we have caused all creation to suffer. But we can learn from our sufferings that God is our Father, that God loves and cares for us as sons and daughters. If we are willing to understand the sufferings of our creaturely finitude as divine instruction, we can learn the love and care of Christ. If we see the sufferings caused by sin and injustice as an education, we can learn of the justice and mercy of our Father. "Suffering," Luke Timothy Johnson writes, "is the sound of the human spirit opening itself to the presence and power of God. It is the very path by which humans become transformed, as was Jesus, into fully mature children of God" (*Hebrews: A Commentary*, p. 60).

This, then, is the content of the deacon's "*new inclination* to serve his brothers and sisters." He seeks to teach sinners and the poor how to fix their eyes on Christ and simultaneously in their suffering to turn from all that is not. The deacon understands, as Raniero Cantalamessa articulated, and wants to teach the poor that one *is* what one looks at (see *The Mystery of the Transfiguration*, p. 7). As the icon of the Suffering Servant, the deacon invites the poor to look upon the suffering Christ and to know in Christ's face, by his wounds, at the font of his pierced heart, that Christ loves them. It is the deacon's natural inclination to educate, that is, to "lead out" and to lead down the path, even to accompany those on it so as to arrive at the knowledge of the mercy and love of God. It is his *new inclination* to accept his sufferings and those of others "for the sake of an education of God, who treats [them] as sons." Suffering for and with others, then, especially sinners and the poor, and bearing both the Lord to the suffering poor and the suffering poor to the Lord, is the highest form of diaconal preaching. It is a gospel that should be proclaimed with joy.

In summary, then, what marks the deacon's passage from the natural to the new inclination to serve is that he understands his service to be a service of suffering, the form of the suffering of love. Like Christ the Suffering Servant, the deacon understands his sufferings to arise from his new friendship with the Trinity and from his *communio* with the church, that is, with his bishop and the priests, on one hand, and sinners and the poor, on the other. Second, the deacon understands suffering differently; he assigns suffering a different *meaning*. Suffering is not punishment but education in the fatherhood of God. Third, as when he first pronounced his "Present" at his ordination and as he willingly prostrates himself before the altar, both at his ordination and on every Good Friday hence, the deacon suffers *freely*, he accepts his sufferings as Christ accepted his. Indeed, with St. Paul, the deacon "rejoices in [his] sufferings . . . and in [his] flesh . . . is completing what is lacking in Christ's affliction for the sake of his body, that is, the church" (Col 1:24).

Created by and Choosing *Communio*

In their groundbreaking work on the psychosocial dynamics of vocation (published in English in 1978 as *Psychological Structure and Vocation— A Study of the Motivations for Entering and Leaving the Religious Life*), the Italian psychologist Luigi Rulla and his colleagues describe a mature person as one who "engages all the dynamic forces of the personality, both conscious and unconscious, in a freely chosen project of life." They continue, "The same is true of vocation maturity, which may be presented as the integration of affective maturity and spiritual maturity" (p. 10).

For his part, the French philosopher-theologian Gabriel Marcel, in his work, *Creative Fidelity*, affirmed that fidelity is rooted in the choice of a relationship with another, a choice that is unending, its assurance neither contingent nor fleeting. Only in being faithful to the other who has been chosen does one find happiness. Marcel writes:

> The fact is that when I commit myself, I grant in principle that this commitment will not again be put in question. And it is clear that this active volition not to question something again, intervenes as an essential element in the determination of what in fact will be the case. It at once bars a certain number of possibilities; it bids me to invent a certain *modus vivendi* which I would otherwise be precluded from envisaging. . . . My behavior will be completely colored by this act embodying the decision that the commitment will not again be questioned. The possibility which has been barred or denied will thus be demoted to the rank of a temptation. (p. 162)

In applying their thinking to the diaconate, what might we draw from these great thinkers, what Rulla calls "the integration of affective maturity and spiritual maturity" and Marcel "creative fidelity" in one's chosen relationships? As a deacon, how does one "invent a certain *modus vivendi*," a discipline to his diaconal discipleship, which is suffering, so that his behavior is completely colored by his choice to be in an unending relationship of new friendship with Christ, to be the icon of the Suffering Servant? To answer, once again we reflect on the Trinity, specifically on the economic Trinity, which reveals itself to its creation and pours itself out in love.

Recall that when the Trinity reveals itself it does not simply reveal things about itself. What it reveals is its very self, its nature, precisely its being as *communio*. The Father desires that every creature know the love he bears for his Son. The Son, in whose image all creation has been fashioned, wants creation to know of his honoring of the Father. The Spirit desires that all creation participate in this loving and honoring of the Father and the Son.

Our own human experience gives us insight into this desire of the Father to be known by his love for his Son and the Son's love for the Father, and to share his *communio*. Consider a man and woman who fall in love and decide to marry. Both have come to believe that neither has a future except with the other; forever they will intertwine their lives with one another and with none other. From that moment, their choice of each other *is* their being and their doing.

Furthermore, a couple who chooses one another wants everyone else to know and forever to judge them by this irrevocable choice. They want everyone, the whole world, even the entire cosmos, first to know that they have made their choice and, second, to know them for the choice they have made. In this way they invite others to share in this choosing. But they are also warning others against incursions or outside interference into it.

By choosing and revealing to others one's life choice, the choice itself becomes the relationship and the relationship is the choosing. Isn't this the greatest need and deepest desire of the human heart—to choose and to be chosen by another in love and honor, and by that loving and honoring to live and forever be known?

Let me offer a folksy example of what I mean. In the movie *Fiddler on the Roof,* the tailor Motel stands to lose Tzeitel, his beloved, to Lazer Wolf, with whom Tevye, Tzeitel's father, has arranged a marriage. Motel, despite his poverty yet desperate for Tzeitel's love and honor, and having pledged his love and honor to her, dares to approach Tevye and request her hand in marriage. Tevye actually gives in; he agrees. Motel, having won Tzeitel's hand, runs off and dances through the forest, singing aloud to the trees, "God has made a man today." He wants all creation to know that that day he himself has been created anew by his choice of Tzeitel and hers of him. And he wants all to know that henceforth his very existence as a man *is* the faithful choosing of Tzeitel, his beloved, and that her very existence *is* her faithful choosing of him.

As Christians, our *modus vivendi,* our discipline of discipleship, takes its shape from God's choosing us *and* from our choosing him in response *and* making that choice known to others. The Father chooses us as sons and daughters; he sacramentalizes that choice in baptism. The Spirit, "Lord and giver of life," dwells in us and chooses us to be bearers of life; he seals his choice in confirmation. The Son chooses us in the church; he covenants that choice in Eucharist. Through fidelity to our baptismal promises, being nurtured by eucharistic food and drink to love and serve the Lord and one another, and by living by the power of the Holy Spirit, we proclaim to others that God is attracted to us, that he has chosen us and we have chosen him.

When the deacon accepts the call to be a new friend of the Trinity, the church, sinners, and the poor, he makes that choice known by "engaging all the dynamic forces of [his] personality . . . in [this] freely chosen project of life" and in creative fidelity to the laying on of hands that he receives. Moving from the natural to the new inclination to serve, an "inclination inspired by grace," the deacon is daily, on one hand, to integrate the promises he made in baptism with those he assumed in marriage (if married) as well as those in ordination. He lives that *communio* in the ever greater integration of a life lived in conformity to the sacramental reality of his Christian initiation together with the three functions of his diaconal ministry, namely, service of the Word, the altar, and of charity.

Integration, Maturity, and Creative Fidelity

St. Paul urged his communities not to grow weary of doing good or to relax in their service to others (see Gal 5:9; 2 Thess 3:13). Diaconal ministry can be trying and tiring. The Lord and the church call upon deacons to minister to persons who more and more come from broken homes; are digitalized, decimalized, depersonalized, and dehumanized; live in a culture that sacrifices substance at the altar of celebrity; work in an economy that increasingly values product and profit over persons; are more and more tempted to value death over life; are depressed; and are likely to die lonely and alone. To be ever a bearer of light to those who dwell in darkness, a source of hope to those who despair, a porter of faith to those who lack faith, is tedious and fatiguing. Constantly to be gathering the dispersed, to place at the heart of the community those who live at its margins, and to be in solidarity with the poor and oppressed of the world can take its toll. To be the cry of the poor and their advocate for justice; to labor for the construction of a social order that frees one's brothers and sisters from servitude and slavery; to feed, clothe, and house the indigent; to welcome the immigrant—in short, to be on the front line of the church's ministries of righteousness and social justice in the world can take its toll, resulting in disillusionment and despair. Deacons who minister in urban settings and in increasingly larger parish communities will especially feel the strain and drain of ministry. This is certainly compounded if in his marriage, family, or personal life a deacon is undergoing trials and bearing the sufferings and more intense heartaches of loved ones. To do all of this as Christ himself, the Suffering Servant, and in the name of the church adds Christ's own cross to the burdens he bears.

Seven Habits of Creative Fidelity

How is a deacon to overcome the temptation to lose hope, if not even faith, and keep the fires of love and service stoked and burning brightly? How does he ever more integrate, mature, and remain creatively faithful to Christ and the church? How does he daily choose the Trinity, the church, and the poor and make that choice known to others? How does he "rekindle" the grace of his ordination (see 2 Tim 1:6) and in grace grow from the natural inclination inspired by grace to the new inclination to serve? How is he strengthened to bear the cross of Christ in bearing the cross of the suffering? As in the first "class" of deacons there were seven reputable men, filled with the Holy Spirit and wisdom, upon whom the apostles laid hands, I propose seven habits of creative fidelity (in addition to those discussed elsewhere in this book), seven *regulae vivendi*, rules of living, that every deacon must practice and perfect.

Joy and Gratitude

First, a deacon must be attentive lest routine and regularity lead to tedium and boredom, and tedium and boredom cause joy to die. A deacon who has allowed joy to die in his ministry cannot luminously represent Christ the High Priest, to whom he has been conformed, and Christ the Suffering Servant, whose icon he has become. Because the world is saved by hope, a hope that is lived in joyful love, a deacon who has lost joy, who is not joy-filled, would not then be able to serve the Lord, the church, sinners, and the poor. A deacon who has lost heart does not serve; he only goes through the motions.

How does one stave off the death of joy? Consider two ways.

As at the wedding at Cana, a deacon should fill the empty stone water jars with the new waters of the daily examination of his conscience. Through the daily examination of his conscience, which requires honesty and humility, he will draw forth the greater vintage of the suffering of love. The examination of conscience is necessary for the ongoing purification of one's motives, the forgiveness of one's sins, a greater holiness of life, and ever greater zeal for serving the church and the poor. Daily he must ensure that the waters of this examination never run dry, as did the waters of the stone jars of Jewish ritual purification. It is very easy to skip the daily examination of one's conscience, occurring, as it should, at nighttime and as part of the Night Prayer of the Liturgy of the Hours. But it is one of the keys to daily growing in the intimacy of a new friendship with Christ and with those whom one serves. (As an aside, I encourage married deacons and their wives to examine their consciences together. It is not only an indispensable tool for living the promises of one's baptism and ordination; it is also an invaluable tool for the living of one's marriage vows and growing in spousal intimacy.)

Next, a deacon must develop the attitude of gratitude. St. Paul speaks of this habit when he urged the Thessalonians, "Rejoice always, pray without ceasing, give thanks in all circumstances; for this is the will of God in Christ Jesus for you" (1 Thess 5:16-18). No matter what suffering he bears or poverty he encounters, a deacon must see the good in others and give thanks "in all circumstances." This is especially true when he believes himself to be the victim of a misunderstanding, injustice, or insensitivity rendered at the hands of a fellow cleric—his bishop, a priest, or a brother deacon. Christ gave thanks even at precisely the moment he knew his betrayer to be at hand and eating his bread. His thankfulness was the grounding of the joy with which he endured such injustice and the shame of the cross.

The deacon should be careful lest he grow cynical, resentful, and angry in life, his relationships with others, especially his bishop and diocesan priests, and in ministry. The only antidote for anger is gratitude. Henri Nouwen wrote an important treatise entitled *From Resentment to Gratitude*. When a deacon finds himself becoming cynical and growing angry, he must sincerely examine his motives for accepting the call to diaconal ministry and examine his conscience, striving to eliminate sin and selfishness where they have crept into his marriage (if he is married) and diaconate. Then, as the psalmist who prayed, "What shall I return to the LORD for all his bounty to me?" the deacon should "lift up the cup of salvation and call on the name of the LORD . . . [paying his] vows to the LORD in the presence of all his people" (Ps 116:12-14).

Community Spirituality

The second habit of creative fidelity is what the church calls "a community spirituality." The church teaches, "By a special sacramental gift, Holy Orders confers on the deacon a particular participation in the consecration and mission of Him who became servant of the Father for the redemption of mankind, and inserts him in a new and specific way in the mystery of Christ, of his Church and the salvation of all mankind. Hence the spiritual life of the deacon should deepen this threefold relationship by developing a community spirituality which bears witness to that communion essential to the nature of the Church" (*Directory* 46). Deacons should not forget that *diaconia*, as Pope Benedict XVI describes it, is "the ministry of charity exercised in a communitarian, orderly way" (*Deus caritas est* 21). It is as much a ministry carried out from the *communio* of the community of deacons as it is the ministry of any individual minister.

By living and ministering out of *communio* with one's brother deacons, deacons witness to the *communio* of the Trinity and of the church. And when diaconal ministry is carried out of *communio* it is for that reason alone more effective. Simply put, what a deacon does in and out of communion with others, especially his clerical coworkers but also the laity, is of infinitely greater value for the church and the poor, even if it is less efficient, than what he does by himself in the cubicle, if you will, of his diaconate. The church instructs deacons that to this end they are to "nourish themselves and their ministry with an ardent love for the Church, and a sincere desire for communion with the Holy Father, their own bishops and the priests of their dioceses" (*Directory* 48).

It has sometimes been my experience that deacons are sincerely desirous of communion with the pope and with their bishop but not so much with their diocesan presbyterate. While it is true that presbyteral-diaconal communion is a two-way street, deacons should seek out opportunities to pray with priests, especially their parish priests; to collaborate under their guidance and with them in ministry, in the parish, deanery, and diocese (and not solely at the altar); and to join them in programs of continuing formation. For their part, priests should extend to deacons their trust and respect for the Christ whom they all imitate and the sinners and poor whom they all serve and, looking upon them as brothers, offer to them willing collaboration in their pastoral care of the Lord's flock entrusted to them.

The next five habits of a deacon's spirituality are expressions of this "community spirituality."

Communal prayer

Third, the deacon must be a man of communal prayer. We have already spoken at length of various forms of prayers. It is not these forms to which I now refer. Rather, I want to emphasize that he must be a man who does not simply pray for the poor but who prays with the poor and leads them in prayer.

Deacons who are men of spousal and familial prayer have discovered a source of great intimacy and joy in life. Similarly, by praying with the poor and not simply for them, a deacon will offer to the poor the intimacy Christ desires to know with them and which the poor can even here and now come to know with the divine bridegroom. Prayer must be the first means by which a deacon enters into relationship with the poor and serves them, even before he otherwise provides for them, for example, through counseling or social assistance. More than anything else, praying with the poor—not only praying for them or offering them succor and social assistance—is the way in which a deacon shows himself to be the "responsible" one, bridging the poor to himself and bridging them both to Christ. In prayer with the poor he not only leads them to Christ but accompanies them on the way.

St. Paul instructs husbands and wives that, even more than sexual intercourse, prayer is the supreme act of intimacy between spouses (see 1 Cor 7:5). Although the context is different, nonetheless, from St. Paul a deacon can learn something vital for his ministry. Married couples tell me how difficult it is to develop and ground their relationship in prayer and to pray together. If they lack intimacy, they know that something is missing, that their relationship is not as it should be. When a married person or couple comes to me and asks for help in healing their breaking or broken relationship, one of the first questions I always ask is, "Do you pray together?" How sad it is that in most instances the answer is no. Perhaps they would like to but they don't know how. More often than not they have never really tried. A married couple that does not develop and maintain a life of prayerful communion is a couple probably afraid of, if not incapable of, achieving intimacy.

If praying with another whom one loves is challenging, praying with the poor can be downright frightening. As with one's spouse, praying with the poor requires that one be open to intimacy with them. Praying with them, therefore, is the most charitable act a deacon can carry out on their behalf. If by the exercise of the virtue of justice one gives to the other his due, then by the virtue of charity one gives *his very self* to the other. Praying with the poor is that most gracious act in which a deacon gives himself to the poor and, in giving himself to them, truly gives Christ to them. Praying with the poor is the supreme means by which a deacon shares the sufferings of the poor and bears the suffering poor to the Lord.

How many times—and I say it to my embarrassment—have I helped the poor, for example, by giving them a handout, money, advice, recommendations, or instruction, and later realized that I did not pray with them and so denied them my intimacy, the one thing that they needed most from me and that as a priest and pastor I should have treasured most in their regard?

Is not the same true by not asking the poor to give, to care for us by praying for us, offering up for us and for the church their poverty, suffering, and shame? Praying with the poor, then, is also the act by which a deacon allows the poor to minister to him. Through prayer the poor educate the deacon in the suffering of love. How? Intimacy is knowing another even as one knows oneself. Intimacy therefore requires that I know and accept who I am. To be intimate with another requires, first of all, that I make an honest judgment about myself without judging the other. To the contrary, I must respect the other, see the other for the truth of his or her being. (The Latin word *respectare* has the roots *res*, truth or reality, and *spectare*, to see.) One can never become intimate with another by judging the other. Intimacy is only possible when it is rooted in mercy. And out of a deacon's prayerful intimacy with the poor he is himself confronted by his own poverty, whatever it may be—physical, emotional, relational, and especially spiritual. In prayer with the poor a deacon comes to know that he too is poor and must be served. And so he comes to know that it is Christ the Lord who serves him, even as he, the deacon, offers his own life in sacrifice for others.

One more comment regarding a deacon's prayer. I very much advocate that bishops, priests, and deacons develop a regular routine of praying in public, even beyond celebrating the Eucharist publicly. Why? By developing a routine of public prayer, a cleric more solidly builds a habit of prayer. The habit itself holds him accountable for his behavior. Furthermore, he develops greater credibility as a man of prayer. What does it say of a bishop, priest, or deacon if he is seen preaching from the pulpit and ministering at the altar but is never seen kneeling before the Blessed Sacrament? Certainly one should not pray simply so as to be seen praying. If that were the case, the people would clearly see one's prayer as nothing more than an act, and one would have already been repaid for his or her performance (see Matt 6:5). When the disciples watched Jesus pray they saw something in him they wanted to imitate and learned something from him of the Father. Similarly, the people of God, seeing a bishop, priest, or deacon at prayer, observe in him something of Jesus and learn from him something of the Father. I would add, too, that if a deacon is married it is good for his wife, children, and him to be seen praying together.

Right Relationships with Bishops and Priests

Fourth, a deacon must have a right relationship with both his bishop and the priests of his local church. Within the sacrament of orders there exists a "subordering" of ministry from the episcopal and priestly functions to the diaconal. From the top down it looks like this: the bishop is ordained to the fullness of priesthood. Christ pours out on the bishop his "governing Spirit" and conforms him to himself as "shepherd and guardian of . . . souls" (1 Pet 2:25). Regarding the priest, Christ pours out on the priest the "Spirit of holiness," conforming him to himself as High Priest and conferring on him a share, but not the fullness, of his own priesthood. Deacons, as the church teaches, are ordained not to priesthood but to ministry. At ordination, Christ the Suffering Servant conforms the deacon to himself and commissions the deacon to serve his people through the diaconates of the altar, the Word, and charity. The deacon's ministry is at the service of Christ's one priesthood, which Christ has shared fully with the bishops and partially with priests, and which Christ has shared through baptism with all the laity, although in an essentially different way.

This point bears repeating. Since the deacon is ordained to serve Christ the High Priest and Christ's priesthood, he is ordained to serve that priesthood not only vertically, if you will, as it is embodied in bishops and priests, but also horizontally as it is embodied in the baptized laity. The Second Vatican Council teaches quite explicitly that "though they differ from one another in essence and not only in degree, the common priesthood of the faithful and the ministerial or hierarchical priesthood are nonetheless interrelated" (*Lumen gentium* 10).

From a different perspective, however, the relationship of the three ranks of holy orders looks rather different. Truly, diaconal and priestly ministries are distinct ministries, as in the Old Testament the office of the prophet was distinct from that of priest, which was itself distinct from that of king. Yet in Christ these three offices have been united and remain forever one. For his part, Christ then shares this united ministry—diaconal/priestly/prophetic—by degrees with those whom he calls into each of holy orders' three ranks. Having been united in Christ and by him in the sacrament of holy orders, therefore, the deacon is not to be seen as belonging to a lesser order (as if deacons have a less important role to play than that of priests, and they one of lesser importance than bishops) but rather as an essential and first order of the threefold tier of Christ's singular pastoral service. Both the prophetic and cultic dimensions of the episcopal and priestly orders are incomplete without the kingly, or diaconal, dimension. The kingly dimension, too, is incomplete without the prophetic and cultic dimensions of orders. To put it practically, bishops and priests, as coworkers with the bishops and under their authority, attend to the Word and sacrament so that the Word and sacrament may be preached to and celebrated for the poor. Deacons, united with the bishop and under his authority, care for the poor that they may hear the Word and be brought to the celebration of the sacraments. Considering the ministries of holy orders within the context of *communio*: bishops define the nature and boundaries of *communio* and teach it; priests offer to the Father the sacrifice of the *communio* and of those brought into it; and deacons bring sinners and the poor to the church's *communio*, that Christ may be "all and in all" (Col 3:11).

Accordingly, for the sake of both the good order of *communio* and its ministry to the poor, the deacon promises obedience to the bishop, who alone exercises the fullness of priesthood in the diocese, and not to the priest. But at times, perhaps most times, the bishop subordinates the deacon and his ministry to the authority of a priest. The deacon's relationship with the bishop is not mediated through the priest; in other words, priesthood is not a mediating order between the episcopacy and the diaconate. Rather the deacon's relationship with the bishop is direct and personal, even one of a filial friendship. But for the sake of the good order of the diocesan church and so that the apostolate may be carried out in a rightly ordered way, the bishop may assign the deacon to a priest in virtue of the office that the latter holds, or he may assign the deacon to other office holders, even nonclerical ones, in the church. In such a case, a deacon's legitimate ecclesiastical supervisor must always respect the special bond of orders and friendship between the bishop and the deacon, and the deacon for his part must understand and accept his subordination to another office holder at the direction of the bishop to be for the good ordering of the diocesan church.

Furthermore, bishops, priests, and deacons enjoy a special relationship, a new friendship, not simply in view of ordination, but because of the apostolic origins of their ministries. Although the theological content of the diaconate is not apostolic, as are those of episcopacy and priesthood, its origins are. A *communio* that shows forth the unity of holy orders because its origins are apostolic ought to evoke among bishops, priests, and deacons a profound and mutual respect and concern for one another. In view of the apostolic origins and demands of priestly and diaconal ministry, as well as the basic demands of Christian living, such behavior as power struggles, putting ministers down or in their place, gossiping among deacons or their wives about the bishop, priests, or other deacons or their family members, and other sinful and scandalous activities that violate *communio* have no place among the ordained, who bear witness to the redeeming death of Jesus and serve their brothers and sisters, and their wives.

Diaconal Friendships

Fifth, to be motivated by the new inclination of service, a deacon must develop and maintain friendships with other deacons and deacons' families, especially those with whom one ministers in the same Christian community, a parish, for example. Friendship among deacons and their families is a source of creativity and joy. "By virtue of their ordination, deacons are united to each other by sacramental fraternity," the *Directory* teaches (6). "They are all dedicated to the same purpose—building up the Body of Christ—in union with the Supreme Pontiff and subject to the authority of the bishop. Each deacon should have a sense of being joined with his fellow deacons in a bond of charity, prayer, obedience to their bishops, ministerial zeal and collaboration" (6). Then again, "[T]he deacon incarnates the charism of service as a participation in the ministry of the Church. This has important repercussions on his spiritual life, which must be characterized by obedience and fraternal communion. . . . The candidate must therefore be educated in a sense of belonging to the body of ordained ministers, to fraternal collaboration with them and to spiritual sharing" (76).

A deacon gains real credibility when he is known to be a man of authentic, joy-filled fraternity with his brother deacons, enjoying their company, contributing to one another's ministries, and especially holding one another accountable for ministry. Active, joy-filled diaconal fraternity cannot be discounted for the positive witness it gives to *communio* and to the care of Christ for sinners and the poor. Would one want to enter more deeply into the *communio* of Christ and the church if one witnessed nothing but aloneness and acting alone, let alone jealousy, rivalry, and politics on the part of the deacons serving that *communio* and bringing others to it? "How very good and pleasant it is when kindred live together in unity . . . . For there the Lord ordained his blessing, life forevermore" (Ps 133:1, 3). Can deacons gather others into the community of the church if they themselves are not participating in, giving to, and receiving from the community of diaconal fellowship? I would even say that a deacon (or any cleric for that matter) who is not in active union with his brother deacons and regularly absents himself from diaconal gatherings is in a right relationship neither with the Lord nor with the church nor with his bishop.

As an expression of diaconal friendship, a deacon might consider belonging to a prayer and support group of deacons (or even of deacons and priests), what I call CDACC communities, that is *Communities of Deacons Accountable to Christ and the Church*. I cannot say enough about the importance of belonging to such communities—meeting regularly and frequently, praying with, and developing over time that security and trust in the love of his brother deacons wherein one is held accountable for his discipleship and his diaconate and holds others accountable in turn. Together with one's bishop, spouse, and spiritual director, a brother deacon is the best person to hold a deacon accountable for life and ministry. The *Jesus Caritas* format, used by many bishops and priests, offers a sound model for CDACC communities as well.

Continuing Formation

The sixth habit of creative fidelity renewing the new inclination for service comes from continuing formation, which a deacon must never neglect. "Personal concern and commitment in ongoing formation," the *Directory* affirms, "are unequivocal signs of a coherent response to divine vocation, of sincere love for the Church and of authentic pastoral zeal for the Christian faithful and all men" (67). The *Directory* specifies, however, that this formation cannot be limited to "updating," that is, simple education or training in better techniques. Rather, a deacon must be formed and reformed continually through a "practical configuration" of his entire life to Christ (67).

What forms might this practical conforming take? The *Directory* and the *National Directory* list many qualities of this practical conforming, among the most important of which are included here.

First, and most important, a deacon must not neglect Bible study and prayer. The Word of God renews all things (see Heb 1:3); it is living and active, able to judge "the thoughts and intentions of the heart," laying bare and exposing everything to him to whom we must render an account (see Heb 4:12-13). A deacon will find it especially valuable if he is a member of a Bible study group (I emphasize member, not leader) or of a small Christian community founded on reflection on the Word of God, together with brother deacons, priests, married couples, and laity. He does well to take advantage of educational opportunities that will deepen his understanding of Scripture (and therefore improve his preaching and teaching), for example, by attending conferences and workshops on Scripture, enrolling in biblical study initiatives, should they exist in his community, and even studying for advanced certification or degrees in accredited theological programs.

Additionally, the handmaid of Scripture is Sacred Tradition, and the handmaid of Sacred Tradition is the hierarchy of the church. A deacon's ministry in the church is a participation in the apostolic ministry of the Roman pontiff and of his own bishop. Therefore, a deacon should not fail to know the teachings of the pope and of his bishop. The former exercises his teaching ministry in encyclical letters, apostolic exhortations, homilies, his Wednesday general audience addresses, and through other means. One might incorporate the pope's encyclicals and exhortations into his daily prayer and preaching. A deacon should familiarize himself with the Vatican website or subscribe to a service making the pope's Wednesday addresses and other addresses available on a timely basis. One should be familiar with his own bishop's teachings, accessing them in whatever form they are made available (newspaper columns, web sites, e-mails, etc.).

In this regard, finally, the deacon should be particularly familiar with the church's social doctrine. He does well to study the Roman pontiffs' social encyclicals, especially those of the popes from John XXIII to Benedict XVI. An invaluable resource for a deacon is the *Compendium of the Social Doctrine of the Church*, originally published by the Pontifical Council for Justice and Peace in 2004. It is an excellent handbook, in some sense *the* handbook of diaconal ministry to the poor.

Spiritual Direction and Retreat

The seventh habit of creative fidelity is spiritual direction and the annual retreat. A deacon must have a spiritual director and, if his director is not a priest, a confessor. Other than one's spouse and one's bishop, there is no one else in a better position to mediate the Word spoken, the Word made flesh, and the Word being echoed. In one's relationship with a spiritual director/confessor, the four dimensions of ongoing diaconal formation, namely, the human, spiritual, intellectual, and pastoral, converge. In spiritual direction a deacon is held accountable to the spiritual program he is to develop annually on his retreat (see *Directory* 70). The deacon should not be hesitant to work out this spiritual program with his supervisor, share it with him or her, and ask his supervisor to hold him accountable to it.

The *Directory* understands that these two expressions of a deacon's spiritual life are really one. The deacon who takes spiritual direction and confession seriously and who lives out his spiritual program demonstrates to his bishop, family, and community that he takes seriously the integration of life and ministry. I believe that spiritual direction, making the annual retreat, and the development of one's spiritual program are necessary prerequisites for the reception and keeping of diaconal faculties.

A Virtue of Integrity

To bind these seven habits of creative fidelity together, there is one virtue of diaconal life and ministry by which, possessing it, the deacon shows himself to be Christian and a deacon of integrity. In Acts 6, the apostles require that the first seven deacons be men who were "full of the Spirit" and "full of wisdom." Why were these the qualities the apostles sought in distributors of bread? One would think that rather than a deep spirituality the apostles would have sought out good bakers, managers of crowds (like Walt Disney, a master of line management, for example), or numbers men. Instead, the first seven were chosen because they had a prayerful relationship with the Lord, a relationship "full of Spirit," and they judged wisely, treated fairly, and acted honestly in their relationships with others.

"Wisdom" in this passage is sometimes translated as "prudence." Prudence is that virtue by which, in one's dealings with another, one most effectively judges and utilizes the means of communicating truth. Prudence is therefore that virtue by which as a deacon one most effectively (not necessarily efficiently) contributes to the good order of the church and serves sinners and the poor. And it was in large part for the sake of the good order of the church that Christ and the apostles established the diaconate. It is of such a deacon that the Lord said, "Who then is the faithful and prudent manager whom his master will put in charge of his slaves, to give them their allowance of food at the proper time?" (Luke 12:42). It is such a deacon who knows how to "bring out of his treasure what is new and what is old" (Matt 13:52).

chapter nine

Acts 6

St. Paul's exhortation to Timothy, found in the second letter he wrote to him, is particularly appropriate for deacons, and with it I wish to begin this penultimate chapter.

> I am reminded of your sincere faith. . . . For this reason I remind you to rekindle the gift of God that is within you through the laying on of my hands; for God did not give us a spirit of cowardice, but rather a spirit of power and of love and of self-discipline.
>
> Do not be ashamed, then, of the testimony about our Lord or of me his prisoner, but join with me in suffering for the gospel, relying on the power of God, who saved us and called us with a holy calling, not according to our works but according to his own purpose and grace. This grace was given to us in Christ Jesus before the ages began, but it has now been revealed through the appearing of our Savior Christ Jesus, who abolished death and brought life and immortality to light through the gospel. (2 Tim 1:5-10)

In light of Paul's exhortation, I want to reflect on the New Testament pericope in which the Holy Spirit reveals the establishment of the diaconate, namely, Acts 6. Then I want to take a very brief look at the meaning of the laying on of hands in the New Testament. Finally, I want to consider more specifically what it means that the deacon is the new friend of Jesus.

Acts 6

Now during those days, when the disciples were increasing in number, the Hellenists complained against the Hebrews because their widows were being neglected in the daily distribution of food. And the twelve called together the whole community of the disciples and said, "It is not right that we should neglect the word of God in order to wait on tables. Therefore, friends, select from among yourselves seven men of good standing, full of the Spirit and of wisdom, whom we may appoint to this task, while we, for our part, will devote ourselves to prayer and to serving the word." What they said pleased the whole community, and they chose Stephen, a man full of faith and the Holy Spirit, together with Philip, Prochorus, Nicanor, Timon, Parmenas, and Nicolaus, a proselyte of Antioch. They had these men stand before the apostles, who prayed and laid their hands on them.

The word of God continued to spread; the number of the disciples increased greatly in Jerusalem, and a great many of the priests became obedient to the faith. (Acts 6:1-7)

We are quite familiar with this story. From the day of Christ's ascension, the apostles understood that their ministry included both the proclamation of the Good News to the poor (the Word) as well as service (sacrament; public work). Then, as now, the Word could not be preached credibly unless the poor were served. In the early days of the church, though, a problem arose. St. Luke tells us that in "those days" the number of disciples continued to grow. What days? "Those days" refers to the previous passage, to Acts 5. There Luke tells us that "every day in the temple and at home [the apostles] did not cease to teach and proclaim Jesus as the Messiah" (Acts 5:42). Simply put, because the apostles were teaching and proclaiming the Gospel, the church experienced great growth.

Because the master of the harvest himself was adding disciples to the Christian community (see Acts 1:47), surely such growth was a great grace for the church. But it was a "mixed blessing," for it resulted in a crisis both in the community itself and in the ministry of the Twelve in its regard. The growth in the number of those who relied on the Jerusalem church for food stretched both the apostles' capacities and the community's resources. Consequently, the apostles were unable to serve effectively. As a result, "the Hellenists complained against the Hebrews because their widows were being neglected in the daily distribution of food." As the church grew, the Twelve were increasingly unable to minister to its members, consequently putting both the church's good order and mission at risk.

The text doesn't explain exactly what the problem was. From the limited information it does provide, it seems to be the case that the Twelve personally, and perhaps without assistance from others, were daily distributing the food to those in need. When their capacities and resources were stretched too thin because of the growing number of persons in need, the Twelve either didn't get the job done, quite simply, or they began to choose who would be served and who wouldn't be. Remember, too, that tensions in the ecclesial community were already high as the church's apostles and presbyters were debating whether or not God was demanding the circumcision of non-Hebrew disciples. For example, after Peter had eaten at table with a Gentile, Cornelius, and rumor of his "irreligious" act had reached Jerusalem, upon Peter's return "[t]he circumcised believers criticized him, saying, 'Why did you go to uncircumcised men and eat with them?'" (Acts 11:2-3). And, according to Eusebius, the Jerusalem community was made up largely of believing Hebrews (*Eccl. Hist.* 4.5.2). The Greek believers might have constituted a small and relatively insignificant number of disciples; they were certainly in the minority. We can begin to imagine just how very complicated the situation must have been.

This being the case, the charges the Greeks were leveling against the apostles are quite damning. At the very least the Greek disciples might have been charging the Twelve with incompetence. Other explanations are possible, though. For example, the Jewish members of the Christian community (and all of the apostles were of Jewish heritage) may have been avoiding certain foods, adhering strictly to Jewish dietary prescriptions and believing the consumption of certain foods to be a violation of Jewish law. Perhaps, therefore, the two sectors of the Christian community—Jewish and Gentile—were simply not sitting at table together. If that were the case, the Greek widows may not have felt altogether included in the provision of the food, the Twelve providing different foods to each group. Perhaps the Greeks were charging the apostles outright with relating unfairly and unequally to disciples of different ethnic and religious origins, that is, with favoring circumcised disciples over the uncircumcised, Jews over Gentiles. But it might not have stopped there. At the very worst, perhaps the Greeks were accusing the Twelve of actual prejudice. Today we might say, harshly, that the Greeks could have been accusing the ones upon whom Christ founded his church of racial discrimination, of racism.

Whatever the basis of the Greek's accusations, and whether they were founded or not, the Twelve took them very seriously; they took the issue to heart. They did not attempt to paper over the problem or deny the charges. They did not become defensive or transfer the problem back onto their accusers or the Greek widows. In response, Luke implies, they considered the matter privately and they prayerfully presented their dilemma to the Lord. We can well imagine them, knowing of their deep love for Jesus and their personal familiarity with him, petitioning him, "Lord, this problem is of your making. You have charged us to provide bread to the poor. Yet day by day you keep adding more and more of them to our number. Help us solve this predicament, that all might receive what they need from the church and at our hands." The Lord heard their prayer and answered them. What was his response, and that of the Twelve?

The Twelve first assembled the entire community of the disciples, both Hebrews and Greeks. In doing so they affirmed that the church was united, one family. The Twelve were also affirming, therefore, that this problem wasn't theirs alone to solve. Neither was it the problem simply of the Greeks, on one hand, or of the Hebrews, on the other. That the widows of the Greeks were not being fed, that the poor were not being served, was a problem facing the entire church. And the entire church, a united church, could and would have to solve it.

In their exhortation, the Twelve greeted both Greeks and Hebrews as "brothers [*adelphoi*]." In the collectivist society that was first-century Jerusalem—a tribal society, a very highly socially stratified and ordered "who is in and who is out" society—to be considered by another as "brother" was a matter of great honor. This honorable title addresses the charge leveled against them that they favored Hebrews over Greeks. All were "brothers." The apostles affirmed that the right relationship among all disciples—theirs with the poor, the Hebrews and Greeks with one another—was brotherhood.

The Twelve informed the community that "it is not right" that they themselves serve the poor at table if doing so meant that they would neglect the Word of God and prayer. The Greek word Luke uses, *areston*, does not technically mean "right." A better translation would be "pleasing" or "desirable." It is the same word Jesus himself used to affirm that he always does "what is pleasing" to his heavenly Father (John 8:29). In his first letter, St. John writes that one whose conscience is clean will receive whatever he asks of the Lord, "because we obey his commandments and do what pleases him" (1 John 3:22).

Using this word to describe the judgment of the apostles, Luke wants to impress upon the reader that the apostles were not facing the either-or choice between something that was important and something that was relatively less so, something that was more pleasing to God (studying his Word—the Word of God here refers to both the Scriptures of our Old Testament and the oral teachings the Lord had handed on—and prayer) and something that was less pleasing to God (serving the poor at table). No, the dilemma the apostles faced was rather how they might be better servants of the Lord, that is, of his word, *and* at the same time better servants of the church. The solution they came to in their prayer and discernment provided first of all for the feeding of the whole church with every word that comes from the mouth of God (see Matt 4:4), *as well as* improving the feeding of the poor with physical bread. From the Lord, the Twelve understood that they themselves should better serve the bread of God's Word to the church by study and prayer while others would be better at serving physical bread to the poor at table (at which, in any case, they were failing). So that everyone could be fed with the bread of God's Word—apostles, brothers and sisters, widows, Greeks, Hebrews—the Twelve concentrated on prayer and the ministry of the Word. That everyone, including the poor Greek widows, could be fed with the bread of wheat, the apostles would choose seven deeply spiritual and prudent men.

Then the Twelve invited their brothers and sisters to look around. Specifically, Luke tells us they invited the community to look to one another. The word he uses is *episkepsasthe*. (Note that this word has the same roots as *episcopus*, which means overseer, and from which we draw our English word "bishop.") In Greek it means more than simply glancing over. It means inspecting and judging. The community was to evaluate one another according to the criteria the Twelve themselves established, criteria that, presumably, they had in prayer received from the Lord and discerned to be his will.

There were two such criteria for which the community was to look and judge. The men whom the community was to recommend and upon whom the apostles would lay their hands were to be judged to be deeply spiritual and wise. This meant that the Twelve understood and affirmed that the needs of the growing Christian community could only be met by men of prayer, men who had grown and would continue to grow in their relationship with the Lord and with their brothers and sisters. Surely, too, the Twelve sought to head off at the pass any cause for accusation against these men such as were earlier leveled against the Twelve themselves. Therefore, by choosing men whom the community's members themselves judged to be deeply spiritual and wise, the Twelve prevented further fractioning and hard feeling in the church and secured its good order and unity, both that of the Twelve with the church's disciples (hierarchically) and that of the Hebrew disciples with the Greeks (the horizontal communion of faith).

Luke then tells us, in verse 5, that this "word [*logos*]" was pleasing to the whole community. Some translations of the text read that the community unanimously accepted or rejoiced at the proposal. This is not exactly the sense of the original Greek. The community rejoiced at the word, the *logos*, communicated by the Twelve. What specifically is the content of this *logos*, or, better yet, over what specifically did the disciples rejoice? First, the whole community was pleased because the Twelve had shown that they understood God's will for the church. They rejoiced, especially, namely, that the Twelve had their priorities straight. The whole community agreed. It was the duty of the Twelve to concentrate on prayer and the study of the Word, not to serve the poor at table. To serve the poor was nonnegotiable; the Twelve did have to make certain that it took place. But the Twelve themselves could better serve the poor if they concentrated on the study of God's Word and on their prayer for them, while providing for the distribution of daily bread from the hands of others, from deeply spiritual and prudent men.

Second, the community rejoiced not as such because the Greek widows would now get to eat their fill of earthly bread. The whole community—Greeks and Hebrews, apostles and presbyters, brothers and sisters, members all—rejoiced because the apostles would no longer neglect prayer and the study of the Word in order to distribute bread and so would feed them *all* with the Word of God. They rejoiced that they *all* would eat of the bread of the apostles' study of the Word and of prayer. The fact that the Greek widows would no longer be neglected in the daily distribution of food was certainly a cause for rejoicing. But it was a secondary cause for doing so when compared to the affirmation that now the whole church of Jerusalem would no longer be neglected in the daily distribution of the Word of God from the table of the apostles' study and prayer. In the history of the nascent church, this was the first truly pastoral solution to the needs of the poor—Word and prayer first but at the same time bread. In this way the good order of the church and its unity were secured. Pope Benedict XVI teaches, "[T]he social service which [the group of seven deacons] were meant to provide was absolutely concrete, yet at the same time it was also a spiritual service; theirs was a truly spiritual office which carried out an essential responsibility of the Church, namely a well-ordered love of neighbor. With the formation of this group of seven, '*diaconia*'—the ministry of charity exercised in a communitarian, orderly way—became part of the fundamental structure of the Church" (*Deus caritas est* 21).

Notice, then, how the story of Acts 6 concludes. It does not conclude, for example: "From then on all of the Greek widows ate their share of food, and everyone lived happily ever after." While verse 7 is sometimes written as a new and separate paragraph, it shouldn't be; it actually concludes the story of the choosing of the first seven deacons. The verse reads, "The word of God continued to spread; the number of the disciples increased greatly in Jerusalem." First of all, we can see how pleased the Lord himself was with this solution. Wonderful, since it was the Lord himself who added disciples to their number! But note: in verse 1, when the apostles were struggling to keep their ministerial priorities straight and before the complaint had been lodged that they were neglecting Greek widows, Luke tells us the number of disciples simply increased. Now, however, thanks to the way in which this crisis had been met and resolved, with the apostles once again focused on the Word of God and prayer and the deacons serving the poor at table, the number of disciples "increased greatly."

Besides this, not only was the Lord adding more and more disciples to the community's number. Luke tells us that even "a great many of the priests became obedient to the faith." He uses the word *ochlos*, which could be translated as "throngs" or "multitudes," rather than "a great many." Because the apostles studied the Word and prayed and because the needs of the poor were being met by the deacons, throngs of Levites—they who, to minister to God in the temple, had kept themselves separated from even their own Jewish brothers and sisters—were now joined to the church and participating fully in the life of the community.

I want to highlight one final point of the story instructive for the ministry of deacons before we turn our attention to the apostolic gesture of ordination, that is, the laying on of hands. The Twelve chose seven deeply spiritual and wise men to assist them in the daily distribution of bread to the poor. In doing so they called on these deacons not only to be distributors of bread. Before they could distribute bread, the Twelve needed these men to assist them in being reconciled with the Greek disciples and in the reconciliation of the Hebrew and Greek members themselves. Then and now, it is crucial that deacons witness for justice and labor for harmony between people of different races, that they combat racism and seek righteousness, that is, right relationships between persons of "every race, language, and way of life" (Eucharistic Prayer for Masses of Reconciliation II).

It is too simplistic to say that in the early church Hebrews and Greeks were of different racial and ethnic backgrounds so that tensions were bound to arise, as they do in any melting pot. Behind this story there was much more. Jerusalem was an occupied capital—occupied by Rome. Civilly, Greeks were strangers in Jerusalem, immigrants and foreigners, and certainly they were in the populace's minority. Nonetheless, at the time, secular Greek culture was dominant in the city. And so there was palatable underlying tension to daily life in Jerusalem, the "capital" city of Jewish faith and life.

Greeks too were increasingly in the minority in the church in Jerusalem as she grew by the enormous numbers about which Luke speaks, numbers that increasingly included many Jewish priests. Within the church, too, there raged a crucial debate regarding circumcision and adherence to the Torah and Jewish ways. Consider also that because of Jewish law, if the apostles preached and prayed in certain precincts of the temple, Greeks who were not circumcised Jews would have been prevented by the Jews from joining in. We know that increasingly the Jewish authorities persecuted more and more Christians of all ethnic backgrounds. Additionally, St. Paul himself clues us in to the fact that the disciples in Jerusalem were quite poor, for he took up a collection on their behalf. Finally, the followers of Jesus lived in an increasingly tense political environment as Judea and Rome came to blows and to war.

By ensuring a fair distribution of the church's resources to the needy in this stressful environment, the seven deacons were agents of the reconciliation of the Hebrews and Greeks to one another and Greeks to the church. Beyond that, as we know from history, the deacons ensured that as the church grew so did its love for and attention to the poor, especially for minorities, those living on the edge, those away from home, the homeless, etc. Today, too, it pertains to deacons in virtue of their ordination, deacons who are the icon of Christ's own suffering servanthood, to care that within the church men and women of every racial, ethnic, and language division, especially the minority, the marginalized, and the immigrant, are united to the church and with its members. The deacon is to ensure not simply that all are fed but even more so that all are gathered in and seated at the table of the Lord's bounty and that of the church.

In the end, the apostles loved the Greek widows, as surely they treasured all of the members of the nascent community who were being born of water and the Holy Spirit. And because they treasured them all, for their sakes they laid hands on seven deeply spiritual and prudent men. From apostolic times until our own, the church, if I may appropriate the language of the 1969 Synod of Bishops, has chosen the deacon as her "preferential option for the poor."

The Laying on of Hands

Neither in Acts 6 nor anywhere else in the Acts of the Apostles does Luke use the noun *diakonos*, "deacon." The word he does use, *diakonia*, he uses to describe either the ministry of the Twelve, on one hand, or of St. Paul, on the other. For example, in Acts 1:17 and then again in 1:25 the apostles look for another to join their ranks and to carry out the ministry (*diakonia*) abandoned by Judas. In 20:24, St. Paul, in his farewell address to the presbyters of Miletus, said, "I do not count my life of any value to myself, if only I may finish my course and the ministry [*diakonia*] that I received from the Lord Jesus, to testify to the good news of God's grace." When addressing James and the presbyters of the church in Jerusalem, in 21:19, Paul "related one by one the things that God had done among the Gentiles through his ministry [*diakonia*]."

Our understanding of what it means that the apostles "appointed" these seven men to be deacons, therefore, comes not from the process by which and the criteria because of which the seven were chosen, or even from a reflection on the ministry itself that they carried out, that is, that they distributed bread. (It goes without saying, though, that from the appointment of these seven the diaconate began to acquire definite theological form and shape.) Rather, we must look to the meaning of the act itself by which the apostles appointed and set these seven men apart for ministry. We look, therefore, to the meaning of the laying on of hands. It isn't possible here, or even necessary, to engage in a historical and theological discussion regarding the laying on of hands. Instead, I want simply to review briefly what this gesture meant as Jesus used it and in the life of the early church. It is this same gesture, together with the prayer of ordination, by which a bishop ordains a man a deacon.

First of all, for Jesus and in the early church the laying on of hands was a gesture of blessing, healing, and even of resurrection. So, for example, Jesus laid his hands on the little children that had been brought to him and in doing so blessed them (Mark 10:16; Matt 19:13). In Luke 4:40, Jesus laid hands on the sick who suffered from all manner of diseases, and he cured them. In one instance, Jesus touched a woman "with a spirit that had crippled her for eighteen years" leaving her "bent over and . . . quite unable to stand up straight." He laid his hands on her and she stood up straight (a symbol of resurrection), immediately praising God (Luke

13:11, 13). In Matthew 9:18, the synagogue leader asked Jesus to come and cure his little girl by laying his hands on her. Jesus did so and raised her from the dead. Jesus taught that those who proclaim the Gospel will be proven credible because, among other things, they will lay their hands on the sick, who will recover (Mark 16:18). Paul himself was cured of his blindness when Ananias laid his hands on him (Acts 9:17-18).

Already in the Old Testament, the laying on of hands was the means of instilling in another the wisdom of God. Thus "Joshua son of Nun was full of the spirit of wisdom, because Moses had laid his hands on him" (Deut 34:9). In the early church, too, the laying on of hands was a gesture of invoking the Holy Spirit on another or on a community. Ananias explained to Saul that the laying on of hands would not only cure his blindness but also fill him with the Holy Spirit. Paul, we are told, was immediately baptized, ate, and his strength returned to him. In Acts 8:17, Peter and John invoked the Holy Spirit on the disciples of Samaria who had accepted the Word of God, "and they received the Holy Spirit." In Acts 19:6, Paul baptized twelve men, laying hands on them; they received the Holy Spirit and began to speak in tongues and prophecies.

That the laying on of hands invoked a "power" is clear as well from the attempt of Simon the magician to bribe the apostles into sharing it with him: "Give me also this power so that anyone on whom I lay my hands may receive the Holy Spirit" (8:19). Peter harshly rebuked Simon, referring to the power received in the laying on of hands as "God's gift" (v. 20).

Finally, the laying on of hands was the gesture for consecrating and commissioning another for mission and service, for transmitting a charge. In the desert the Israelites laid hands on the Levites, thus setting them apart from all of Israel and presenting them to the Lord for priestly service. Aaron so consecrated the entire tribe of Levi "as an elevation offering from the Israelites, that they may do the service of the Lord" (Num 8:11). After Moses laid his hands on Joshua, "the Israelites obeyed him, doing as the LORD had commanded Moses" (Deut 34:9). In the church, Paul himself was commissioned through the laying on of hands to bring the name, that is, the person, of Christ, to the Gentiles (Acts 9:15-17). The seven deacons, as we have already seen, were appointed to their ministry and to the task of distributing bread by the laying on of hands. Paul and Barnabas were set apart and sent off "for the work" to which the Holy Spirit called them (Acts 13:2-3).

Concluding this brief survey of the laying on of hands in the Scriptures, what can we conclude in regard to the deacon, whose life and ministry have been the objects of our reflections? The church teaches,

"The sacramental act of ordination surpasses mere election, designation or delegation by the community, because it confers a gift of the Holy Spirit enabling the exercise of sacred power which can only come from Christ himself through his Church" (introduction to the *Basic Norms* and the *Directory*). Through the laying on of hands the Trinity chooses a man, whom the church has set apart, and invites him into their very personal *communio*, recreating him anew. The Lord himself used the gesture to bless, to heal, and to raise to new life. Through it he still blesses, heals, and gives new life to the deacon, gracing him for his ministry and strengthening him so that he might bear the sufferings of the poor. Through the laying on of hands Christ invites the deacon into a new friendship.

The Holy Spirit used the gesture to confer his presence and charisms, his gifts. So through the laying on of the bishop's hands, the Spirit gives to the deacon his charisms of charity and service. The invocation of the Holy Spirit upon the deacon at his ordination is these words prayed by the bishop: "Lord, send forth upon them the Holy Spirit, that they may be strengthened by the gift of your sevenfold grace to carry out faithfully the work of the ministry." "These are the gifts of the Spirit given to the Messiah, which are granted also to the newly ordained," the church teaches (*Basic Norms* 6). The apostles laid hands on one another and on their assistants to send them to proclaim the Gospel and to assign the tasks of ministry. From those apostolic days to our own time, through the laying on of hands the bishop has chosen his deacon-assistants and sent them to announce the Good News to the poor. Today, no less, and perhaps more urgently than ever before, deacons are sent, as Christ, "who made himself the 'deacon' or servant of all" (*CCC* 1570).

A New Friendship

Concluding our reflections on the diaconate, I want to consider the nature of the new friendship that Christ extends to the deacon. We have already reflected on various spiritual and ministerial aspects through which this new friendship is lived out. In this reflection, instead, I want to look at the very special friendship Jesus had with John the Baptist. Although in the Scriptures their physical presence to one another occurred on occasions that were few and far between, nonetheless we can say most assuredly that theirs was a bond of deepest friendship and spiritual intimacy. Of Jesus, John said, "He must increase, but I must decrease" (John 3:30). Of John, Jesus said, "Among those born of women no one is greater than John" (Luke 7:28). Surely John the Baptist is the servant who suffered most for his friend, the Suffering Servant. In their friendship we will find the image of the new friendship between Christ and his deacons.

I direct your attention to John 3:22-30.

> After this Jesus and his disciples went into the Judean countryside, and he spent some time there with them and baptized. John also was baptizing at Aenon near Salim because water was abundant there; and people kept coming and were being baptized—John, of course, had not yet been thrown into prison.
>
> Now a discussion about purification arose between John's disciples and a Jew. They came to John and said to him, "Rabbi, the one who was with you across the Jordan, to whom you testified, here he is baptizing, and all are going to him." John answered, "No one can receive anything except what has been given from heaven. You yourselves are my witnesses that I said, 'I am not the Messiah, but I have been sent ahead of him.' He who has the bride is the bridegroom. The friend of the bridegroom, who stands and hears him, rejoices greatly at the bridegroom's voice. For this reason my joy has been fulfilled. He must increase, but I must decrease."

John the Baptist's disciples had come to him, pointing out, almost, so it seems, with a certain jealousy in their voices, that "all are going" to Jesus (v. 26). (As an aside, it is interesting to note that John the Baptist still had disciples, even after having recognized Christ as the Messiah and after having pointed him out to others as the Lamb of God.) John answered his disciples, affirming that Christ's ministry was indeed "from heaven" (v. 27). He then added, "He who has the bride is the bridegroom. The friend of the bridegroom, who stands and hears him, rejoices greatly at the bridegroom's voice. For this reason my joy has been fulfilled. He must increase, but I must decrease" (vv. 29-30).

In the original Greek, the word the Baptist used to refer to himself is *philos*, friend. This friend is the *shoshben* of Jewish tradition, "the groom's closest friend" who enjoyed his "special trust" (see Raymond Brown, *The Gospel According to John I–XII*, p. 152). In Jesus' time the *shoshben*, or, as the Baptist refers to himself, the groom's friend, was not he who, as in our own tradition, simply stood alongside the groom, witnessed a couple's exchange of consent, and then cosigned the license. Rather, as marriages were arranged, the friend of the bridegroom was he who on behalf of the bridegroom acted as the go-between for the groom and the father of the bride and arranged the groom's nuptials. He was the one who drafted and arranged the agreement between the two families because of which the bride could be taken from her family of origin and "embedded" into the family of the groom. (To use two other images to which we have already made reference, the friend of the groom acted as a bridge between the groom and the bride, a sort of vicarious representative of each to the other.) John the Baptist, by referring to himself as the groom's friend, acknowledged more than simply that he himself was not the Messiah. He proclaimed that Christ, the Messiah, was a bridegroom, that Christ was the fulfillment of the prophecies of the marriage of the Lord God with Israel, and that his manner of redeeming was marital love.

In his relationship with Christ and in this discourse to his disciples, John the Baptist identified three qualities of a friend of the groom. First, a *shoshben*, because he is entrusted with his friend's future and in this case particularly because the friend is "from heaven," must be trustworthy. Second, a friend of the groom must be patient, for he waits, listening for his friend's arrival. He knows not when the bridegroom may arrive (Mark 13:33). The bridegroom may delay his coming (Matt 25:5). He may come at midnight or before sunrise (Luke 12:38). He may come when he is least expected (Matt 24:50). Third, when the bridegroom does arrive his friend is overjoyed. In fact, as John the Baptist said of himself, his joy was complete when finally at Christ's arrival he heard his voice.

There is one little detail in John the Baptist's description of his role as the bridegroom's friend, though, that tends to get lost in the English translation. John says of himself, "The friend of the bridegroom, who stands and hears him, rejoices greatly at the bridegroom's voice. For this reason my joy has been fulfilled" (v. 29). In Greek the Baptist uses the word *histēkōs* for standing. *Histēkōs*, from the verb *histēmi*, indeed means to stand up, but not simply as one might stand up from a sitting or lying position, as, for example, from a chair or bed. More specifically, *histēmi* means to stand in the presence of others, especially as when standing before another of higher authority. But *histēmi* also means to acknowledge and uphold the authority of the one before whom one stands, something that one does, for example, by standing when the pope, the president, a judge, a jury, or a person of higher rank enters a room or when one's boss comes into one's office. *Histēmi* is the coming to attention and the salute of a military inferior when a superior officer comes into his or her presence. (Interestingly, Matthew uses this verb to refer to Jesus "standing" before Pilate, in 27:11, but John does not.)

Using it here, the Baptist is teaching us not simply that one must be attentive to the coming of the bridegroom so as most readily to hear his voice, or simply that one must be ready to act, as a soldier standing at attention is more ready to obey his or her commanding officer's orders than one who is seated or lying down. John the Baptist is teaching us that even while waiting for the bridegroom to arrive, he recognized Jesus' authority, that Jesus was from on high, that his authority was of God. As Jesus' *shoshben*, truly it was with the Lord God himself, that is, Jesus' Father in heaven, with whom the Baptist had arranged the nuptials. And John's joy was complete not simply because the Messiah had come, but that the Messiah was the bridegroom who had the bride. The friend of the bridegroom "rejoices greatly," he continued. "For this reason my joy has been fulfilled. He must increase, but I must decrease" (3:29-30).

It is this image of a bridegroom's friend that best describes the new friendship into which a deacon is invited. A deacon's relationship with Christ is not a sort of commercial transaction by which, in exchange for being conformed to Christ, he agrees to perform certain duties, if even in Christ's name. Nor is it a sort of commercial partnership with Christ and the church on behalf of the Gospel and for the sake of the poor. Rather, because of the laying on of hands the deacon enjoys a loving partnership, a loving friendship with Christ, the church, the bishop, and the bishop's priests. As the bridegroom's friend, as Jesus' *shoshben*, the deacon is entrusted with the proclamation that Jesus' saving mystery is "from heaven." And Jesus turns to the deacon as his friend to "arrange" his nuptials, not only by proclaiming his Word and serving at the altar, but by going before him and, especially, by going out in his name to gather to his nuptial table all whom he himself has invited there. Above all, then, because the deacon is the bridegroom's new friend, his best man, his *shoshben*, he stands and waits so that when the bridegroom comes he will hear his voice and at his coming escort him into the wedding banquet which he himself, the deacon, has arranged and prepared.

Standing, the deacon serves him who is from on high. Standing, the deacon acknowledges his authority as the Suffering Servant. The deacon is the bridegroom's friend. He must decrease while the Lord must increase. Standing in diaconal life and ministry, the deacon's joy is complete.

Martyrs of Charity

The *Basic Norms for the Formation of Permanent Deacons* concludes with these words.

> The *Didascalia Apostolorum* recommends to the deacons of the first century, "As our Saviour and Master said in the Gospel: *let he who*

wishes to be great among you, make himself your servant, in the same way as the Son of Man came not to be served but to serve and give his life as a ransom for many, you deacons must do the same, even if that means giving your life for your brothers and sisters, because of the service which you are bound to fulfill." This invitation is most appropriate also for those who are called today to the diaconate, and urges them to prepare themselves with great dedication for their future ministry. (89)

This is quite the charge the church repeats to those who would seek to be ordained and to her deacons. No less than she called deacons to do in the first century, the church continues to call deacons in the twenty-first century to be formed and prepared to give their lives in the service of Christ and in her own service. She is not calling deacons simply to work hard, to be prepared to put up with a little hardship or headache, or simply to donate a few weekly hours of diaconal service to the parish or other church ministry. The church ordains deacons to be full-time, 24/7/365, luminous icons of Christ the Suffering Servant—that means at home, work, at play, in addition to the parish or church setting. The church calls deacons to love others as Christ has loved them—that means unto the cross. Deacons are called to be, as Pope John Paul II declared of the life and witness of St. Maximilian Kolbe, "martyrs of charity."

In the end, to be a martyr of charity is the greatest witness of love that a deacon can put forward to the poor. St. Paul wrote to the Romans, "Indeed, rarely will anyone die for a righteous person—though perhaps for a good person someone might actually dare to die. But God proves his love for us in that while we still were sinners Christ died for us" (Rom 5:7-8). Applying St. Paul's words to deacons we can say that they prove their love for the poor, that while they were still poor the deacon was willing to care, to sacrifice, to die for them.

"[O]ne does not presume to take this honor, but takes it only when called by God, just as Aaron was" (Heb 5:4). The church believes that Jesus is today calling men, young and old, celibate and married, to be deacons. No one should enter this ministry unless he is prepared to enter into the mystery of Christ's own suffering servanthood, to be educated as God's son through the discipline of suffering, and to serve as Christ's and the church's vicarious representative in the ransom, expiation, and exchange of sacrificial love. I stand in awe at this mystery and before its implications for all whom Christ invites into his suffering servanthood and whom he asks to give their lives as a ransom for others.

As we have seen throughout these reflections, the church's service to the poor is the sign of the credibility of the Gospel she proclaims. By seeking out the poor, who will always be with us, and uniting them to Christ and to the church, thus building up the community, the deacon witnesses that Christ has been raised from the dead and will be with us always even until the ends of the age (see Matt 28:20). By feeding the poor with the Word of God and the Bread of Life, as well as with the bread of their physical sustenance, the deacon bears witness that Christ himself is serving the least of his brothers and sisters.

Now, as much as in the first century, the church and the world are in need of deacons. I pray the Lord to raise up many more after his own heart to announce the Good News to the poor and to feed them. Through these reflections I hope in some small way to contribute to the understanding of the diaconate and thus to its renewal in the pastoral life of our churches and Christian communities, and especially in the many places in which the poor live and are to be found—vacant lots, prisons, detention centers, rest homes, addiction centers, hospitals, etc. Above all, I hope for a greater appreciation of "the value of that precious gift of the Spirit which is diaconal service" (*Basic Norms* 90).

chapter ten

A Word to the Wives*

The adage goes, "Behind every great/successful man there stands a woman." The *Cambridge Advanced Learner's Dictionary* explains that this is "said to emphasize that men's success often depends on the work and support of their wives." This is absolutely true for a married deacon. As a gesture of my appreciation and support, I want to address a word or two to the spouses of those who might consider the diaconate, to the wives of deacon candidates, and even to wives of those already ordained.

Dear wives, you supported your husband's application for formation for the diaconate. In doing so, in your own right you gave witness to your love for Jesus and the church and to your trust in them. As your husband was accepted into candidacy, promoted through lector and acolyte, and now has been called by the bishop to the diaconate, your continuing support has expressed your judgment that his diaconate is a call, a vocation from the Lord. Now he stands at the threshold of ordination. Undoubtedly you are very proud of him. But now what? What about you? In the years of your husband's formation, now at the time of ordination, and truth be told even after ordination, you have felt and

---

* I originally offered the following reflection to the wives of the men who had made the ordination retreat and were soon to be ordained deacons. The wives were invited to join their husbands on the last morning of the retreat. It is addressed directly to them.

will continue to feel many emotions and ask many questions. What are your place and role within the vocation of your husband's diaconate? If the Lord has called your husband to be a deacon, what is he calling you to become and to do, if anything?

During formation—his as a deacon and yours as a deacon's wife—you and your husband may at times have experienced misunderstanding and tension. Each may have approached formation and begun to experience his ministry differently. The time he spends in prayer, study, and apostolic work may have competed with your own needs and interests and those of your family. Often, too, the questions, concerns, worries, and needs of your children and the broader family about their father, son, or brother were projected on to or voiced through you.

Then there are some questions that simply cannot be asked and some whose answers cannot be known until after your husband has been ordained and your family has begun to live in the wake of the bishop's laying on of hands. By then, though, will it be too late? For example, he takes a promise of obedience to the bishop. Will a time ever come when that promise will conflict with the mission of your family? What will happen if your husband is assigned to a parish other than your own home parish? In many dioceses a deacon is required to put in so many hours every week of active ministry in the parish or ecclesial community to which the bishop has assigned him and which, therefore, has a claim and a right to his attention, time, energy, and service. Will your husband and you be able to reconcile his responsibilities as a deacon in active ministry with his responsibilities as husband, father, and grandfather? Will you, will the two of you, be forever forced to navigate between the proverbial rock of marriage and family life and the hard place of his ministry?

All fear is in some way a grappling with the unknown, especially the unknown that regards diminishment, loss, and even, ultimately, death. It is these fears that I would wager probably best characterize what you experienced in the discernment leading up to your husband's application and acceptance into diaconate formation, during formation, and now at the threshold of ordination itself. That these fears will manifest themselves again must be acknowledged up front and dealt with in the crucial first months, perhaps even years, following his ordination, as the two of you and your family adjust to life now lived for two Christian communities, namely, your family, on one hand, and the church, on the other. Truth be told, some of these will be ongoing concerns that, as every deacon and his wife know, you will also experience anew whenever you face the prospect of a new assignment or the assumption of new ministries.

In these reflections I want to address some of these fears. Concretely, there are three questions with which you and your children might find yourselves grappling when your husband and their father is ordained to the diaconate.

Will I Still Like Him?

First, you may fear that ordination will change your husband, or you may fear that it will not. Does ordination change a man? Will he be the same person after ordination that he was before? If it does change him, will you even like him? If it doesn't change him, shouldn't it? How does a deacon's wife or how do children love a deacon?

Yes, the laying on of hands does change the one ordained. Ordination changes him sacramentally, configuring him to Christ. Through a new relationship with the divine bridegroom, as Jesus' *shoshben*, the friend of the bridegroom, ordination establishes him in a new friendship with the Trinity itself and with the church. With the laying on of hands, your husband is given a new blessing of life: he is strengthened for service to sinners and the poor. He is commissioned to announce the Good News to the poor and assigned new responsibilities on their behalf. If he co-operates with its grace, ordination may indeed change your husband's character. It should, however, make him better, not worse. If he does not grow in holiness it is because he is not cooperating with the Holy Spirit, who has been poured out into his heart and whose sevenfold gifts are strengthened within him with the laying on of the bishop's hands.

As for personality, your husband-deacon will still be that same Prince Charming you married but whom everyone else now knows as Deacon Joe. Ordination will not make him a more successful businessman or sportsman, or a better driver. It won't make him change behavior that you yourself haven't been able to make him change since the day you met him. He'll still throw his dirty clothes on the floor and not put his dishes in the dishwasher. He'll still have the same annoying quirks and make the same disgusting noises in bed. After ordination he'll be the same mediocre lover that he was before! In and of itself, without his cooperation with its grace, ordination won't even make him a better husband and father. By itself it won't cause him to stop sinning.

Christ's humanity is the vessel through which he reveals his divinity and through which he redeems us. He had to become like his brothers and sisters in all things but sin so as to be constituted high priest on their behalf. Similarly, Christ, after his resurrection from the dead, neither lost nor gave up his humanity. Fully human, he ascended into heaven. Analogously, so too at ordination the deacon neither abandons nor loses his humanity but brings it fully into the new friendship he enjoys with Christ. That is part of the mystery and greatness of sacramental ordination, as it is with those two other great sacraments that change a person's character, namely, baptism and confirmation. In some sense these sacraments "deepen" a person's humanity, restoring us by grace to that state of life that was ours in Christ and in the Holy Spirit before the fall of Adam and Eve and their "birthing" of original sin. Your husband's humanity is the very vessel Christ uses to shine forth as from an icon, to shine forth as the Suffering Servant. Your husband cannot shed it but, to the contrary, must be fully human, fully himself, fully alive, fully "present" to be fully a deacon and most luminously an icon of Christ the Suffering Servant.

The church needs and wants deacons who are more human, not less. If anything, ordination should do just that—make your husband more human, not less. As the French philosopher-theologian Gabriel Marcel wrote, "The more my existence takes on the character of including others, the narrower becomes the gap which separates it from being; the more, in other words, I am" (*The Mystery of Being: II. Faith and Reality*, p. 33). In other words, at his ordination your husband "takes in" the person of Christ the Suffering Servant, as well as the church and the poor in a new friendship. Following his ordination, then, the more he incorporates these new friends into his relationship with you—his spouse with whom he is already one flesh—and into your family life, the more his very being "is" in God, the more human he becomes.

Widows and Orphans?

Together with the fear that ordination will or will not change your husband, you may very well fear, on one hand, the loss of intimacy with him and, therefore, on the other hand, the loss of the family's mission. Because the Lord and the church may be calling your husband to serve the daily bread of the Gospel at the tables of widows, orphans, and strangers, you may fear that you yourself will become a "widow," your children "orphans" and "strangers," without the daily staple that is your husband and their father.

You may find it difficult to articulate this fear to your husband, worried that he will interpret it as lack of support for his vocation, ongoing formation, ministry, or taking of a new assignment. You don't want to be the one who stands in the way of doing what he believes Jesus and the church are calling him to do, something you may have both agreed to when he applied for formation but subsequently about which you have developed doubts. You don't want to seem selfish, as if thinking only of yourself and not of Christ and of the church. Too, oftentimes you are the first to see through what may be his less-than-pure motives. But you are afraid to articulate those insights to your husband or to his formation superiors because you don't want to cause conflict in your marriage. You don't want to be responsible or, worse, blamed by him or by others (especially his mother!), for extinguishing his dreams.

You must address these fears in prayer, especially in your spousal and family prayer, and in honest communication between the two of you, the members of your family, and those responsible for his formation, as well as the bishop and your husband's pastor and yours. In spousal and family prayer and in talking things through, though, you and all those discerning his vocation must bear in mind two basic principles. First, your husband's prior vocation, his moral vocation, if you will, is to the truth. Second, his ecclesial ministry is in the first place directed to your family. The Lord calls him to be a good husband and father, and then a good deacon.

God himself founds all families, including yours. God himself bestowed on your family his own name (see Eph 3:15). Your family, your *ecclesia domestica*, is your husband's first church and prior obligation. God will not call a man to the diaconate if his diaconate were to diminish his vocation as a husband and father or compromise the integrity of his family. Your husband can only be a good deacon to the extent that he is first of all your good husband and a good father to your children. It should go without saying, moreover, that a man who seeks to be a deacon because he is afraid of or incapable of intimacy in marriage or because he wants to avoid the responsibilities of family life is not called to be a deacon. Nor is a man called to be a deacon who believes that in becoming one his children will be better off—that if their father is ordained then his children will be better Christians and Catholics. A father who is incapable of raising his children in the practice of the faith as a baptized and confirmed layman will do no better at it as an ordained deacon. What is sure is that the children of a deacon face greater challenges in the wake of their father's ordination than do children of those who are not ordained, including the social pressure of being known or always having to act as "a deacon's son," "a deacon's daughter."

In addressing these fears, you do well to recall St. Paul's exhortation to the Galatians. "Whenever we have an opportunity," he wrote, "let us work for the good of all, and especially for those of the family of faith"

(6:10). St. Paul called on Christians to be good to all people, but especially to their fellow church members. Analogously, we could say that your husband is called to do good to the fellow-members of the church, but especially to the members of his own family. Your husband must first and foremost be dedicated to his family. He is saved by being faithful to his baptismal promises and his marriage vows as well as by the promises of his ordination. Christ does not declare those vows null nor does he dissolve them when he ordains your husband to the diaconate or renews within him the grace of his holy order.

Moreover, the church teaches that a deacon is to use the love he has for his family, a love that has become service, "as a stimulus of his diaconia in the Church" (*Directory* 61). You see, then, that your husband's faithfulness to you, his spouse, and to your family is a prior obligation to carrying out ministry in the church, which in any case he does not bind to himself as a spouse, unlike a bishop and even a priest. As John Paul II instructed, "*In particular* [emphasis added] the deacon and his wife must be a living example of *fidelity and indissolubility in Christian marriage* [emphasis original] before a world which is in dire need of such signs" (Allocation to the permanent deacons of the USA in Detroit, September 19, 1987, quoted in *Directory* 61). So, if either your husband or you before ordination or, after ordination, your husband, you, and the bishop conclude in conscience that there has arisen a contradiction between his marital and familial obligations and those of his diaconate because of which he can no longer remain faithful in love and service to his family and which threatens your marriage, then your marriage and family take precedence. Graver harm is done to the very institution of marriage and to one's family, and therefore to the church itself (for the smallest cell of the church is the family), should a deacon "introduce disorder into the family and into society" (CCC 2385) by choosing to serve the local church over and above his domestic church, sacrificing and jettisoning his wife and children in the process. Contrarily, if your deacon-husband is faithful to you and his family, is a good husband, father, and family man first, he will bring you and your children to know "with all the saints, what is the breadth and length and height and depth, and to know the love of Christ that surpasses knowledge, so that you may be filled with all the fullness of God" (Eph 3:18).

It must be acknowledged, too, that since a deacon is a *shoshben*, a friend of the Divine Bridegroom, there would be something incongruous about a separated or divorced deacon continuing publicly to serve the bridegroom's bride, the church. This would be especially so if the cause of the breakup of the marriage was the inability of the couple to incorporate the diaconate into their marriage, or if in any way the fault of the breakup lie with the deacon. Certainly this would be much more out of keeping with the witness of both the sacraments of marriage and the diaconate than a deacon who has with integrity admitted he cannot serve both the church and his family and so, "be[ing] subject" to his wife out of reverence for Christ (see Eph 5:21-28), receives the bishop's permission to withdraw from public ministry, perhaps even to be dispensed from his diaconal obligations altogether.

I want to offer here a word of counsel regarding spousal intimacy. The Trinity, in virtue of our creation and especially in baptism, invites us into his own divine intimacy, into that unhesitating and complete loving and honoring, giving and receiving that characterize the divine relationships, that is, in other words, into *communio*. Informed as it is by trinitarian intimacy, therefore, our own experience of intimacy in Christ, at the physical, emotional, and especially at the spiritual level, by its very nature is never exclusive. Christ himself is never exclusive in intimacy, and one's intimacy with him never excludes another from sharing in it. Indeed, since the greatest intimacy that a husband and wife can achieve is in fact spousal prayer, as St. Paul teaches (see 1 Cor 7:5), intimacy with Christ is the foundation and possibility of true, abiding intimacy with one's spouse. Likewise, true intimacy, that is, the sharing of the good, the beautiful, and the true with one's spouse, is an expression of one's intimacy with the Lord, who is himself "the way, and the truth, and the life" (John 14:6). For this reason, for example, the use of artificial contraception, because it directly contradicts and violates the ends of marriage, is more dangerous to the intimacy of your marriage and to the effectiveness of diaconal ministry than diaconal ministry ever could be to marriage and family life.

This is to say that if the intimacy you and your husband experience as baptized Christians and in marriage is authentic, altruistic, fertile, and honorable, so too will be the intimacy you experience as deacon and wife. If prior to ordination your intimacy as husband and wife is deeply rooted in complete openness to the other, and in prayer with the other completely open to God, then, even after the bishop has imposed hands on your husband, if you both remain open to and cooperate with grace, intimacy is not only possible but also deepened.

But What about Me?

Third, you might fear the loss of yourself, your own identity, your own ceasing to be. Will my husband's ordination change me? Will it mean the loss of my friendships, my lifestyle? Will I have to sacrifice my own interests so that he can serve the Lord and the church (although the interests of every baptized person in some way should be in service to the Lord and to the church)? Henceforth will I be known for who I am and what in my own right I have accomplished, or will I only and forever be known as "the deacon's wife"?

Here, too, the answer I give is both no and yes. No, you won't be changed. You will still be that same beautiful princess who swept her Prince Charming off his feet. After his ordination you will still be the same great lover that you were before! What you are not before his ordination you won't become afterward because of it. How you grow as a Christian wife and mother will be rooted in your own cooperation with the graces of your baptism, confirmation, the Eucharist, the sacrament of reconciliation, the anointing of the sick, and marriage, not his sacramental ordination. For example, what you yourself have failed to bring into the marriage and to the family prior to his ordination you cannot withdraw afterward. If there is a loss of friendships or relationships because your husband is a deacon, it might be just as likely because your friends and acquaintances, and not you, changed the terms on which the friendship had been built.

But, yes, you too will be changed. Married persons, as Christ taught, are no longer two but one flesh with their spouses (Mark 10:8). You can't help, therefore, but be affected by the grace your husband receives at ordination, which he brings into your marriage and with which you yourself in turn can cooperate. Building on the graces received in your own baptism and confirmation, by which you yourself have been configured to the resurrected Christ, and building on the graces of marriage, by which you were united with your husband as one flesh, you will be the first to benefit from the graces of his ordination and his diaconal ministry. And by the simple fact that you are married to a deacon, if not through your own active apostolate, you yourself do become a partner with him in announcing the Word of God to sinners and the poor.

Married in Ministry, Not to It

How, though, does this happen? How as a baptized Christian do you cooperate with the grace your husband receives at ordination and participate in his ministry? To answer we must look to Christ.

God never acts alone in his work of creating, redeeming, and sanctifying. God the Father is always at work through the Son, whom he has constituted as high priest. God the Son is always at work through the Holy Spirit, the soul of the church. God the Holy Spirit is always at work through the church on behalf of the world, over whose waters he hovered at creation. For its part, the church is always at work through its priestly and ministerial hierarchy on behalf of the lay faithful, and the church is always at work through the exercise of the baptismal priesthood of the laity for the sake of her bishops, priests, and deacons, and for the sake of the world.

Christ has taken the church to himself as a bride, with whom he has become one flesh. On her behalf and through her he exercises his own high priesthood. Bishops particularly (in the Catholic and Orthodox traditions bishops are always celibate) and priests too in imitation of Jesus have also taken to themselves the church as their bride, with whom they spiritually become one flesh. As is true for Christ himself, for them, too, the church is the mediator through which they exercise their priesthood. Their ministry is at one and the same time both personal and communal; it is ecclesial. When they preach, if their preaching is faithful to the Gospel, it is both Christ and the church who preach; when they celebrate the sacraments, Christ and the church herself are sanctifying her children. When they govern, the church herself is shepherding her flock and guiding them to Christ.

Since restoring the diaconate as a permanent ministry and opening it to married men, the church has required two things of a candidate's wife. Lacking one or the other of these, a bishop is not to ordain a man to the diaconate. First, a deacon-candidate's wife must consent to his husband's ordination. In virtue of the sacrament of marriage, then, by which the two of you have become one flesh and a spiritual bond has been forged between you, when your husband ministers, his ministry is rooted in your consent, both that of marriage and to his ordination, and is a fruit of your marital love and service. Second, you yourself must possess "the Christian moral character and attributes which will neither hinder [your] husband's ministry nor be out of keeping with it" (*Sacrum Diaconatus Ordinem* III, 3, quoted in *Basic Norms* 37). In offering your consent to his ordination, you offer the agreement of your will, your spiritual agreement to his vocation. By possessing "the Christian moral character and attributes which will neither hinder [your] husband's ministry nor be out of keeping with it," you offer the agreement of your own life to his ministry; you give evidence that you are both consecrated by your believing (see 1 Cor 7:14-15), of your own desire to be holy, and to live in peace with your husband. Through your agreement of both will and life, you do not simply give your husband permission to be ordained a deacon and to exercise the diaconal office. You also join yourself personally and actively to him in ministry.

Let's talk concretely about four expressions of such consent of will and life. How practically is your consent expressed?

First, your consent is an expression of trust. You must trust the Holy Spirit, whom you believe is calling your husband to be Christ's deacon. You must trust the church, who confirms the Lord's call and judges that your husband, like the first seven deacons, is "full of the Spirit and of wisdom." You must, of course, trust your husband. Prudence is that virtue by which one knows how to wed truth with charity, to draw out from Christ's storeroom "what is new and what is old" (Matt 13:52). Your husband will be forever tested in the virtue of prudence, but not simply in his ministry. He must know, and with you he must continually learn anew, how to balance the demands of his *ecclesia domestica* against the needs of his *ecclesia locale*.

Second, by the very fact that you are married and simply by being a good wife and mother, you are the partner who gives a certain credibility to your husband's ministry. What God has joined no one can rend apart; therefore, once ordained, your deacon-husband and you remain "one flesh." Pronouncing his "Present" at ordination, your husband brings to ordination all he is and has in virtue of baptism and confirmation, as well as marriage. When Christ ordains him, he configures a married man to himself, not one who is single and celibate. The laying on of hands does not annul or diminish in any way the sacrament of marriage, nor does it establish a barrier to its grace. Therefore, although you yourself are not configured sacramentally through orders to Christ the Suffering Servant, in virtue of the sacrament of marriage, which the church describes as a partnership of the whole of life (see canon 1055), you are partnered to your deacon-husband in ministry. A deacon's wife would mitigate her husband's credibility if her own behavior is itself incongruent with what he as a deacon is called to be and to do, for example, if she is a busybody, a gossip, if she has a reputation in the parish as one who came to be served and not to serve, does not respect the privacy of others, etc.

Third, the most effective and tangible participation that you can have in your husband's ministry is through your common prayer. Shared spousal prayer is first of all the most effective means of integrating the various and sundry elements and requirements of marriage and family life with those of diaconal life and ministry. "Since family life and professional responsibilities must necessarily reduce the amount of time which married deacons can dedicate to the ministry," the *Directory* teaches, "it will be necessary to integrate these various elements in a unitary fashion, especially by means of shared prayer" (61).

Shared spousal prayer, moreover, is a primary agency through which a deacon's wife actively participates in his day–to-day ministry. In *Five Books on Consideration: Advice to a Pope*, St. Bernard of Clairvaux taught his former monk, Pope Eugene III, that the command of Christ is not to cure all but to care for all. But how can one care for all? Prayer is the only way, for in prayer alone can all be included in one's ministerial care and by prayer alone can all be gathered to the Lord. When a deacon and his wife pray together they exercise the greatest cooperation possible in caring for the sinners and the poor whom the church entrusts to him. Your prayer is truly shared ministry. And it is ministry that you both carry out in the name of your own *ecclesia domestica*, the family.

Finally, you join in your husband's ministry simply when you deeply love each other. In other words, to the extent that you are deeply in love with one another and you grow daily in your marital love, you serve the Lord and the church. No less an authority than Pope John Paul II said exactly this when addressing deacons and their wives and families, in Detroit. "The nurturing and deepening of mutual, sacrificial love between husband and wife," he taught, "constitutes perhaps the most significant involvement of a deacon's wife in her husband's public ministry in the Church" (quoted in *Directory* 61). The love of husband and wife, the *Directory* itself continues, "fosters a mutual self-giving which soon becomes evident in ministry. It eschews possessive behaviour, undue pursuit of professional success and the incapacity to programme time. Instead it promotes authentic interpersonal relationships . . . and the capacity to see everything in its proper perspective" (61).

Dear wives, your husband's new friendship with Christ, the Divine Bridegroom, and with his bride, the church, should be reflected in your own new friendship as husband and wife. You have chosen one another forever and you want the whole world to know of that choice. You hear the Word spoken; you eat and drink the Word made flesh, you echo the Word. United in marriage you shine forth in the church and for the world as an icon of Christ the Divine Bridegroom. Because you do so, your deacon-husband shines all the more brightly as an icon of Christ the Suffering Servant.

And to your families, especially your children, I add a final word.

Dear children of our deacons, the church and her communities, especially her parishes, are enriched by the life and ministry of your fathers and by your own love and partnership in their ministry. A deacon who is passionate about his ministry to sinners and the poor, who makes himself available with a gracious generosity of heart, time, and energy, and who serves faithfully and well, and, perhaps even at personal cost and expense to his career and personal interests, is a great gift to the church. In many ways—through your prayer, by living a virtuous life, by agreeing to your father's ordination and supporting his ministry, and particularly through the sacrifices you make that your father might serve—you give him as a gift to the church and especially to the church's poor. Jesus teaches, "Whoever gives even a cup of cold water to one of these little ones in the name of a disciple—truly I tell you, none of these will lose their reward" (Matt 10:42). In some way your deacon-father ministers in your name. May Jesus reward you. May you, too, know a disciples reward.

Bibliography

Papal Teaching and Magisterial Documents

Benedict XVI. *Deus Caritas Est*: Encyclical Letter God is Love. Washington, DC: USCCB Publishing, 2006.

Bishop's Committee on the Liturgy. *Study Text VI: The Deacon: Minister of Word and Sacrament*. Washington, DC: United States Catholic Conference, 1979.

Catechism of the Catholic Church. Collegeville, MN: Liturgical Press, 1994.

Code of Canon Law. Washington, DC: Canon Law Society of America, 1983.

Congregation for Catholic Education and Congregation for the Clergy. *Basic Norms for the Formation of Permanent Deacons*. Washington, DC: United States Catholic Conference, 1998.

———. *The Directory for the Ministry and Life of Permanent Deacons*. Washington, DC: United States Catholic Conference, 1998.

General Instruction of the Roman Missal. Liturgy Documentary Series 2. Washington, DC: United States Conference of Catholic Bishops, 2003.

John Paul II. *Domincae Cenae*: Letter on the Mystery and Worship of the Holy Eucharist. Washington, DC: United States Catholic Conference, 1980

———. *Dominum et Vivificantem*: Encyclical Letter on the Lord and Giver of Life. Washington, DC: United States Catholic Conference, 1986.

———. *Salvifici Doloris*: Apostolic Letter on the Christian Meaning of Human Suffering. Washington, DC: United States Catholic Conference, 1984.

Paul VI. *Humanae Vitae*: Encyclical Letter on the Regulation of Birth. Washington, DC: United States Catholic Conference, 1968.

———. *Ministeria Quaedam*: Apostolic Letter Laying Down Certain Norms Regarding the Sacred Order of the Diaconate. Washington, DC: United States Catholic Conference, 1972.

———. *Sacrum Diaconatus Ordinem*: Apostolic Letter on the Sacred Order of the Diaconate. Washington, DC: United States Catholic Conference, 1967.

Rites of Ordination of a Bishop, of Priests, and of Deacons. Second Typical Edition. Washington, DC: United States Conference of Catholic Bishops, 2003.

Sacred Congregation of Rites. *Eucharisticum Mysterium*: Instruction on Eucharistic Worship. Washington, DC: United States Catholic Conference, 1967.

Synod of Bishops (1969). *The Ministerial Priesthood/Justice in the World.* Washington, DC: United States Catholic Conference, 1972.

United States Conference of Catholic Bishops. *National Directory for the Formation, Ministry, and Life of Permanent Deacons in the United States.* Washington, DC: United States Conference of Catholic Bishops, 2005.

Vatican Council II. *Apostolicam Actuositatem*: Decree on the Apostolate of the Laity. In A. Flannery, ed. *Vatican II: The Basic Sixteen Documents.* Northport, NY: Costello Publishing Company, 1996.

———. *Gaudium et Spes*: Pastoral Constitution on the Church in the Modern World. In A. Flannery, ed. *Vatican II: The Basic Sixteen Documents.* Northport, NY: Costello Publishing Company, 1996.

———. *Lumen Gentium*: Dogmatic Constitution on the Church in the Modern World. In A. Flannery, ed. *Vatican II: The Basic Sixteen Documents.* Northport, NY: Costello Publishing Company, 1996.

———. *Sacrosanctum Concilium*: Constitution on the Sacred Liturgy. In A. Flannery, ed. *Vatican II: The Basic Sixteen Documents.* Northport, NY: Costello Publishing Company, 1996.

Other

Barron, Robert. *Eucharist.* Maryknoll, NY: Orbis Books, 2008.

Bernard of Clairvaux. *Five Books on Consideration: Advice to a Pope.* Kalamazoo, MI: Cistercian Publications, 1976.

Brown, Raymond. *The Gospel According to John.* Garden City, NY: Doubleday and Company, Inc., 1966.

Congar, Yves. *Lay People in the Church.* Westminster, MD: The Newman Press, 1965.

Deck, E. M. *The Baltimore Catechism, No. 3 with Explanations.* Buffalo, NY: Rauch & Stoeckl Printing Co., 1933.

Johnson, Luke Timothy. *Hebrews: A Commentary.* Louisville, KY: Westminster John Knox Press, 2006.

Kasper, Walter. *Leadership in the Church: How Traditional Roles Can Serve the Christian Community Today.* New York: The Crossroad Publishing Company, 2003.

Marcel, Gabriel. *Creative Fidelity.* Noonday Press, 1964.

———. *The Mystery of Being: II. Faith and Reality.* Chicago, IL: Henry Regnery Co., 1951.

Merton, Thomas. *The Ascent to Truth.* Dublin: Clonmore & Reynolds, 1951.

Nouwen, Henri. *From Resentment to Gratitude*. Chicago: Franciscan Herald Press, 1986.

———. *Jesus: A Gospel*. Maryknoll, NY: Orbis Books, 2001.

Ratzinger, Joseph. *Behold the Pierced One: An Approach to A Spiritual Christology*. San Francisco: Ignatius Press, 1986.

———. *Ministers of Your Joy: Spiritual Meditations on Priestly Spirituality*. Ann Arbor, MI: Servant Publications, 1989.

Rulla, Luigi M., Franco Imoda, and Joyce Ridick. *Psychological Structure and Vocation: A Study of the Motivations for Entering and Leaving the Religious Life*. Dublin: Villa Books, 1978.

Vanier, Jean. *Drawn into the Mystery of Jesus through the Gospel of John*. Mahwah, NJ: Paulist Press, 2004.

Yarnold, Edward. *Cyril of Jerusalem*. New York, NY: Routledge, 2000.